THE CASE FOR GREATNESS

THE CASE FOR GREATNESS

Honorable Ambition and Its Critics

ROBERT FAULKNER

Yale University Press   New Haven & London

Copyright © 2007 by Yale University.

Designed by James J. Johnson and set in Janson type by The Composing Room of
Michigan, Inc.
Printed in the United States of America.

Library of Congress Cataloging-in-Publication Data
Faulkner, Robert K., 1934–
   The case for greatness : honorable ambition and its critics / Robert Faulkner.
      p. cm.
   Includes bibliographical references and index.
   ISBN 978-0-300-12393-7 (alk. paper)
   1. Ambition.   I. Title.
   BJ1533.A4.F38 2007
   179'.9—dc22
                            2007023112

A catalogue record for this book is available from the British Library.
The paper in this book meets the guidelines for permanence and durability of the
Committee on Production Guidelines for Book Longevity of the Council on
Library Resources.

10 9 8 7 6 5 4 3 2 1

To Margaret

Mankind has never been in this position before. Without having improved appreciably in virtue or enjoying wiser guidance, it has got into its own hands the tools by which it can unfailingly accomplish its own extermination. . . . It is therefore above all things important that the moral philosophy and spiritual conceptions of men and nations should hold their own amid these formidable scientific evolutions.

—Winston Churchill, *Thoughts and Adventures* (1932)

Contents

Acknowledgments

I'm grateful to Christopher Breull, Susan Meld Shell, and Margaret McConagha Faulkner, who read earlier versions of this book. It benefited from their comprehensive advice. Other friends, colleagues, and students helped with this or that part; I'll acknowledge them along the way. Here I wish to add thanks to the anonymous readers for Yale University Press, to my editor at the Press, Keith Condon, who contributed in ways big and small, and to Thomas Schneider for an exacting final review.

Boston College granted fellowships and periods of leave essential to my studies and writing. For these, for its support over many years, and for harboring serious scholars from whom I have learned much, I am very grateful. I warmly thank the Earhart Foundation, whose fellowships enabled me to begin and then to complete the writing, and thank also Rowman and Littlefield Publishing Group, Inc., for permission to draw from previous work. A version of chapter 6 appeared as "John Marshall and the False Glare of Fame," in Peter McNamara, ed., *The Noblest Minds: Fame, Honor, and the American Founding* (Lanham, Md.: Rowman and Littlefield, 1999), 163–84. Part of chapter 5 appeared as "Justice Overruled: The Ambition of Xenophon's Cyrus the Great," in Svetozar Minkov, ed., *Enlightening Revolutions: Essays in Honor of Ralph Lerner* (Lanham, Md.: Lexington Books, 2006), 289–308.

THE CASE FOR GREATNESS

CHAPTER ONE

Introduction:
Honorable Statesmen and
Obscuring Theories

His ambition was a little engine that knew no rest.

— HERNDON, *Life of Lincoln* (1888)

Every man is said to have his peculiar ambition. Whether it be true or not, I can say for one that I have no other so great as that of being truly esteemed by my fellow men, by rendering myself worthy of their esteem. How far I shall succeed in gratifying this ambition is yet to be developed.

— ABRAHAM LINCOLN, 1832

THIS IS A BOOK ABOUT GREAT POLITICAL AMBITION and especially its good version, honorable or statesmanlike ambition. Statesmanlike ambition is well known, of course, unless one could maintain that Nelson Mandela or Winston Churchill does not differ from the tyrant Joseph Stalin or the dangerous mediocrity Neville Chamberlain. Mandela and Churchill appeared larger and better than life to many of their free contemporaries. They attract as a matter of course attentive political historians who size up their efforts at defending, reforming, and founding a free country. But what seems obvious to the public-spirited is not so obvious to many scholars, thinkers, and intellectuals. There is a big divide between the easy acknowledgment of greatness that arises among thoughtful citizens and appreciative historians (I'm not talking of foolish hero worship) and the doubting cynicism of many contemporaries who generalize about human affairs. Among the theorists, too often, skepticism as well as cynicism prevails. Why is it that social scientists speak much of rational maximizing, power seeking, self-interest, and popular voice, but not much of extraordinary judiciousness, honorable aims, and knowing justice? Or that influential professors of philosophy and literature talk confidently of autonomy and equal dignity, while deprecating ambition for office and accomplishment as elitist domineering or a remnant of repressive culture? The contrast between our experience and our theories set my inquiry in motion.

I begin with the obvious thing, the ambitions all around us. You see the candidate running for office, the representative vying for the television lights, and the mayor trying to improve the schools. But how to understand the underlying motives and the different kinds of motive? The ambitious candidate wants to rise, we tend to say; he or she wants to get ahead, to succeed. But that description, familiar in our mobile democracies, is even there loose and inadequate. It doesn't catch what distinguishes the ambitious candidate from the careerist or moneymaker, who also wants to get ahead. It doesn't even catch what distinguishes the politically ambitious candidate from the time-server or the candidate on the take. If he or she is in it for lifetime security or graft, he or she is not politically ambitious, except in an imprecise sense. Who, then, is ambitious in the precise sense? It is the candidate who wants not so much the security or the money as to be in charge, to have his name in the papers, to make a difference. These three objects, superiority in power, reputation, and notable accomplishment, are crucial to the disposition we call political ambition. If present on a grand scale, they distinguish grand ambition as well. Napoleon sought kingly command, imperial fame, and enlightened empire over all Europe and farther. (He also got riches on an imperial scale, although not job security.) And if the aims are honorable and just as well as grand, they mark a truly grand ambition, ambition good as well as great. George Washington, the American icon, sought command in just and necessary battles, honorable fame, and the establishment of his country as an exemplar of popular self-government.

In our everyday experience we distinguish all the time between good and bad ambition. It is too obvious that Mandela, who liberated his fellow citizens while working for a free and multiracial country, differs from the twisted despot Idi Amin, who slaughtered hundreds of thousands of his countrymen. Justice, judgment, the common good, honorable conduct—these make a big difference. Which is not to deny cases, such as that of Julius Caesar in a decayed republic, in which the merits are complicated and disputed. Here it is enough to remind of the American congressman's simple distinction between the show horse and the workhorse. The show horse shines at press conferences and in the media; the workhorse does his duties, even as he appreciates a good reputation among his knowing peers. Doing one's duty, and if one seeks grand office and famous command, then doing one's grand tasks there, too—that is the obvious key. I illustrate the point with some reflections on two famous descriptions, quoted at the start, as to Abraham Lincoln's ambition.

Lincoln's law partner and friend, William Herndon, characterized Lincoln's ambition as a powerful drive, like an unceasing mechanical force: "His ambition was a little engine that knew no rest." The phrase reminds of a popular and rather cynical opinion: politicians are always out for themselves, and the stronger ones more strongly. Lincoln's own description, at twenty-three, when he first sought office as a representative in the Illinois Assembly, is more complex and revealing: "Every man is said to have his peculiar ambition. Whether it be true or not, I can say for one that I have no other so great as that of being truly esteemed by my fellow men, by rendering myself worthy of their esteem. How far I shall succeed in gratifying this ambition is yet to be developed." Let us suppose that this published view is Lincoln's true view. (Whom would one believe more?) What does it show about his ambition?

Lincoln disavows talk about some universal force or ambition in men generally, while talking of a certain kind of ambition, his own, that he might certainly know. He seeks office, that is, to be (to an extent) in charge. But he also seeks the good opinion of his countrymen, and he wishes to be worthy of their good opinion. The wish to be deserving, not only to win a name but also to do things worthy of such a reward, is important. Otherwise put: Lincoln seeks the true "esteem" of his fellowmen. To seek esteem is not to seek notoriety, as by crimes or spectacles, since those who esteem someone have a good opinion of him. Lincoln seeks the good opinion of his fellow citizens, not their shock and awe. He seeks their reasoning, discriminating approval. He does not have in mind the now-fashionable notions of charisma or prestige, which involve dazzling or blinding people rather than obtaining the appraisal one deserves. (According to the *Oxford English Dictionary*, *prestige* originally meant an illusory impression.) Nor does Lincoln mean here mere image making, although that certainly has its place in politics, not least in mass democracy. Consider Honest Abe the railsplitter, of his first presidential campaign. While Lincoln was extraordinarily shrewd as to the ways of political success, he sought something more reasonable than mere victory and more to do with his merit or deserts. He wants to be "truly esteemed," not merely esteemed. I take this to imply a wish for approval not by mere public opinion, but rather by the opinion of a discriminating public. Lincoln would not characteristically describe himself as seeking glory, which glows blindingly. Esteem warms one with intelligent honor, bestowed knowingly and deservedly. This is what Lincoln seeks for himself.

Admittedly, this preliminary description of truly great ambition is drawn from small evidence, although the full facts do place Lincoln among the most commanding, knowing, and morally serious of liberal democratic statesmen. Admittedly, too, the ambition so described is more just and wise than that of the vast majority of the ambitious, in any time or place. But this is the point. I am suggesting that Lincoln's kind of ambition sheds indispensable light also upon the lesser kinds, including the ambition of decent but more ordinary leaders, and not excluding that of the tyrant and the time-server. That is the reason to clarify ambition at its best; it illuminates what we most often find lacking. It sheds defining light. Alternatively, it helps explain the admiration of discriminating citizens for grand statesmen, those who make, defend, or preserve a decent country. Theirs can be a deserved fame, imprinted in the hearts of their countrymen as well as on streets, cities, states, and public buildings.

But can such a rather simple and old-fashioned analysis still be true, given the pluralism, moral skepticism, irrationalism, historicism, and egalitarianism of this sophisticated age? Many decades ago Churchill urged the special need in modern times to hold fast to "the moral philosophy and spiritual conceptions of men and nations." He was confronting new ideological tyrannies and new scientific and industrial powers of destruction. Great victories have now been won over the twentieth century's fascist and Marxist tyrannies, partly owing to his inspiration and leadership. But has his plea for preserving moral and spiritual standards been successful? I fear not, at least if one judges by the intellectual fashions of the enlightened West. Seven or eight decades later one sees a pervasive relativism as to values and, what is more, a positive project to liberate from traditional values, especially moral restraint and high character. Modern skepticism and postmodern liberation make up a strange tag team of beliefs, beliefs in one way or another ratified and broadcast by the universities, by most novelists and playwrights, and by much of the media. These intellectual fashions now penetrate a mass public, and in such broadening circles, at least, things moral and spiritual seem less sustained than systematically undermined. This, even as the movements of doubt and liberation provoke a moral and religious backlash, especially among Muslims but also among a Christian right and other circles in the democratic West.

What follows might be called an attempt to refresh a reasonable understanding of human excellence. To speak more within compass, I attempt to revive a once-celebrated understanding of honorable ambition, in particular, by returning to the seminal accounts of the classical political philosophers. This will seem to many a strange step. I shall contend that it is a necessary step. While along the way I address contemporary critics who say it can't be done or shouldn't be done, the core of this book does it. In the three most important chapters I investigate the accounts of political greatness by Aristotle, Plato, and Xenophon. Whatever the differences, all three diagnoses are variations on the Socratic beginnings of moral and political science as we know it. All three, I mean to show, have the freshness of beginnings. Here is the key contention. These old accounts illuminate our experiences of a Mandela or a Margaret Thatcher far better than the critical and doctrinal theorizing that is more familiar and has been in the works for three or four centuries. This is what I seek to prove.

Nevertheless, mine is an inquiry, not a screed or a creed, and I also address the critics. The last two chapters review the leading objections, that so-called grandeur of soul is really mere vanity and desire for domination, and that the old philosophic defenses only gild an inhumane, impracticable inequality. These discussions are in small compass, and they offer less rebuttal than genealogy, an account of the philosophic developments underlying our intellectual predicament. But there is some rebuttal, if only to exhibit the doubtful premises in the family tree. I also confront relevant theoretical objections and plainer political doubts throughout, especially in the remainder of this introduction and in the following chapter, which examines Aristotle's proposal, now often disdained, of the gentleman-statesman.

In general, the book begins by considering an honorable and just form of grand ambition, the statesman who works within the laws of his free country. The focus then moves to the political dangers and psychological dynamics of the less bounded and less just forms, the ambitions of those who seek empire and rule for themselves. I conclude by weighing certain modern theories that obscure these moral-political phenomena and make them peculiarly alien to our apprehension and sensibilities.

Aristotle's model of grand ambition is a distinctively moral interpretation, at least in the *Nicomachean Ethics*. It treats of a special virtue, magnanimity (or greatness of soul: *megalopsuchia*), and this, plus other virtues such as justice, shape the gentleman-statesman that he encourages. I concentrate upon this discussion of moral virtues, although I acknowledge less rosy remarks in the *Rhetoric*, and I make much of subsequent developments, within the *Politics* and *Ethics* both, that would subordinate such a man to the laws and politics of his country.

Magnanimity, in Aristotle's version, is the disposition to claim great honors because one is worthy of them. Lincoln, to repeat, sought not only the esteem of his fellowmen, but also to be worthy of their esteem. Attention to true worth, which means concern not for honor and glory but for being honorable and just in what one does, becomes a leading theme in the *Ethics'* analysis of the great-souled man. This is not simple or trite moralism, partly because the account proves more subtle and the soul in question much more strained, than is usually observed. If at first Aristotle describes a rather general, honorable, and reasonable disposition, he then outlines particulars that manifest a powerful passion for one's own superiority. Aristotle's proves to be a remarkable moral psychology that shows us the tensions within such a soul (as well as the promise). Nevertheless, the efforts of the *Politics* as well as those of the *Ethics* go to foster neither a radical adventurer such as the Alcibiades portrayed by Thucydides and Plato, reaching beyond any free country, nor the Cyrus that Xenophon analyzes, who so ranks greatness over goodness as to become a world conqueror and despot. On the contrary: Aristotle fosters ambitious men good as well as great, and he would subordinate their greatness to the service of their country. Besides, he encourages a certain knowing resignation before the lawful limits and harsh necessities of political striving. The first serious biographer of George Washington was the American chief justice John Marshall, himself no mean statesman, and the character sketch that concludes his *Life of Washington,* on which I shall occasionally draw, virtually paraphrases the *Ethics'* description of the great-souled man.

The next two chapters draw out the problems for free politics of unbounded grand ambition and then go more comprehensively into the psychology. Both discussions involve the Athenian general and politician Alcibiades. I focus on Alcibiades partly because of his spectacular if questionable ambition, but mostly because, like a brilliant comet, he attracted observers of the highest capacities. While I examine chiefly Plato's diagnosis of the psyche, I introduce that with Thucydides' account of the political exploits. In Alcibiades one sees grand ambition writ large in imperialism, civil strife, and even treason. But one sees also daring strategy and victories, brilliant policy, a certain justice, and a moderation from the heights, that is, an equable judiciousness above vengeance and the usual animosities of class. An Alcibiades poses insoluble problems for free societies, I conclude, and free societies pose insoluble problems for an Alcibiades.

The discussion of the political effects sets the stage for the Socratic cross-examinations in Plato's two *Alcibiades.* These little dialogues develop the psychological complications, not least the tendencies to both masterful tyranny and Oedipus-like self-hatred. I look to the two *Alcibiades* as one whole, which is rarely done, partly because Plato's authorship had been denied for a couple of centuries. Whatever the authorship (I shall argue for Plato or some follower of equivalent powers), together they shed a light perhaps unparalleled upon such a man's desires, pleasures, opinions, scruples, and internal contradictions. They show extra-ordinary ambition, first in the hopes of youth and then in the gloomy obsessions of frustration. The Alcibiades of both treat-ments is moved most by one extraordinary desire: love of honor and rule. He desires to "fill practically all people with his name and power"; he would have everyone in the world perceive him as tyrant. Yet in each dialogue Socrates makes Alcibiades prove that he knows what he is doing. He cannot, and in the course of the cross-examinations he comes face to face with other inclinations and devotions, such as a certain nobility, justice, and patriotism. The paradoxes shake his pride and shake him almost to the core. These two examinations, together with relevant passages from other dialogues, exhibit grand ambition in the capacious mirror of Platonic wisdom about the soul.

The last of the chapters on classical diagnoses looks at ambi-tion on an imperial scale, and the subject seems more the stuff of historical novels than of some allegedly profound argument from a philosopher. I examine the now-obscure account by Xenophon of Cyrus the Great. One could be excused for thinking that doubts about the imperial type, from the famous Plato and Aris-totle, are here replaced by a simple picture of imperial ambition on the march. The *Education of Cyrus* seems a how-to book on conquering the world. However, Xenophon's engaging work, once thought the first and authoritative "mirror of princes," proves not so simple, not merely practical, and not so adoring. Under the guise of an adventure story starring the founder-con-queror of the Persian empire, Xenophon shows the most rational and moderate way to empire. You can do it with a minimum of oppression and killing and a maximum of benefiting and clever-ness. Yet instrumental rationality is not enough. Xenophon shows more quietly the defects of such an imperial ambition. In the *Education of Cyrus* Cyrus's desire for superiority edges aside justice, love, nobility, and friendship as well as deep thoughtful-ness—all. The edging aside of these good things becomes my chapter's leading theme. What seems in many ways a grand and defensible project managed with extraordinary generosity and consummate skill narrows toward cold despotism. That is an outward and political sign of the narrowing within: Xenophon's is also a psychological study, albeit within a marvelous tale. I argue for the superiority of Xenophon's political psychology to that of Niccolò Machiavelli, who admired the *Education* most, perhaps alone, of ancient political-philosophic books.

Having discussed various forms of grand ambition, I weigh in the three final chapters certain modern theories that obscure or deny such things. Chapter 6 discusses interpretations of the iconic American gentleman-statesman Washington. I contrast Marshall's account, which focuses on character, with the historian Douglass Adair's influential interpretation of the founders, which focuses on fame. The founders generally were moved above all by desire for fame, according to Adair, albeit as channeled through a complicated republican tradition. That tradition encompassed ancient as well as modern theories, Plutarch as well as the Enlightenment philosopher Francis Bacon, all in one basically seamless web. On the contrary, I argue, there is a crucial seam, and the failure to open it muddies the differences and a Washington's distinctive grandeur of character. I pit Adair's account against Marshall's attention to honorable pride and devotion to duty, and Bacon's interpretation of fame seeking, on which Adair relies, against Cicero's account of the priority of duty, which Marshall recommends. The point is to bring out the differences between the classical account and the enlightened account, and to bring out too the practical bearing as to a very great statesman still more or less familiar. Washington, like Lincoln, exhibits the importance of high character, especially duty, to liberal democratic statesmanship.

Objections far more sweeping and theoretical are the topic of the two concluding chapters. Chapter 7 lays out the most influential contemporary critiques of the ancients' diagnoses. I sketch first John Rawls's extended argument against any politics of greatness and then Hannah Arendt's effort to restore a certain greatness without the inequalities of classical rationalism. This prepares the final topic, how we arrived at these critiques. Chapter 8 samples the key stages, starting with Thomas Hobbes's slashing critique of pride, ambition, and virtue itself (I include an occasional darting comparison with Machiavelli and other Enlightenment thinkers). There follows an outline of the Kantian reaction, both the critique and the construction. In the face of Machiavellianism and Hobbism Kant would restore a moral teaching, albeit a novel version compatible with equal rights. He supplies a searching critique of Aristotelian magnanimity as well as of Hobbist power seeking, and he devises the famous idealism of equal moral dignity and self-respect. I conclude by reminding of Friedrich Nietzsche's extreme reaction against bourgeois security seeking and democratic idealism both. Confronted by difficulties arising from earlier modern premises, Nietzsche was led to develop historical and value relativism and to resort to an irrational and willed greatness, the notorious superman. This has for good reason given grand ambition a bad name.

In short, mine is an inquiry into a perennial moral-political phenomenon that turns for help to now-unfashionable but once-admired political-philosophic thinking. Thoughtful help is what I seek; the reader will notice that the classical diagnoses yield no panacea. While taking account of political greatness, they measure it soberly. I'll close this introduction by distinguishing what I attempt from two similar efforts at recovery and then by confronting, in a popular formulation, the usual objections to any such efforts.

I'm not trying to restore a comprehensive "honor culture" in war and peace, with its "old-fashioned, even primitive, notions of honor." That task James Bowman set himself in *Honor: A History*, an independent, pungent, and wide-ranging contribution.[1] My task is a measured appreciation of the honor-seeking life, not simply a revival of it. That leads me to distinctive and outstanding examples, not everyday cases, and to penetrating thinkers, not a common and amorphous culture. It leads me also to focus on character and true worth. Bowman dwells on retaliation and "the honor group," that is, on the social need for members to stand up against threats to their closed community. He fears that a focus on "inner" honorableness, on desert or worth, dilutes the real thing. He fears, despite our secular age, Christianity's under-mining of spirited ambition in the name of inoffensiveness and pious humility. But can one understand Lincoln, Washington, and Mandela without appreciating their desire to do good things and thus to deserve the honors they get? Besides, the classic authors themselves separate their moral and intellectual doctrines from the woollier extremes of religion, as I point out. In any event, in our circumstances I worry less about the dangers of Christianity and more about modern theories that undermine uprightness al-together, especially the noble pride that disdains base conduct. My last chapter confronts these theories, whereas Bowman dis-misses them as unimportant adjuncts to an alleged historical process, one started by the Christian "bias against honor."

On the other hand, I'm not merely seeking a more effectual interior "agency" on behalf of equal rights, as is Sharon Krause in *Liberalism and Honor*.[2] Worrying that liberal democrats may not risk their necks for diversity and the rights of minorities, she looks to a sense of honor as spur to moral courage, thus to oppose an oppressive majority or government. Krause supplies some re-freshingly precise arguing. She also supplies invaluable sketches of honorable character in plainer wrapper: Lincoln, yes, and Martin Luther King, but also Frederick Douglass ("the soul of honor") and Susan B. Anthony. These sketches should be con-sulted, for they supplement with less orthodox examples of pro-test my own focus on figures such as Washington, Lincoln, and Mandela. But do her theories do justice to the admirable and honorable pride that she praises? Or do they decapitate the phenomenon? Krause's chief authority is the Enlightenment phi-losopher Montesquieu, and she acknowledges that Montesquieu advanced "false honor"—a passion for distinction "detached from moral virtue"—as incentive enough for political purposes. Another of her authorities, Alexis de Tocqueville, explained honor similarly: it is chiefly an opinion of right that serves a class or caste, as opposed to the true "moral rules" serving the "perma-nent and general needs" of the human race.[3] Krause herself thus recommends a new type of honor that disavows any connection with perfection of soul. But this beheads honorable uprightness.

It may also mix incompatibles. An honor oriented neither to up-rightness nor equality is married to a Kantian moral agency that upholds moral rules prescribing equality.

My own effort is to recover honorable ambition in its fullness, not as demoralized, and to look to thinkers open to the phenom-enon, not to those who explain it away or introduce a substitute, however politic. Which is not in the least to deny the troubling tendencies that provoke these two impressive efforts at recovery. As Tocqueville put his own apprehensions about mass democ-racy: what is "most to be feared is that in the midst of the small in-cessant occupations of private life, ambition will lose its spark and its greatness; that human passions will be appeased and debased at the same time. . . . This same man, who can tolerate neither subordination nor equality, nonetheless despises himself to the point that he believes himself made only to taste vulgar plea-sures. . . . I should want one to strive to give them a vaster idea of themselves and of their species."

This introductory summary would perhaps suffice, especially since objections to Aristotle, Plato, and the others are addressed in the relevant chapters, were it not for a widespread contempo-rary prejudice against any such return to ancient philosophers. This is the Great Intellectual Barrier. Arguments against going back are in the air. Everyone has heard them. Some contend that ancient diagnoses are historically obsolete; others, that ancient rationalism (unlike ancient tragedy) is dry, repressive, and impe-rialistic. Some maintain that the old rationalism is naïve and sub-jective, compared to scientific accounts of leadership; others, that attention to classical virtue is at odds with popular government and the equal dignity of persons. Some contend even that human nature has changed, or does not exist at all because of social con-ditioning. These criticisms are often combined, whatever the contradictions.

Still, such arguments are easier to assert than to live by. They cannot be lived by. To make the point in a plain way at the start, while avoiding unneeded detail, I examine briefly a book that ad-vances these objections and more, Leo Braudy's *The Frenzy of Renown*.

Braudy's big volume came out in 1986 and was republished in

1997 essentially unchanged (except for an afterword), and it ranges from the passion for glory of the heroic Homeric Achilles to the celebrity worship of modern mass democracies. The author aims for a comprehensive "history of fame." But he also seeks reform. He seeks, that is, lessons in moderating precisely contemporary celebrity worship. In our individualistic mass democracies, status depends on one's success in rising, and Braudy would allay the "frenzy" to stand out as unique, to seek personal validation, "to stand out of the crowd, but with the crowd's approval."[4] Nevertheless, whatever the defects of contemporary fame seeking, Braudy rejects any return to some ancient outlook that puts honor and "true achievement" at the core of a serious desire for distinction. He gives arguments why we cannot go back. But he cannot sustain these arguments, and he contradicts them.

The very meaning of fame differs historically with the development of society, according to Braudy, and for that reason one cannot update an old outlook (however thoughtful) for a modern time. Actually, Braudy does not much believe in superior thoughtfulness, at least among the big thinkers. He writes history instead of philosophy or political science, and among a plethora of vignettes about fame he does not even bother to include the diagnoses of Thucydides, Plato, Aristotle, or Cicero. The poet Homer, the conquerors Alexander and Augustus, and imperial Rome—these suffice for his picture of the classical view, as if serious rational analysts were but typical parts of a historical process of changing eras. Yet Braudy cannot stick to this historicism. Despite his disdain for the philosophers, he allows that Hobbes turned "classical honor into modern fame by removing any justification beyond an inner desire to be appreciated."[5] Despite his insistence that desire for fame is defined by "the context" and that it is but "a nexus of more generalized forces," he speaks of "perennial contradictions" within the desire for fame, explains Alexander by his "enormous desire to achieve," and finally seeks a new understanding of fame that corresponds to the underlying needs of human nature.

According to Braudy, the ancients' recommendations of honor, honorable conduct, and serious achievement were "un-

real" and at most but class oriented. "Golden Ages of true worth
and justified fame" never existed, and any such pretension to purity was an attitude of the unjust aristocracies and monarchies of
a now-forgotten past. To measure ambition by enduring achievement merely marks someone nostalgic for fixed values. But
Braudy himself contrasts the contemporary preoccupation, with
self-image, with an older version of honor, when "appreciation
by a few" or even self-appreciation of "achievement" was "sufficient." Is, then, the wish for discriminating judgment and true
achievement not mere nostalgia? Indeed, by the end of his second
edition Braudy goes farther in this direction than any ancient
philosopher would have thought realistic. He envisions even the
"end of fame," when a media-induced contemporary frenzy will
be replaced by devotion not to fame but to others. Devotion will
be less to self-consciousness than to self-awareness, not to one's
unique self but to "selflessness," and not to other-directed alienation but to "the intrinsic satisfaction of acting for others." This
seems an extreme version of the old self-appreciation, and of the
achievement, earlier dismissed. "We have forgotten the elements
of selflessness in honor and renown as well as the elements of
community good in any worthy definition of individualism." In
short, Braudy urges something foreign to his individualist and
self-indulgent historical era, something always good as opposed
to mere selfishness, and something good apart from the pretense
of image and fame. "Where now, for example," Braudy asks, "are
the models of a truly disinterested and principled patriotism like
that embodied by Lafayette?" Contrary to the antiphilosophic
bent, the historicism, and the egalitarianism, Braudy advances
what he supposes to be a true diagnosis of his era's fame seeking
and a true corrective of democracy.

Admittedly, these are proposals more asserted than argued,
and they are asserted in the manner of a prophet, albeit a secular
prophet of progress. Over the horizon is a "new individualism
not yet defined," in which people will concentrate not on themselves but on others. The end of fame is part of a vision of "socialist individualism," a new "commonality of shared desires." We
are given little supporting argument, let alone a properly socialist argument. Are these visions any more than unconsidered

residues of a secular faith in historical progress? Enough. Without pretending to a full accounting of this big book, it is enough
to have brought out some typical prejudices against recurring to
a classical philosophic diagnosis, the difficulty of living by them,
and the costs of avoiding thinkers, modern as well as ancient, who
considered these matters with sobriety and clarity.

Admittedly, mine is thus far a most preliminary weighing of
objections. Books such as *The Frenzy of Fame* hardly enter into
the telling arguments on which they depend, relying lazily on
an eclectic mix of premises drawn vaguely from more serious
thinkers. One can discern some hazy combination of, say, Hegel
and Marx on history and civil society, the early Enlightenment's
critique of common sense and ancient philosophy, Kant's defense
of the equal moral dignity of everyman, and Nietzsche's development of relativism and his call for secular prophets of a transformed humanity. I address contentions of this quality in my final
chapter as well as in the accounts of grand ambition that follow,
especially in the next chapter on Aristotle's diagnosis.

CHAPTER TWO

The Gentleman-Statesman: Aristotle's (Complicated) Great-Souled Man

Trusting to the reflecting good sense of the nation for approbation and support, he had the magnanimity to pursue its real interests in opposition to its temporary prejudices; and, though far from being regardless of popular favor, he could never stoop to retain, by deserving to lose it. In more instances than one, we find him committing his whole popularity to hazard, and pursuing steadily, in opposition to a torrent which would have overwhelmed a man of ordinary firmness, that course which had been dictated by a sense of duty.

—JOHN MARSHALL, *The Life of George Washington*

GREAT VIRTUE AND ITS CRITICS

GREATNESS, RESOLVE, a wish for the public's esteem, but governed by duty, by public duty in particular, and by a height of soul that would not stoop. So Washington's "magnanimity" appeared to his protégé Marshall and to others, Jeffersonian as well as Federalist, who knew the man at first hand. Washington seems to have been great as well as good, and good as well as great. Whereas Xenophon's Cyrus turns justice, honor, and duty into instruments of imperial ambition, Washington's ambition served justice, honor, and duty. Whereas Thucydides' Alcibiades ranges beyond his country's laws and limits toward glorious victories and empire, Washington defended his democratic republic, accepted its limitations, and framed and settled its fundamental laws. Napoleon, an authority on imperial ambition, is supposed to have lamented on Elba: "They wanted me to be another Washington."[1]

The combination of such goodness with such greatness is hard to understand. This chapter investigates the classic exposition, that of the "great-souled man" in Aristotle's *Nicomachean*

Ethics. ("Magnanimity" is Latinate for Aristotle's *megalopsuchia:* "greatness of soul.") Such a man is great because he claims great honors and offices and he deserves them. He is good, for his is a lofty ambition to benefit others on a grand scale.

Abraham Lincoln once hoped that he understood "the inside of a gentleman," however deficient he might be in the "outside polish."[2] Aristotle, we may say, is *the* philosopher of the inside of a gentleman. His *Nicomachean Ethics* is the first and probably the wisest philosophic explication of good character and good judgment, which he, drawing upon and adapting common usage, called the traits of the gentleman (*kalokagathia,* lit. noble and good).[3] Aristotle is the philosophic portraitist of the serious gentleman at his best. Such a man claims the superior places due his superiority, as did a Washington and a Lincoln, and he finds them in the activity of governing. The phenomenon of the gentleman-statesman or gentleman-ruler—that is what Aristotle sought to portray and to foster. His is no mere eulogy, nevertheless.

The Aristotelian account reaches to the complications and the dangers issuing from such a soul's inclinations. There are intractable forces and problems, within and without. In the face of these Aristotle would provide reasonable guidance and thus both an intellectual clarification and a political moderation and purification. This is partly through his treatment of the virtue magnanimity itself, and it is partly through subsequent discussions, in the *Politics* as well as the *Ethics,* of justice, political necessity, a philosophic outlook, and gentlemanly cultivation. Aristotle begins with an opinion admiring greatness of soul and ends with a surprising depreciation of that and of great politics generally. That is the drama of his account, the drama that the following sections investigate. First, however, I outline the distinctiveness of the account and confront some contemporary objections to taking it seriously.

The Aristotelian turn to moral virtue is distinctive even among the classical philosophers famous for their attention to virtue. His ethical treatises, especially the *Nicomachean Ethics,* seem to be the first sympathetic philosophic elaborations of good character. He has even been called the philosophic discoverer of moral virtue.[4] Plato and Xenophon, for their part, had agreed on the Socratic premise that clear thinking begins with taking seriously claims to right conduct and the good life. But they had not gone Aristotle's route. While beginning with justice, courage, and so forth, they ended up with doubts about merely moral virtue; they tended to treat it as but politically useful. Compared to prudence, the moral virtues could seem unthinking, moralistic, and indefinite. Compared to a life of clear thinking, of the activity of man's distinctive intelligence, the practical virtues could seem means to lesser goods such as safety, riches, and honor. Only Aristotle does otherwise, taking the moral virtues as obviously good. Only he among the three treats great ambition within a moral context that seems to stand on its own. Among the seminal ancient accounts of human excellence, I suspect, only his adequately illuminates the mixture of greatness and goodness to be found in, say, Washington or Winston Churchill.

The contrast is graver with that succession of modern philosophers, still somewhat familiar, who from the start rejected an orientation by opinions as to what is right and good. Bacon, Hobbes, and their followers in modern enlightenment rejected altogether an orientation by what men think they ought to do, whether intellectual, moral, or pious. They sought a foundation for political science more reliable than mere opinion, especially diverse beliefs as to justice, truth, and the good. These giants would "put such principles down for a foundation, as passion not mistrusting, may not seek to replace," as Hobbes put it at the start of his first book of political science, the *Elements of Law*. If these thinkers looked to greatness (as had Machiavelli with his prince), it was to a worldly greatness without goodness, with a *virtù* not morally virtuous. Machiavellian virtue is an industrious and versatile opportunism, the famous ability to mix force and fraud, the arts of the lion and the fox. While surely targeting biblical charity, righteousness, and innocence, it was aimed also at the classical "writers" whose attention to what was right and rational ended in talk of utopian republics and kingdoms. These utopias are but "imagined," not the result of clear thinking about the implications of what decent men seek (*Prince* 15). Machiavelli turns from an orientation by "what men should do," from duty and the best life, to "what men do," to common motives and their management. The new "great" are instructed not in justice and in deference to divine thoughtfulness, but in the arts of advancing themselves and their peoples in wealth and power.

It was against such enlightened systems of liberated self-interest and national empire that Jean-Jacques Rousseau, Immanuel Kant, David Hume, G. W. F. Hegel, and others reacted, raising universal moralities of compassionate sympathy and rational duty. But those sentimental and idealistic projects accepted something of their predecessors' insistence on realizable political plans and of their skepticism as to traditional morals. Besides, they condemned especially ambition for one's own superiority and honor; it was perhaps the worst of vices. And if Nietzsche reacted later by restoring a noble "will to power," he attempted this in a half-Machiavellian spirit by liberation from good and evil and, more radically, by liberation from the restraints of reason itself. In him and his semifollower Martin Heidegger, modern philosophy turns on itself, blaming the whole tradition of philosophy.

Amidst the rational paradoxes and moral-political ruins left by such attempts, Aristotle's teaching could seem an oasis of sober good sense. There is reason for the efforts to revive his accounts of virtue ethics, political judgment, citizenship, and other such moral-political phenomena. That quiet movement of restoration has been afoot for at least a half century now, and this chapter is intended as a contribution to the effort.[5]

Today's admirers of Aristotle's ethics, however, often neglect the priority he himself gives to greatness of soul. They concentrate on the moral disposition as such, on some variant of happiness, or on the virtue of justice. A prominent recent collection of twenty-one essays on the *Ethics* contained many on moral knowing, three on happiness, one apiece on justice and courage, and none on magnanimity.[6] This is un-Aristotelian in a big way. As to moral matters, Aristotle insists, there is more truth in particulars than in generalities ($1107a27-35$). As to particular virtues, he ranks greatness of soul as the "crown" ($1124a1$) needed to perfect all the virtues, including justice.[7]

Aristotle does not mince words on this topic, and neither should we. No greatness without goodness, yes, but also no true goodness without greatness. The great-souled human being, in claiming a worthy stage, claims for human excellence the prominence and tasks it deserves (1123b18–23). Accordingly, while greatness of soul "cannot exist without" such other virtues as moderation and justice, it also "enhances their goodness." A man of such virtue is too noble to stoop, or to accept the second best, especially in his own conduct. Aristotle calls greatness of soul a *kosmos*. It is an ornament of good character that is also an exalting order: an ordering heightened by an awareness of the grand activities such a soul calls for and is owed.

This outlook is rather foreign to our ears. But is it foreign to the character and to competent observers of the character? Consider another extended remark in John Marshall's old biography. Washington displayed an "unaffected and indescribable dignity, unmingled with haughtiness, of which all who approached him were sensible. . . . In him, that innate and unassuming modesty which adulation would have offended, which the voluntary plaudits of millions could not betray into indiscretion, which never obtruded upon others his claims to superior consideration, was happily blended with a high and correct sense of personal dignity, and with a just consciousness of that respect which is due to station."[8]

Still, such recommendations may now sound like praises from a bygone era. To many modern and postmodern readers Washingtonian pride has to seem pretentious. It seems that of a prig, as some say directly of Aristotle's magnanimous man. More seriously, the character and the doctrine are thought politically dangerous. I will address some of these concerns and touch in a preliminary way on Aristotle's own responses. Later I bring out Aristotle's powerful provisions both for the usual objections and for other dangers now less acknowledged.

The most obvious objection is to alleged elitism. Do such claims to superiority justify power in the strong to exploit the weak? Aristotle, however, distinguishes sharply between virtuous pride and the arrogance of the usual few distinguished by riches, power, and family. The merely privileged consider themselves worthy of great things, but "unjustly," for "in accordance with truth, only someone good is honorable" (1124a25). Aristotle acknowledges that the merely prominent are all too honored. But in fact they are "arrogant and insolent" precisely because without virtue; they do not deserve the name great-souled. While a truly great man may look "down on others justly (since he holds his opinion truly)," "most people are disdainful at random" (1124a21–1124b6).

Neither is this man of justifiable pride exploitative. He disdains not least exploitation, especially injustice to the weak. Superior generally in character, he is superior not least in discerning true deserts as opposed to differences in class, wealth, or other such marks of fortune. Frederick Douglass saw this kind of superiority in his first meeting, in 1861, with Lincoln. Lincoln showed an "entire freedom from popular prejudice against the colored people. He was the first great man that I talked with in the United States freely, who in no single instance reminded me of the difference between himself and myself, of the difference of color." The great man Lincoln, "as great as the greatest,"[9] saw Douglass for what he was, that is, for the man, indeed the great man, that he was. Aristotelian magnanimity is not prejudiced pride or snobbery.

Nor is it domination, in the sense given by certain familiar theories, whether postmodern, Nietzschean, or even Machiavellian. These theories authorize being out for oneself alone (becoming "autonomous," a "self," or *uno solo* [as Machiavelli put it]), and from this it follows that governance of others amounts to mere domination. But Aristotle's is not a self-proclaimed Machiavellian "departure from the orders of others," with a foundation beyond morals. It is not a self-proclaimed Nietzschean "transvaluation of values," toward a will beyond good and evil. Aristotle presents a version of the moral virtues actually praised and admired among people of honest character, with greatness of soul a crown, and justice, often thought "the chief of the virtues," the other peak (1124a1–2, 1129b27–28). Actually, I shall show that justice seems to take over priority in Aristotle's full account. Justice seems "the greatest or strongest" of the virtues, in part because the good of one's country seems "more noble and divine" than that of oneself alone (1094b9–10, cf. 1129b31–1130a8). Washington and Lincoln were very great men, in part because of their devotion to equal rights, popular government, and, in Lincoln's case especially, the destruction or at least the limitation of slavery. Aristotle elaborates the outlook of a statesman devoted to his country and its justice, not that of a Cyrus or Napoleon who for his own glory destroyed his republic. Compare to that Washington's successive actions as liberating but republican general, lawmaker of republic and nation, and establisher of a popular government capable of governing.

Still, perhaps such a man's claims to superior place and honor reflect a "self-absorption which is the bad side of Aristotle's ethics," as the distinguished scholar W. D. Ross put it years ago. Is there something "smug and comfortable" in Aristotle's teachings on magnanimity, as Bertrand Russell contended; do they forget "everything that makes men feel a passionate interest in each other?"[10] The answer to both questions is no, if indeed such a man is law abiding and seeks to benefit his fellow citizens. Still, the critics' underlying concern seems to be whether magnanimity is sufficiently idealistic and oriented to humankind. If the great-souled man claims superior opportunities on the basis of his own superiority, is he devoted enough to the dignity of every man and woman, or compassionate enough toward suffering humanity?

To this question I return a question. Were not Washington, Lincoln, and Churchill superior in concern for the common good to the common citizen, not to speak of the freeloader or the criminal? If one denies this, one denies what is obvious to most thoughtful and public-spirited citizens. If one grants their superiority in justice, one respects superior human being as well as universal human being. But if a person were superior in this way, he would be dishonest and false not to claim what he deserves. It would be hypocritical not to claim his due. It would be worse, if Aristotle is right. To be self-effacing is bad for human excellence, *especially if one has superior powers*. Better to be vain than small souled, he contends, for the latter, which is the more usual vice, makes a man shrink from demanding his just deserts. It makes him shrink from accomplishing in life what he might, including what he might do for the public (1125a20–35).

Besides, such an idealistic altruism seems unrealistically and artificially selfless. While it demands moral conduct, it neglects the problem of the self's motives and satisfaction—and pleasure! —in doing the right thing. Aristotle's moral teaching, by contrast, is above all an account of moral habits, that is, the dispositions or character that cause good conduct. In short, Aristotelian magnanimity is far from exploitation or self-absorption, especially compared to the now-familiar doctrines of self-reliance, self-expression, individuality, and autonomy.

There is naiveté political as well as moral in these objections. For the great-souled man claims as tasks what no one else can do or do as well, and this service is at least as necessary in democracies as in other political orders. The doctrine of equal dignity may be easily professed in settled democracies. It is impossible to live by. It is never lived by. It should not be lived by. Superior founders, preservers, and statesmen are needed there, too, and thoughtful citizens give them superior respect. The Second Continental Congress chose Washington unanimously as commander in chief, the members of the Constitutional Convention chose him unanimously as their president, and the electors twice chose him unanimously as president. They did this rightly and wisely. Washington was probably the only man who could have done any one of his famous accomplishments: win the Revolutionary War, obtain the state delegations' agreement to a rather strong government, and turn the new plan into an actual government.[11]

Granted, those of powerful passions are too likely to seek mere superiority over others. Aristotle himself fears this danger, as I will emphasize. He recommends, for most circumstances, a powerful middle class, middling virtues, and a democratic republic. Those who paint him as elitist seem ignorant of all that. Nevertheless, these arrangements, too, are difficult to get, keep, and defend. All the more important, then, is what Aristotle does: the fostering in powerful souls of magnanimity, of law-abidingness, and of loyalty to one's regime. Aristotle encourages pride in one's virtue, rather than in one's honors, riches, and family, and law-abiding sobriety in one's expectations from politics. He fosters a gentlemanly attitude, a patriotic attitude, and what can loosely be called a philosophical attitude.

Nevertheless, we must grant that such a man may be dangerous in established republics, whatever his services in extreme situations. Thomas Jefferson worried about the precedent of precisely Washington for popular self-government in America. There is a genuine problem here. If "the great-souled looks down on others justly (since he holds his opinions truly)" (1124b5–6), can he be devoted to his country if it denies what he deserves? But if this is a problem, it is not to be wished away by some false allegation of equality. It is a problem, and Aristotle addresses it. His *Ethics* encourages a gentleman-statesman within his country's laws and with moderate expectations from his (or any) country. The *Politics* dwells on the inevitable variety of governmental forms, dwells not least on the prima facie claim of democracy, and is soberly hesitant about the claim of the best to rule. It even allows that ostracism of outstanding figures possesses a certain "political justice." Such considerations help explain Aristotle's counsel that the truly great-souled hold themselves "moderately" toward "power" as well as toward wealth and indeed toward "every sort of good fortune and bad fortune" (1124a13–16). This genuine moral-political problem is also a genuine complication for the soul of an outstanding human being.

Apart from such moral and political objections, finally, there is the modern relativistic challenge. We can have no more than subjective values, it is said, because our science can only describe facts or because all our opinions (including our science) are relative to historical epochs. I address this now-familiar contention in the concluding chapter. Here I merely assert that the sophisticated grounds of such skepticism are less evident than an honest man's awareness of the difference between a fair official and one who feathers his nest or lords it over the weak. This awareness of good and bad, writ small, is also present as to leaders, writ large. What of a Franklin D. Roosevelt and his helpmeets Churchill and Charles de Gaulle in the great twentieth-century struggle to defend modern free government? They, like their ally Stalin, could seem bigger than life in charm, force, and shrewdness. But these gentlemen-statesmen, unlike the obsessive despot Stalin, were bigger also in justice and honor. The difference is evident to even many sensibilities once distorted by Marxism.

As to Aristotle in particular, he was open to the variety of common opinions about virtue and justice without being doctrinaire as to their certainty or generality and without ever believing in the possibility of universal agreement. (How on such matters could good people agree with bad?) His is not the skeptical-foundational style of morals, which occasions modern relativism and is the special target of postmodern critics. He begins with an admittedly circular reliance on decent opinion (on a certain common sense of a moral kind), and he is well aware of the fragile beginnings and of the dialectic of clarification that takes him beyond. But his is also the confidence that goes with the sobering lesson of Socrates. No study of decency, and no truly scientific study of human affairs, can begin other than in this dialectical way. One fruit of this lesson is openness to what is closed for contemporary orthodoxies, the outlook of great and honorable human beings.

Greatness of Soul as a Virtue

Most of the philosophers of antiquity, who treated of human nature, have shown more of a delicacy of sentiment, a just sense of morals, a greatness of soul, than a depth of reasoning. They content themselves with representing the common sense of mankind in the strongest lights, and with the best turn of thought and expression, without following out steadily a chain of propositions, or forming the several truths into a regular science.

— David Hume[12]

Greatness of soul, even from its name seems to be concerned with great things, and let us first take up what sort of great things they are; it makes no difference whether one examines the disposition or the person with the disposition. Now the person who seems to be great-souled is one who considers himself worthy of great things and is worthy of them.

— *Nicomachean Ethics* (1123a34–1123b1)

The distinguishing mark of Aristotle's greatness of soul is that it is a moral, an ethical, virtue. It is the correct and habitual disposition with respect to the desire for great honors, as the virtue temperance is with respect to desires for food, drink, and sex, and courage, with respect to fear. Someone could say, in the words of Hume, that Aristotle begins with "common sense." Aristotle does not say this. He himself begins with the special opinions that articulate what such a man feels and what equable people of intelligence see in the flesh. His is not a universal explanation for common humankind. Accordingly, Aristotle's way catches the distinctive outlook of a Washington or a Nelson Mandela, the statesman who stands out in goodness as well as greatness.

Indeed, Aristotle makes a point of distinguishing the virtue greatness of soul (*megalopsuchia*) even from the virtue ambition (*philotimia*, lit. love of honor). Ambition is a more ordinary virtue, the virtue of those who seek rightly the common sort of honors and offices. The great-souled man, however, disdains the usual and seeks the tribute and high offices that are "great things." A concern for greatness puts him above honor seeking as such. Actually, the *Ethics* at first makes greatness of soul alone *the* defining excellence as to honor and dishonor (1107b21–23). It at first fails to distinguish a lesser virtue. While eventually the distinction is made, the virtue of (ordinary) ambition is left nameless, discussion of it is very brief, and the content is hazy. Aristotle concentrates on greatness of soul. This, the *Ethics* spells out at length, first its general outlook (1123a34–1124b6) and then the various particular attitudes (1124b6–1125a17).

Perhaps the reason for the differential treatment is that greatness of soul is linked with a human completion that can be defined, that is, with a standard that rises above political and cultural differences. If this is true, it as a crown can define both individual excellence and rightful political authority, whereas appropriate ordinary ambition varies with the powers and laws of different countries. Ambitious liberal democrats should exhibit different restraints from those seeking to rise in a politburo. Nevertheless, I should say immediately that Aristotle's radical equation of magnanimity with excellence and justice, which seems to follow from book 4's thematic description, is by no means his last word. Even his thematic little treatise makes this virtue not so simple and not so simply good.

The great-souled man seeks great positions and honors from others as well as virtue of soul for himself, and this proves to complicate both his disposition and his relation to others. Indeed, the greatest thing for the great-souled man is honor from others. So Aristotle's thematic account virtually begins and ends. But such a man also holds that "nothing is great" (1123b33–34, 1125a14) besides his virtue, and he seems to regard any honor as less than what is due a soul of such worth (1124a9). So which is greater, his honor or his virtue?

Another and related difficulty shows itself among the particulars. Aristotle's initial picture in book 4 focuses on general and high-minded opinions. It attends to such a man's knowledge of himself and to his preoccupation with honor, virtue, serious judges, and true opinion. The second part of the description, on the particulars, brings out another side: a powerful passion for superiority, with its resulting complications. The particular attitudes are mostly about the great man's relations with other people, especially as they involve this inclination for moral as well as political superiority. To leave it now at the key complication: in his superiority the great-souled man is "incapable of leading his life to suit another," and yet he seeks "great honors" from others and "great deeds" that require others (1124b31–1125a1, 1124a5–7, 1124b25). Can there be honors from others that involve no needing of others, and deeds requiring others but not depending on others? Or does the great man's desire for superiority harbor an impulse that can be called monarchical or despotic, or even suprahuman (cf., e.g., 1124b10, 14, 20)? The answer to the last question is yes, although one must add that precisely for the great man, virtue gives to this impulse something of an honorable and just direction.

A later passage from the *Ethics* clarifies the general relation between natural desire, such as the passion for superiority, and true virtue. Children and beasts have the natural dispositions, but not the virtues. These natural dispositions by themselves, without intelligence (*nous*), are harmful for human beings. That is, while virtues are to some extent given as natural passions and desires, these must be shaped in a correct direction to make them fully human. Such passions may contribute to the moral virtues. Some people are naturally more spirited and therefore inclined to be courageous; others, more naturally gentle and inclined to be just. But "the governing [*kurios*] good is different, and belongs to us [*huparchein*] in another way." Aristotle's example is a heavy body, which, when moving while blind, will suffer a heavy fall (1144b1–12).

Apply this to the man possessed by a "heavy" passion, such as that for great superiority. While he is by nature more powerful than others in his desire, his force can be a blind force. He can fall with great consequences to himself and to those who depend upon him. But if one "acquires intelligence," one may guide one's actions wisely (1144b12). Acquiring intelligence means not merely cleverness, in the calculation of means, but cleverness guided by an "eye of the soul," which calculates means in the light of what is fair and admirable (1144a30). Aristotle's moral reasoning is not merely instrumental rationality. Magnanimity is that virtue that brings intelligence to those who passionately want superiority. Consider Washington again. As a young soldier he was "too desirous of acquiring all the honor," complained Britain's agent for Indian affairs. Even as president, Jefferson recalled, when Washington's temper "broke its bonds he was most tremendous in his wrath." Still, the eruption over, Washington restored the bonds. Bonds—guiding restraints present within, and restorable when breached—were needed. They were present.[13]

Perhaps it is this tension, between things intellectual and the passions, that occasions the division in Aristotle's account between a rather intellectual general outlook and the practical reconciliations of such an outlook with an immense desire for superiority over others. While the whole can work, it can also break, but character tells, and sound character tends to restore the whole.

Consider Washington yet again. After the presidency had been constituted his friends worried that he might refuse nomination from fear of sullying his lustrous fame. Washington's comment was curt. He was by no means so "solicitous of reputation" as to "seek or retain popularity at the expense of one social duty, or moral virtue." If the "good of my country" requires "my reputation" to be risked, so be it.[14] He needed to know where his duty lay. The evidence, at least from his private letters after the Constitutional Convention, shows him less a claimant to supreme honor than the indispensable man who reluctantly acquiesced in that fact. It is nevertheless true and consistent that as president he reacted with barely controlled fury to imputations of dishonor, that is, to aspersions cast upon his impartiality and character. Washington, said Jefferson significantly, felt attacks from the press "more than any person I ever met with."[15] Great in his desire for honor, Washington was greater in his animus against dishonor and especially imputations as to his virtue. It is the priority of virtue and honor, so understood, that largely distinguishes Aristotelian greatness of soul and a Washington.

What Is Greatness? Honor, Knowing, and Worth Clarified

I know from my experience how incomprehensible and foreign Aristotle's concept of *megalopsuchia* was to me originally, and *now* I not only theoretically, but also practically, *approve* of it. A man like Churchill proves the possibility of *megalopsuchia* exists today *exactly* as it did in the fifth century BC.

— Leo Strauss to Karl Löwith, 1946[16]

While Aristotle asks what great things are sought by the great of soul and affirms the answer "honor," he does not proceed directly, and his full conclusion amounts to a distinct reduction of the status of honor. The important steps are four. Before elaborating on what the great things are, Aristotle first emphasizes that the great-souled man must be knowing, knowing, that is, as to his own deserts. Else he would be foolish, and no one "who answers to the description of virtue" is foolish (1123b2–4). After affirming that honor is the greatest thing for the worthy claimant, second, he holds that true worth is virtue. "It is necessary for one who is great-souled in the true sense to be good," and the greatest man is the best man (1123b28–29). These two steps prepare the third and fourth, an explicit depreciation of honor itself and especially the usual honors given to the rich and powerful. The great-souled man is pleased only with honors from serious (*spoudaios*) people, not from anyone, and he is not all that pleased even with these. For since he is moderate as to all bad and good fortune, he takes even honor "as a small thing" and "not the greatest thing" (1124a14–15, 17–19). Nevertheless, Aristotle is compelled to acknowledge that fortune plays a role, that those fortunate in power and riches are in fact honored, and that their fortune makes them "more great-souled." All this, despite the fact that, "in accordance with truth, only someone good is honorable" (1124a23–25). A quiet contrast appears, between what in truth should be honored and what people do honor. This is a high point of clarification, although it is immediately modified by an acknowledgment that those to whom both virtue and riches or power belong are more worthy of honor (1124a25–26). One sees foreshadowed the difference between true virtue and the compromised political forms, a difference that prepares the way for later clarifications. I will spell out these first clarifications and rectifications of ordinary opinion.

First of all, the truly great man must know himself, that is, have a true estimate of his worth. This criterion leads to the definition of appropriate choice (the mean) and erroneous choice (the extremes). Someone who in claiming great things overestimates his worth is vain; someone whose claims underestimate his worth, small-souled. Vanity and pusillanimity are the opposite extremes or vices, and both are based upon a "foolish or senseless" judgment as to oneself as a whole (1123b3). Claiming too much, one looks foolish. Claiming too little, one misses out on great things one deserves. The middle or mean is the man who knows himself as great and claims accordingly.

Is it arbitrary, this move, in Aristotle's account of a human peak, toward "know thyself"? Could it, however, be otherwise? Suppose a fool were accidentally great by inheriting a dukedom. Something like this happens all too frequently. Still, must not a serious judge call him great not as such—he is a fool—but only qualifiedly, as great in family and power?

This sort of self-awareness differs from the self-reliance now familiar. While self-reliance in our sense also involves a correct self-assessment, it is of one's powers to get on in the world, not of one's virtue or worth of soul. This is not to deny that great-souled men must know the necessities of life and often bow to them. The *Ethics* and *Politics* remind repeatedly of the difficulties confronting high aspirations. But Aristotle, to his everlasting credit, does not forsake those aspirations.

Still, if virtuous self-knowledge is not merely knowledge of one's abilities to get on in the world, it is not self-knowledge in the full Aristotelian sense either. The great-souled man of the *Ethics* is not an opportunist, but he is also no philosopher. The knowledge relevant here is of a particular thing, his worth for great things and especially for great duties and deeds. But such a man is not given over to knowing. Indeed, he is in his pride above such things. Nothing is great to him (apart from himself, that is, his virtue), and he "is not much given to wonder" (1125a2–3). Indeed, Aristotle intimates a certain problem by revising his praise. Such a man merely "opines truly" as to his worth (1124b6). From the more knowing point of view the great-souled man's knowledge of himself is an opinion, one unexamined by the great man himself.

There are some commentators who argue that the true great-souled man is indeed the philosopher. They rely on a brief passage, in the *Posterior Analytics*, in which Aristotle uses Socrates to illustrate a certain version of greatness of soul (97b15–26). The topic is equivocal terms. Socrates exemplified the ability to endure turns of fortune, one meaning of the term "greatness of soul"; Achilles, Ajax, and Alcibiades showed an inability to tolerate dishonor, the other meaning.[17] Still, the passage is brief, hypothetical, and enigmatic. Besides, it illustrates the ability to endure bad fortune also with a political man, Lysander, the superior Spartan who was haughty abroad while long acquiescing in humiliating subordination at home. Be that as it may, the *Ethics* itself obviously describes a political type who claims great honors and yet will also "hold himself moderately" toward "good fortune and bad fortune," even "honor" (1124a13–15). While Aristotle helps prepare such a man within for the slings and arrows of political life, he does not forsake him or his distinctive knowledge for either a Machiavelli's single-minded cleverness or a Plato's single-minded philosophizing.[18] He remains faithful to such a man's distinctive if hazy knowledge, his eye for the right action that is "an extreme by reason of magnitude" and a mean by "doing things as one ought" (1123b13–15).

Then what, second, should such a person seek?

The answer is obvious, says Aristotle, since the prominent seek honor most of all. And is it not obvious? The young Washington sought distinction and rank in soldiering, rose among Virginians like a rocket, and then resigned in indignation when he felt dishonored, that is, when a new regulation subordinated his colonial rank to British officers of lower rank. Nevertheless, the answer proves not so completely obvious. For the "great thing" to be sought is raised as a question, as if there remains some doubt as to whether honor satisfies such souls. And while Aristotle falls in with what seems obvious, he first proffers an argument that clarifies and purifies. Honor must be the "great thing" since it is the tribute paid to the gods, most sought by the prominent (*hoi en axiomati*), and awarded for the noblest deeds (1123b18–20). What can we make of such a remark? It seems that such men are to seek above all a tribute in speech, that is, they seek to be the object of men's respect, esteem, or even reverence. It is a human tribute; they do not seek the favor of the gods as such. It is a tribute in reason or speech; they do not seek ruling as such or even noble actions as such. So wishing honor, they are at once superior and respectful. They are respectful of the speech, the *logos*, that is the superior thing in human beings, especially in the serious ones.

Aristotle thus encourages what he knows to be rare. Elsewhere he notes that the great-souled man thinks "it great to rule" (*Eudemian Ethics* 1233a30; cf. *Politics* 1281a30–35; 1278a36–37). Another work, by Aristotle or some follower, even defines a lover of honor as "one who seeks to be sole possessor of something and by such means to surpass all others" (*Magna Moralia* 1205b32–34). This hunger for superiority, moreover, is usually a passion for wealth and power that overcomes love of the noble— except in the serious (*spoudaios*) (*Eudemian Ethics* 1205b32–34, 1212a36–1212b2).

The *Nicomachean Ethics* adopts and examines the rare outlook. While the great-souled man desires superiority, he also acts in light of what is honored "by the serious" (1124a6). He does not fundamentally seek divine favor, tyranny, victories, or even rule. As to the pleasures attending divine favor, victories, and so forth,

Aristotle is surprisingly reticent. He abstracts from them. The exception proves the rule. The account of the great-souled man mentions one deed of war. It concerns the ways the great-souled man retreats, not the glory of victory. This is conjoined with a remark that such a man could not be unjust (1123b31–32). There may be Socratic irony here, but there is also truth. This great-souled man "is fond of conferring benefits, but ashamed to receive them, because the former is a mark of superiority, the latter, of inferiority" (1124b9–10 and *seq.*). His is superiority from the heights of inner independence. He has bigger fish to fry than his own glory. We are reminded of Washington's laconic remark after the glorious victory at Yorktown. The glory was not the point. The victory is "an interesting event that may be productive of much good if properly improved, but if it should be the means of relaxation . . . , it had better not have happened."[19] Bigger fish, indeed.

For similar reasons, I suspect, the section on magnanimity gives little prominence to things noble. This might seem surprising, since in his discussion of courage Aristotle had asserted conspicuously that the noble is "the end that belongs to virtue" (1115b12–13). While there are a couple mentions of "noblest things" in the discussion of magnanimity, they are pretty insignificant: among things commonly honored (1123b19) and within a discussion of the vice of smallness of soul (1125a25–27). But nobility as a model aspiration or the end, as well as particular things noble, goes unmentioned. (I discount the magnanimous man's preference for beautiful [*kalon*] rather than useful possessions and the word for gentlemanliness [*kalokagathia*, 1124a4].)

I suggest this explanation. Noble actions have especially to do with particular spectacular or glorious actions, which are typically deeds of war, and they typically put one at risk. Magnanimity differs in both respects. It shows itself in more rational and comprehensive actions, and these are to result in one's superiority.

Courage always involves the possibility of the ultimate sacrifice, which seems shining and admirable (some variant of "noble" occurs sixteen times in the thematic discussion of courage). The courageous man prefers "what is noble in war" above "the greatest goods," including life itself. This disparity between noble actions and the good is aggravated for the superior man, since the more nearly he has all virtue and is happier, "the more painful death will be" (1117b9–15). Magnanimity, on the other hand, involves great goods for oneself.

Also, magnanimity is more involved with a complete human good. Courage shows itself especially in particular deeds and in battle; magnanimity, in achievements involving a more comprehensive prudence. A noble charge on the enemy is one thing; comprehensive generalship, another. The spirited young Washington was eager for the field, famously daring, appallingly endangered, famously lucky in not being hit by the bullets whistling around. But as commander in chief, Washington would have been criminally foolish as well as rash to risk his neck with the abandon of a young officer. While General Washington risked his neck at Monmouth, Trenton, and Princeton, and on a white charger, he did so only because his intervention alone prevented defeats catastrophic to his army and the patriot cause. More generally, the nobility of particular actions is conditioned by the larger whole, the policy and regime of which they are part. While the noblest death may be dying in battle, at least according to "the honors given in cities and by kings" (1115a31–32), the courage of Nazi soldiers evokes a mixed response; it is affected by what they fought for. But the great-souled man is a standard of goodness, not of sacrifice for law or ruler. If less a tragic spectacle, he is more serious in his task, more an end in himself, and more to be honored for himself rather than for a particular action or service.[20]

Still, if glory or nobility of action is not the prize to be sought by the great-souled, it is not clear that honor should be an adequate prize. Does not concern for the esteem of others make one other-directed and conformist, rather than independent and serious? Whatever the truth in this objection, it misses the fact that the honor in question is a tribute to some accomplishment or strength. It marks someone independent in judgment and in strength, not subordinate to a social process. The objection confuses honor with certain familiar nonequivalents such as prestige, charisma, and celebrity or even with social approval, public opinion, and majority values. But honor in Aristotle's sense is not won by imposing on people, as are prestige, charisma, and celebrity. Nor does honoring someone amount to mere approval, preference, or validation by some powerful group. It is obtained as a man's due by people looking up to him, not by people emotionally swept away by him. True honor is paid by serious judges, not by some power whether wise or foolish, and is a tribute to something that a man knows or believes he is, not itself a defining validation or recognition.

Yet there is some truth in this objection, according to Aristotle himself. Honor seems too superficial to be the human aim, since it depends on others and is sought less for its own sake than as confirmation of one's virtue (1095b22–30). Still, honor thus responds to a wish to excel. The great man himself may hold honor so secondary to concern for his virtue that he can regard it as nothing, but he looks, nevertheless, if not to any judge, then at least to serious judges. Thus he not only looks up to a kind of thought—honor—as his prize, but he also looks to judges who are thoughtful. I must add here that Aristotle finally guides his own account by the especially thoughtful. His authority is finally not common sense or common moral opinion but those who examine the virtues (1123b33–34). Whatever one is to make of such important qualifications, Aristotle never loses sight of the obvious fact that outstanding men seek the offices that allow them to shine as well as to perform.

If a man must be knowing as to his worth for great honors, and serious honor is what he seeks, it remains to inquire, third, as to what makes him worthy. Here Aristotle is clear and emphatic. Virtue is the measure of worth. "The great-souled man in the true sense" must be "good" (1123b29). No more "seemings." "Honor is the prize of virtue," period (1123b35). The true way of life is of the true character. If the thematic discussion of courage mentions the noble sixteen times, it never mentions the word "true." If the thematic discussion of magnanimity rarely mentions the noble, it mentions six times the true or truthful. True virtue is the measure of a man. Politics and fighting for a polity are demoted. The true crown is within.

No greatness without goodness, then, and the goodness must be comprehensive. A person great-souled "in the true sense" must be great in all of the virtues (1123b29–30). He must be great in courage, justice, and wit, for example, but also in such other virtues as temperance, generosity, and candor. He is distinctively great in claiming superior opportunities to put his virtue on stage and in action. Greatness and goodness culminate in a ruler who is a model for human striving, the gentleman-statesman. It is "difficult" to be "truly great-souled without complete gentlemanliness" (*kalokagathia*; 1124a4–5). If anyone is worthy of honor it "must" be the "best man," for the better "is always worthy of more," and it "is necessary" for a man great-souled "in the true sense" to be good in every respect (1123b28–29).

Now this turn to virtue, to true greatness, is marked by a new prominence for the knowing examiner of these topics. Here we find inferences, not observations. Anyone "who examines" each of the virtues would find it "completely ridiculous" that a man lacking any virtue is nevertheless worthy of the greatest honor (1123b33–34). Is then the truly correct attitude to be supplied by a knower? Not quite, for the big point is obvious rather than in need of inquiry. A Washington who cheated at cards would not be the great Washington we admire. And yet, the matter is not so simple. Other and conflicting goods appeal to such a man, including rule by himself. Is it that the philosopher confirms for the decent man the priority of his decency? The decent man lacks sufficient reason for his choice. He only "opines truly" as to his worth (1124b6). Perhaps the philosopher's reasoning is designed to strengthen such men in their virtue, in light of the temptations of wealth and power. Or is there a more substantive contribution? I will return to the relation between the great man's virtue and the knower on whom he is to a degree dependent.

Whatever its underpinnings, the effect of virtue's priority is to reduce the great man's dependence on honor as well as on wealth and power. Since no honor could be adequate to "complete virtue," the great-souled man is measured (*metrios*) even as to honors that are great and from the serious man (1124a6–7, 28–29). The reduction goes far. "Nothing is great to him" (1124a15), and the phrase is repeated. This assertion seems doubly paradoxical, since the great-souled man holds honor to be "the greatest thing" (1123b16, 20), and he is also aware of the greatness of his soul and deserts. The explanation, I believe, is this: greatness of honor or even of character is subordinated to spotless character, that is, to true virtue. Better that a man be truly honorable than that he be greatly honorable. The light shone on the priority of true virtue and a true sense of one's worth raises a doubt about the importance of the desire for superiority and honors. There seems to be a grave tension in such a soul, between being serious about what one does and being great and honored for it. Consider the very tense soul of a great man, T. E. Lawrence (Lawrence of Arabia). "There was a craving to be famous; and a horror of being known to like being known," he confessed in his masterwork, and the result was extreme: "Contempt for my passion for distinction made me refuse every offered honour."[21]

To summarize: in his developing description Aristotle moderates the great man's desire for superiority, even as the discussion remains (equivocally) within such a man's horizon. The great man is directed above the seeking of honor and also above intolerance of dishonor. Imputations or slights "will not justly apply to him," since he does nothing truly dishonorable (1124a11–12). Unlike Alcibiades, Achilles, and Ajax, the examples in the *Posterior Analytics*, he need not be driven, by an inability to tolerate dishonor, to war, wrath, or suicide (97b19–20). Precisely in this context Aristotle reminds us that honor is but an "external good"(1123b20–21). He reminds us, that is, of the philosophers' classification of book 1 and of his own depreciation there of honor. While honor is the aim of political men, it is too superficial to be the true human end. It is sought to assure us of our goodness or virtue (1095b23–24, 26–29). Looking to a wise depreciation of honor, encouraging the great man in his virtue, Aristotle makes him less dependent on others and less dependent also on riches, power, and "every sort of good fortune and bad fortune"(1124a14). Knowledge of his virtue helps uphold the great man amidst changing fortune. Unlike Machiavelli's great man, his measure is not ambitious mastery of fortune, but living well amidst fortune's gifts and trials.

It is after this purification of grand ambition that Aristotle sharply separates true pride from the all-too-common arrogance of the privileged. "In truth," "rightly," "justly," only the good should be honored (1124a5). The others exhibit insolent disdain without internal measure. The context is politically crucial, bearing as it does on relations among the few and between the few and the many. The great-souled man is like the philosopher in this: he is distinct from both the usual few and the usual many. From heights of inner virtue the great-souled man looks down on others "justly (for he opines truly), while the many are disdainful at random" (1124b5–6).

Still, the full picture contains more shadows. Aristotle's full portrayal shows a man not so superior to fortune, and especially to honor and to slights, as this part of his outlook seems to demand. The great-souled man *is* concerned with honor ("and dishonors") (1123b21–22, 1124a4–5, 12–13). Birth, wealth, and power *do* contribute to greatness of soul. The attention to virtue must be blurred with such a man's natural or necessary concerns. While "in truth only virtue should be honored," Aristotle says in his own name, "someone to whom both belong," goods of fortune as well as virtue, "is more worthy of honor" (1124a25–27). Aristotle's clarifications cannot depart either from the moral-political medium, including the wealth and power that enable such a man to live without much dependence, or from the powerful passion that virtue is to moderate.

OTHERS, FORTUNE, AND THE PASSION FOR SUPERIORITY

The second part of Aristotle's little discourse on magnanimity lists nearly twenty separate attitudes involving the relation between the desire for honorable superiority and various necessities. We get a catalogue of distinct observations without much visible order, although some are linked by conjunction and others by groupings about a tendency, say, to be superior by bestowing rather than receiving. What can one make of this?

Ethics as clarified moral opinion comes to its first peak with these particular opinions of the magnanimous man. Whatever the reach of moral generalities, remarks as to particulars are more truthful (1107a29–31), and the maxim applies to the great-souled man. This catalogue is unparalleled in the *Ethics:* no account of another virtue contains such a list. (While the discussion of courage lists five resemblances to true courage, these are not parts of the true disposition.) These attitudes, along with the later discussion of justice, show crucially the problem of reconciling truth in living with superior practical life. Magnanimity is not partial, like courage, or subordinate, like temperance, or about secondary things, like generosity, or instrumental for society with others, like friendliness, wittiness, and aspects of justice.

Since complete goodness requires greatness, an attitude of almost godlike superiority pervades these particular attitudes. It overshadows similar conduct seen from the point of view of other particular virtues (1124b18–31, 1125a11–12). What might appear as noble sacrifice to the courageous man, for example, the great man appraises in terms of risks to himself. Avoiding small risks, he reserves himself for great ones, since life is not worth living at any cost (1124b6–9). He weighs the greatness of the actions in light of his own worth. Similar variations exist as to gentleness, candor, friendliness, generosity, and, of course, love of honor and justice. The great-souled man does not bear grudges: he is above feeling dishonored since he knows he is above the dishonorable. He is more than honest in speaking of himself, and he is only qualifiedly friendly in his general demeanor. For he is haughty with his equals in prominence or worth, must be open in love and hate, and must speak and act openly, since he prefers the truth to mere opinion, shuns timidity, and despises other men. His special attitude toward property is not about giving to others: he would own things beautiful and useless rather than useful and profitable, since they show better his self-sufficiency (*autarchia*, 1125a11–12). But it is also true that we see the (somewhat ridiculous) relation of his godlike pride to our quite ungodlike body: the great-souled man moves slowly, has a deep voice, and speaks steadily, "since one who takes few things seriously is not anxious, and one who thinks nothing great is not intense" (1125a12–15).

As to the crucial object, honor, he reserves himself for things great and notable. This goes so far as to condition his justice (in the usual political sense). Not only will he not compete for the (usual) things esteemed or where others take first place, he is idle and slow in engaging in actions except for the few actions that involve "a great honor or work," which are, that is, "great" and give "great repute." He does not put his shoulder to any ordinary wheel, especially if he must take a secondary role. Neither is he eager for reciprocity: Aristotle says twice that while the great-souled man does not ask for assistance from others (or asks only reluctantly), he assists others eagerly. He would benefit others but "is ashamed to receive," and if he receives he would return a greater benefit, since benefiting "belongs to one who is superior," receiving, to one "who has someone superior to him" (1124b9–15). As to ordinary necessities, such a man "never" would ask for help, or "only reluctantly," or, at least, not "in small matters."

As to matters of truth, he disdains the common judgments about himself or others; he is no gossip. Above all, he cannot defer to others in what he feels, thinks, or does. "It is necessary" (in this discussion the only express instance of necessity as controlling) that he be open in loving and hating and in speaking, since he prefers truth to what others opine and would not be timid in expressing himself (1124b26). In his way, if not the philosophers' way, he is moved to truth and by truth. His way is with others. To repeat the summary aphorism: the great-souled man is unable to suit his living to others (lit. toward others he is without power to live), except for a friend (1124b31–1125a1).

This pride, then, tends toward solitariness out of superiority (except for friends). Such a person is at once above those below and aloof from those who might think themselves equals. Contemptuous of others, he will not bully the weak, since that is too easy. But he is "great" with those prominent (*axiomati*, 1124b19), since that is difficult and worthy of his superiority. He is then aloof from much. The list mostly details what the great-souled man will *not* do. He is not inclined to small risks and will not be beholden to others. He is not concerned enough with others' judgments to bear grudges for harms to himself, or to complain about small troubles, or to worry about others' flaws or his own merits—except to insult his enemies.

Such a man is then austere as well as proud and solitary. His pride is august. There is little here about deeds that shine, that are a noble spectacle. He himself is not prone to admiration (or wonder: he is not a *thaumastikos*, 1125a2–3). He is then august (*semnos*; 1124b21), a word, with connotations of the sacred, that occurs here and more prominently in the parallel discussion in the *Eudemian Ethics* (1232a25–31). Such a man could seem to himself suprahuman. Is this why Zeus is one of only two examples of magnanimity in the *Ethics'* thematic discussion? One is reminded of Shakespeare's Julius Caesar: "But I am constant as the Northern Star, of whose true-fixed and resting quality, There is no fellow in the firmament" (III, i, 60–62).

Still, the Aristotelian portrayal is not of some figure simply solitary or simply above human affairs, any more than is the strained Caesar of Shakespeare's play. Apart from concern for a friend, which Caesar had, such a man seeks the greatest honors from men, as Caesar did, and he would benefit others, as Caesar would. While he reserves himself, he also gives himself for great honors and notable deeds. Besides, his virtues include justice (he is a gentleman and part of his country), which is questionable as to Caesar, and he will ask for help in event of great necessities.

Above all, the great-souled man is driven to others by a need to show his superiority over them. This is not some simple domination. Such a man needs especially to show his superior goodness. He would benefit others (*eu pioein:* be a cause of good) and not receive benefits (1124b9). For this instance Aristotle supplies the cause: because the former makes him superior (*huperechon*, lit. rise above), the latter, inferior (1124b10). Benefiting others makes him superior in virtue, and on this the great-souled man insists. If benefited, accordingly, he returns a greater benefit and thus leaves the erstwhile benefactor owing something as the one who gained. The virtue greatness of soul, then, seems above justice. It is more generous of soul, as are the virtues liberality and magnificence (as well as friendship).

But such greatness is also in conflict with justice, at least justice to fellow citizens of similar pride. While giving more in some ways, the great-souled man takes more of what is primary to him. He obtains superiority in being grand and independent, that is, as a benefactor rather than a dependent. Not from magnanimity, but only from noble friendship, will he give up the opportunity for noble deeds or for honor and office (1169a30–1169b1, 1124b31–1125a1, cf. 1162b11–13, 1167b33–1168a12).

This sense of himself as grand and independent proves to be in conflict with truthfulness as well as justice. Such a man remembers the good he has done for others, we are told, but he forgets the benefits he has received from others. Aristotle repeats the cause: the recipient is the inferior, and the great man would rise above the other (*huperechein*). He is pleased to "hear about" benefits he has given; he is displeased to hear about those he has received. This very important literary turn to distorted judgment is marked by a mention of pleasure and, tacitly, pain.

These and graver dangers are indicated by Aristotle's singular examples: Zeus and the Athenian empire.

Why are these two the only examples of magnanimity in the *Ethics*' discussion? Admittedly, one must speculate. The context is a certain distorted awareness that accompanies greatness of soul. The great-souled forget their dependence and, like Shakespeare's Caesar, incline to imagine themselves gods. Or, acknowledging *their* dependence, they (like Plato's Alcibiades) imagine truly omnipotent gods. A godlike kingship is one approximation of such longing. But such a culmination is impossible, if only because of the recalcitrance of others. The others must be compelled to be inferior. This leads toward kingship and also toward empire. Perhaps it leads less to kingship as such and more to republican or democratic empire. Such a man would benefit men, not tyrannize them, and voluntary followers are better than compelled followers.

Empire comes almost naturally to such a man. This Aristotle explains in book 7 of the *Politics*, near the end of his development of moral and political science. If the life of great action is best, "one might conceive that having authority over all is best, for in this one would have authority over the greatest number and noblest of actions" (1325a34–36). That concludes Aristotle's sober reconsideration of the best that politics has to offer. It is probably borne out by experience. Churchill and de Gaulle, for example, were imperialists, although held back by the decline of their countries. Jefferson sought "an empire of liberty," and Washington, who would protect lands for Indians and incorporate them decently if possible, was fundamentally a patron of American expansion to the west.

The example concerning Zeus involves the figure absent from Aristotle's account and yet surely in his mind: the wrathful Homeric hero Achilles, himself a kind of god to the Greeks. In Homer's *Iliad* the goddess Thetis pleads to Zeus on behalf of her son Achilles. King Agamemnon had taken Achilles' "meed of honor," the prize girl Briseis, and then taunted him: thus you "might well know how much greater I am than thou" (*Iliad*, I, 184–86). Achilles, "honored not at all as the best of the Achaians," had vowed in return the destruction of them all (I, 414). Zeus, king of the gods, had been set against Achilles at the behest of his wife, Hera. Thetis seeks to turn him around. From Aristotle's very quiet presentation we can infer, I think, a lesson in theology as well as in the moral equanimity he obviously fosters. One will not moderate *hubris* and wrath by invoking the Olympian gods, if only because they exemplify jealousy and the passion for superiority. Consider the contrast with Shakespeare's Caesar, who compared his constancy not to some personal god but to the northern star. Aristotle had moved in this direction. While the *Ethics* eventually subordinates practical concerns to wisdom about a horizon of "things far more divine in their nature than man," these are the things of "the cosmos" (1141a34–1141b2; cf.1141a 20–22). This philosopher, like Plato in the second *Alcibiades*, theologizes so as to encourage urbane judgment and to allay the lurking passions for godlike superiority and revenge.

The great-souled man is above all "not capable of leading his life to suit anyone else." Note the negative. His desire for superiority culminates less in the desire to rule than in a more negative impulse: to keep from being ruled by anyone else. Among the particulars, to repeat, negatives predominate.

We are led to a significant conclusion. The great-souled man inclines less to be free to rule than to be free from others' rule. Disdainful of the usual objects of human striving, despising other human beings, he is nevertheless pained "to be dishonored and ruled by someone unworthy" (*Eudemian Ethics* 1232b12–13). The great-souled man is less drawn to people than impelled above people, except for his concerns to benefit them and to avoid subordination to them. He is a lover of honor but moved more to be intolerant of the dishonor that means subordination to his inferiors. He is impelled to be at a distance above if only to *avoid* sullying his superiority. Whom should he admire if "nothing is great to him"?

Aristotle's diagnosis comes to this: the great-souled man is at once drawn above humanity and drawn to humanity. He exhibits his superiority by aiding his fellows, and yet his wish is less to aid them than to avoid being or appearing dependent on them. He would in his virtue be independent of them, and yet he depends upon them for distinguishing himself. The list of particular attitudes complements Aristotle's first and general account, in which honor is at once the greatest thing to such a man—and almost nothing to him. Neither benefits to others, nor praise from others, is an adequate expression of the great-souled man's superiority, even in his own eyes. What then is?

Great Man as Just Statesman

Despite all I have just suggested, Aristotle in his *Ethics* surely shows a path toward political satisfaction, a path moral as well as political. For the great man is inclined to politics not only by his desire for honor but also by other virtues, especially justice. Book 5 on justice is five times as long as the few pages on greatness of soul. Also, Aristotle elsewhere shows political opportunities above the usual politics, opportunities as the indispensable man, whether as saving general (Brasidas, 1134b23–24) or as founding lawgiver (Solon, 1141b24–26, *Politics* 1296b18–21). Still, the full account shows certain limits to even such extraordinary accomplishments, and it shows most the ordinary situation in which the great man is both a danger and endangered.

With book 5 on justice we seem finally to arrive at the locus of the "great things," "great deeds," and "great honors" hitherto left notably undefined. This is consistent with a certain political direction that appeared in accounts of other moral virtues. Courage at its peak deals with the battlefield, and magnificence expresses itself principally in contributions to one's country's defense, theater, and worship. Among the virtues discussed after magnanimity, politics becomes thematic. Ambition, the lesser form of honor seeking, is given more stature. It involves "moderate" (*metrios*) as well as "small" honors (1125b5), contrary to what had been said before (1107b27–1108a4), and concerns "noble" causes (1125b11–13), which had not been said before. What serves the community obtains a new priority. Contrary to a common opinion, "gentleness" is the mean with respect to anger, for the gentler respond to reason better and the "harsh-tempered" are "worse to live with" (1126a2–3, 31) as well as more common. Then Aristotle brings on stage the social virtues of friendliness, candor, and wittiness with one's fellows. The Aristotelian gentleman is urbane and political, not an isolated and rural warrior like Achilles.

This political moderation of the pride and solitariness of the great-souled man culminates in the treatment of justice, a second and perhaps superior peak. The obvious form of justice is the law, and Aristotle proceeds to eulogize law as the most authoritative and comprehensive of moral-political phenomena. Since law can prescribe the actions of all the virtues, not merely this one or that, it is then perfect virtue, albeit as displayed to others. It seems the greatest (*kratiste*, lit. strongest, 1129b27–28), most enlightened, and most comprehensive of virtues. Neither evening star nor morning star is so wondrous, as the poet puts it; justice sheds light on all actions. We get further testimony from a proverb and from one of the ancient sages (1129b25–33). Ushered along by revered poets, maxims, and wise men, the superior man is led toward government according to law as *the* superior activity worthy of his striving. The gentleman-statesman who defends, upholds, and in general benefits his country—that is the obvious legacy of this mixture of sober respect for law with honorable superiority.

Which is not to say that this impression of perfect harmony is Aristotle's last word. Despite the simple and inspiring first directions, book 5 of the *Ethics* also shows the downside of both justice and politics, especially for the great-souled man. While Aristotle surely fosters patriotic statesmanship, he also moderates political zeal. He moderates the outstanding political man's hopes for politics in light of the limitations inherent in politics. A certain philosophical outlook complements politically his magnanimous man's equableness in good and bad fortune.

To begin with, there is the problem of the quality of law. Aristotle indicates that it may or may not guide rightly, or aim at the common good, or at that of a ruling class selected for "virtue." Actions generally just are "mostly" those prescribed by law. Besides, the law prescribes actions good for "others" and the common good, not for one's own (1129b14–18, 24–26, 1130a3–5, 1130b23–24). Such questioning, gently put, leads Aristotle to question quietly but radically the apparent premise of the whole *Ethics*, that it is a political subject in a sense (1094b11). "Whether the education of each that makes a man simply good is the business of politics or another (study), will be determined later" (1130b26–28). The political good may not be so good.

Besides, Aristotle calls attention to problems in all law, apart from the quality of the lawmaker. True justice involves a fair disposition of soul—"is he honest?" But the law prescribes actions, not motives, and many obey the law only from fear of punishment, not from a just motive. As the chapter proceeds, skepticism mounts. "Justice in the primary sense" differs from "legal justice," and indeed "the actions prescribed by law are only accidentally just actions" (1136b34–35, 1137a11–12).

In addition, law and politics must in good part attend to rather pedestrian things, that is, to trade, retribution, and security. These considerations come to sight when Aristotle turns from justice as law, which prescribes all virtues, to the particular virtue justice, that is, the fairness involved in taking and distributing no more than a fair share. That involves both distribution of community goods such as honor, rule, and wealth, "distributive" justice, and the putting right of private transactions, which Aristotle calls "corrective" justice.

It is significant that the treatment of distributive justice, the more political and grand kind of justice, is very brief. Think of the importance of honors and offices to the great-souled man. While distribution should be according to desert (or worth: *axia*), judgments of desert differ among the leading political classes. Democrats hold that freedom is the measure of desert; oligarchs, wealth or perhaps good birth; upholders of aristocracy, virtue. That is all Aristotle says. Having set forth the (inevitable) variety of claims to rule, he says nothing special as to the superior claim of virtue. He puts even this bit, moreover, in one long sentence. It is a sentence in turn submerged in an interminable account of arithmetical and geometrical proportions for calculating what is fair, whatever the prevailing principle of worth or desert. There is the point, I suspect. In so tolerating the prevailing principle of distribution, whichever it may be, Aristotle does his part for the rule of law and for stable regimes. He subordinates the fiery question of who rightly should get the honors and privileges. He moderates in particular the fiery resentment of the grandly ambitious at the dishonor of being ruled by their inferiors. Justice in any country is largely shared by and determined by who is in power. His topic here, he eventually acknowledges, is both justice and "political justice."

Most of book 5 is given over to corrective justice, and the discussion would tend to cool a thoughtful man's resentment at being passed over. Corrective justice is of the judge who "corrects" a transaction, whether by civil "damages" or by making the criminal "pay" for his crime. This equalizing of parties is more or less without regard to the parties' virtue or vice. But it is vital. Everyday "reciprocity" in everyday transactions is absolutely necessary in any society, for people think themselves slaves if they cannot exchange their products for a fair price or return evil for evil.

Such insistent claims to protection extend into claims to govern, and free people have power to enforce their claims. This is where Aristotle supplies his sober reminder: do not "forget" that his topic is at once justice simply and political justice. Here is a sobering limitation upon justice: between people not free and equal, politically, "justice cannot exist" except in a metaphorical sense ($1134a24-30$). This has big political consequences, not only for slaves but also for those seeking superiority. Equals are not likely to look favorably upon those who claim superiority for themselves. Besides, even where inequality is respected, those who specially contribute to wealth and security, the basic necessities, are thought the deserving ones. The great honors go especially to the great defenders, not as prize for complete virtue. In Aristotle's discussion of natural justice the sole example is Brasidas, the great Spartan warrior-general who gave the Athenians fits in their war with the Peloponnesians ($1134b33-34$). Such necessities affect who and what obtain political honor and power, and therefore the kind of virtue honored. The *Politics*, of course, does equate the best life with active governing. Yet it adds a poet's characterization: "no subtleties for me, but what the city needs" (1277a19–20). These considerations qualify Aristotle's eulogies of law and the political life. They teach in particular of the necessities that pervade selection of who rules and for what. "Justice is for others," not simply for oneself, and rule partakes of the opinions and necessities of others, whatever their quality (1130a3–4).

It follows that an extraneous reward must go to the man who does serve the public. "Some sort of compensation must therefore be given, and this is honor and reverence; those for whom such things are not sufficient become tyrants" (1134b6–8). Politically construed, honor is recompense by citizens for the leadership bestowed on their concerns. Honor and sacrifices to a Brasidas are *necessary* because political actions in themselves—just actions in themselves—will not satisfy the political man's inevitable wish for his own good.

Why this mention of "reverence" as well as honor? Whatever be the case with the ambitious, do the great-souled require some "divine" reward akin to reverence for the gods? Honor in the usual sense proves insufficient in light of the sobering bath we have been given. It originates in all-too-human opinion and is often awarded for limited achievements. We can connect some dots. Why should great men, who seek superiority like that of Zeus (one of the two examples, to repeat, in the thematic discussion of greatness of soul), be content with admiration from their inferiors? They may seek from men something like the reverence paid gods—and thus a confirmation of their status above humankind. They may want lordly stature, even the stature of tyrants.

Here, nevertheless, I insist that Aristotle's account of justice opposes the tendency he exposes. His account of justice is no exhortation to claim one's deserts in lordly superiority or to subject oneself humbly to lordly superiors. It concludes with "equity." Equity, in Aristotle's interpretation, is a correction of the law that follows the intention of the law, or at least of the lawgiver. Correction of the law, then, is subservient to the law and the lawgiver.

It is basically subservient to the existing regime. Indeed, the equitable man is also one who does not necessarily stand on his rights, but who is content upon occasion to take the smaller share (1137b12–1138a4). In treating of justice Aristotle shows a way for judicious men and statesmen to correct law without violating legal fundamentals and fundamental powers. But he also makes more reasonable a great man's disposition and expectations, especially Alcibidean expectations of power bordering on kingship and honor bordering on worship.

GREATNESS SUBORDINATED: PHILOSOPHY AND THE REGIMES

In the *Ethics* and *Politics* Aristotle encourages such sobriety in many other ways. I close with two important examples, the wary account of regimes, especially in the *Politics*, and the subordination of practical life to philosophic life, at the end of both books.

Ostracism of the outstanding has a certain "political justice." This grim conclusion, to a grim little discussion in book 3 of the *Politics*, reminds of how unwelcome in most regimes great men often are. The account ranges from the exile of the prominent, by democracies and oligarchies, to their exile or destruction, by tyrants. The rise of a Caesar or a Napoleon threatens any free country, democratic or oligarchic, and the threat is to good regimes as well as bad ones, and from outstanding figures as well as tyrannical ones. The great-souled man, who seeks a place worthy of his superiority, is not only generally unwelcome but also justly unwelcome and justly gotten rid of, at least according to a certain political justice.

It is of course true that Aristotle's account of politics is not generally so grim. At its start, indeed, it seems that man is naturally political and that the superior man is possessed of a natural claim to rule. But if politics is a partnership in advantages and in justice, then the advantages and the justice must be shared. Aristotle's account of regimes is not least an account of the claims of the poor, rich, and wellborn to share. It educates to the reasonableness of such claims—given their respective contributions of military strength, wealth, and upbringing of offspring.

This is not to say that Aristotle forgets his natural standard.
He strives for a true account of politics despite the disparity between most rulers and true virtue, truly good rule, and even truly
shared rule. Should the rule of an outstanding man be just and
possible, moreover, all should obey such a man, not in turn but
simply (1284b25–34, 1288a24–29). He should rule by himself.
But this astonishing claim, to such extraordinary rule, is beyond
politics in the usual sense, that is, beyond the partnership in
power and justice that is a political regime. It is kingship and like
unto paternal authority. Such a king rules as a father in a household, rather than by law and as an equal (1285b31–33). He is beyond the political community in which any citizen is but a part.
Instead, he is the "whole," in the sense of a completed human being, while the community is but a partial body that should subordinate itself to human completion (1288a24–29).

While Aristotle does not forget the best man's claims, he presents them very briefly and as rarely just. He presents them,
moreover, only after defending at length the more common and
political claimants to rule. There are long defenses of the multitude (especially), the law, the wealthy, the wellborn, those of ordinary political virtue. Monarchy seems rarely just, perhaps only
in barbaric countries or countries emerging from barbarism
(1284b35–1286b40). Yes, Aristotle finally reminds of the justice
(and the necessity) of great political virtue. But he backs up toward such political heights, keeping his and his reader's eyes
trained on the lower altitudes in which politics generally takes
place. The treatment of ostracism is part of Aristotle's unvision-
ary vision.

This political sobriety leads to a revised and more political account of virtue itself. Defending in book 4 the moderation
brought by a class of middling property, the *Politics* praises the decent or equable man (*epieikes*) over the great man. "If virtue is a
mean, as the *Ethics* held," then it is "necessary" that the "middle
[*meson*] life is best" (1295a35–38). One must attend not only to
the best regime in theory, according to noble speaking, but also
to a regime possible or easy to institute in practice, according to
useful speaking (1288b36–39). It is useful to advance practicable
regimes and especially a middle class that can hold a moderate

balance. This, after Aristotle reminds us of the tyranny that often arises from the strife of rich and poor. The rich and powerful themselves tend to be "arrogant and base on a grand scale"; the poor and weak, malicious and base in petty ways.

In this context of stern political likelihoods the *Politics* recommends a virtue possible for the citizen not overly strong, rich, wellborn, and the like, while not overly weak, poor, and so forth, either. Rich and poor alike tend to injustice and are opposed to sharing power. A large middle class, not needy of necessities but needing to work for them, is less inclined to factional strife. It can check and moderate the others. Such a class fits politics, at least free politics. Any community of citizens "wishes to be made up of equal and similar persons to the extent possible," and this homogeneity is most present with the middling class (1295b25–26). Equal claims and needs, an underlying force in all cities and countries, are most easily satisfied in a democratic republic. To such a regime middling virtue can come quite easily. Not high-toned aristocracies, but moderate democracies—that is Aristotle's most general recommendation. Thus one gets safe politics, if not great politics. Aristotle proves doubtful about great politics. Middle-class republics are "the safest of regimes" (1296a22–1296b2; 1302a13–15).

Near the end of the *Ethics* Aristotle had prefigured the *Politics'* elevation of a rational middle class and its depreciation of great deeds. Private persons seem to perform "decent actions . . . even more" than "powerful people" (1179a6–8). While the argument recurs to the need for politics and political science, the return comes out of necessity, not greatness or justice, and only after this elevation of private over public life. The language is of decency and law, not of nobility and justice. The language is of rational guidance. Politics seems less a stage for great actors than an instrument for breeding a certain rationality in the governed. While education should be to perfect gentlemanship (*kalokagathia*, 1179b9–11), such virtue is now presented as a means. Young people with such an outlook can better respond to "speech [*logos*] and teaching" (1179b3, cf. 1180a5–7). The argument recurs to the necessities, but now not with respect to popular claims. Force and law are necessary for dealing with "most people," the uneducable who are not moved by the "noble or the truly pleasant" and who obey only out of fear (1179b11–16). Reform of them is not possible or at least not easy. Law is thus needed to govern those who will do right only by "compulsion"; it adds compulsion to a certain thoughtfulness and intelligence. This is, however, also for the benefit of the governed. Thus and only thus can many people's lives be conducted with some intelligence and correct order (1180a18). Law imposes most upon most people, but it is also for their decent and reasonable life. The depreciation of politics, rule, and great deeds has gone far.

Indeed, now the *Ethics* tells us that moral education itself may be better done privately than publicly. In the household a judicious man's words and habits can set the tone and be suitably tailored to each person. Besides, a father's family, unlike the usual multitude, is already loving and obedient (1180b3–7). Aristotle, architect of the full political art, again educates the political man to reduced expectations from the usual politics. He also educates to the good to be done within one's private political sphere, so to speak.

In the *Politics* Aristotle supplies an even stronger (and more rational) political defense of the middle class. Being likely to "follow reason," it is the likely source of the most thoughtful political men. More than law-abidingness and decency is at stake. It is from such a class, we are now told, that Solon, Lycurgus, and most other great lawgivers come. In light of this, and of the prevalence of rich and poor, it is then of "the greatest good fortune" if those active in politics have a "middling and sufficient property" (1295b39–40). Against the grain of the usual classes, Aristotle encourages a "custom" that lawgivers favor the middle class. Thus, too, he encourages the lawgiver's planning as the greatest of deeds, more thoughtlike and less deedlike than deeds of war and of rule. It is another sobering lesson for the great of soul, a lesson in the priority of political reason as well as of political justice. True superiority and greatness are oriented not to splendid deeds but to the true political art. Let the great-souled man be a legislator like Solon, who regulated poor and rich, especially the rich, with a view to a more stable and just mixture of power. Or one could instance again Washington, whose immense efforts of war and founding were given over to the cause of "popular self-government."

I close by noting Aristotle's most striking effort to subordinate political men to reason: his subordination, in the *Ethics* and *Politics* alike, of practical deeds to a philosophic or at least cultivated life.

The *Ethics* contains a famous paradox. It conspicuously exhorts to moral virtue, in books 2–5, but it conspicuously denigrates moral and political virtue in favor of philosophy, in the concluding book 10. According to book 10, *the* defining activity is that of the intellect. From intellectual activity come true pleasure, true happiness, and even the most power. By comparison with such a "noble and divine" activity (1177a15), moral virtues afford only a "secondary" happiness. The key argument clarifies a distinction left undeveloped in book 1, that between activities good in themselves and those instrumental. Thinking for its own sake is now said to be alone loved for itself (1177b1–2). Practical actions are for something outside the actions: "power [*dunasteia*], and honors, and happiness" for oneself or one's fellow citizens (1177b13–14). Now war and politics appear not as the sphere of great things and great deeds, but as unleisured, that is, as done out of necessity rather than for their own sake.

While any life requires some attention to the necessities, the life of greatness requires excessive attention. Wealth and power are needed for "actions greater and more noble" (1178b1–3), but they distract from the contemplation that is alone loved for itself (1177b1–2). Aristotle draws a big conclusion from his big step. Even preeminently "noble and great" actions, those sought by the magnanimous man, are of less seriousness than "activity [*energeia*] of the intellect" (1177b12–24). Nevertheless, despite all these exhortations to intellectual activity and despite all the authorities and eulogies, *the* lesson here is practical. Greatness, especially great power, is overrated as the way to even a serious practical life. That is the lesson. For "self-sufficiency does not consist in excess, any more than action does, and it is possible for one who is not a ruler of land and sea to perform noble action" (1179a1–5). Here is a concluding caution for the grandly ambitious.

Such a man needs such a caution, as the *Politics* emphasizes in its culminating remarks on ordinary political life. I touched on this before. The great-souled man inclines to think that "authority over everyone is best, since one would have power over the greatest number and the noblest of deeds" (1325a34–36). But Aristotle also brings out here the special danger of this: the great man's tendency accentuates a general political tendency. Not only the great tend to excess. Any country that gets itself organized, that manages to have its "laws look to any one thing," looks especially to "domination or strength" (*kratein*, 1324b5–7). "The people" in general think "the political art" to be "despotic" (1324b32–33). Here, I suspect, the people consists of all who are not philosophic. While everyone admits some importance for virtue and the soul, these are not the priority. All seek most of all "wealth, goods, power, and a name" (1323a36–37). Justice, then, inclines to be an instrument of domination or empire. While countries "demand just government for themselves, they pay no attention to it without" (1324b35–36). The great man's bent exacerbates this almost natural tendency. This seems to confirm our earlier discussion. Aristotle had used Zeus, king of the gods, as one example of greatness of soul, and democratic Athens, the greatest empire of Greece, as the other. The great-souled seek a godlike kingship, but this, I suggested, leads perhaps toward tyranny and especially toward empire. It leads less to tyranny than to republican empire, since the great-souled man would benefit men and since republics supply voluntary followers. Now we learn that the followers are distinctly voluntary.

Precisely in this context the *Politics* questions political activity fundamentally, especially the great man's preoccupation with superiority over others. "An active life is not necessarily to be regarded as being in relation to others" (1325b16–17); imperialism is an "impediment" to the good life (1324a38). Like book 10 of the *Ethics*, book 7 of the *Politics* questions practical activity as such, not simply excessive desire for wealth, power, honor, and great deeds. Practical thinking is not alone active; indeed, it is comparatively passive. "Much more" active is that "thinking [*dianoia*] and contemplating [*theorizein*] which is for itself and complete in itself" (1325b16–21). Aristotle now calls practical actions merely "external actions." This questions the great-souled man's occupation with deeds, not alone his wish for honor. Nevertheless, the conclusion here, as in the *Ethics*, is practical. It is, however, politically radical. The true political life is a means to protect intellectual life. Political life at its best is instrumental to *the* internal activity. Even as to external actions "we speak of as authoritative [*kurios*] those who by their thought [*dianoia*] are master craftsmen or architectonic" (*architectones* 1325b21–23).

At the start of his moral-political inquiry Aristotle had called politics the most authoritative (*kuriotate*) and architectonic (*architektonike*) of the sciences and capacities (1094a26–27). Here, near the end of his inquiry, we learn its decisive end and the decisive architect. The political animal is partial compared to the rational animal. Politics is finally instrumental to the whole man in the true sense. It is instrumental to the philosopher, most obviously the political philosopher who can examine and correct the virtues and regimes. The *Politics* like the *Ethics* retains a practical bent: both encourage gentleman-statesmen. Still they also encourage them to look up to the liberal arts, as we say, and even, in a diluted way, to great books, thinkers, and philosophic legislators. Greatness of soul is to defer somewhat to greatness of mind, and that taste and tact helps keep the great-souled man limited in his ambition, for himself and for his country.

This political culmination was prepared by the developments in the *Ethics* that I have recounted. In treating of magnanimity, Aristotle had elevated virtue for its own sake and was quiet about the glories and pleasures of victory, empire, and rule. In treating of justice, he elevated law, justice, and equity and was quiet about the great man's claim to rule over others. In treating of intellectual virtue and its priority, he subordinated "politics or prudence" to wisdom (1141a20–1141b3) and the life of moral virtue and politics to the philosophic life. And yet all of this is part of a teaching that begins by holding moral virtue as primary and politics as natural and good. Aristotle's effort is a clarifying and a purifying of practical virtue, not an obliteration or replacement of it. Practically speaking, this means a fostering of seriousness, reasonable limits, law, and respect for the most thoughtful, while retaining for political life virtues that sustain both politics and a good practical life.

The end of the *Politics* gives us a summary view of the proper role of this much-moderated great-souled man as well as his proper subordination. It sketches a best regime in which he has opportunity for the deeds of rule and force that are necessary in any regime, including the best.

This is a regime shared by urbane gentleman-farmers. There is no multitude, although there is a slave population (a big injustice is needed even here). This city, like any city, must be "formidable" (1327a10) and prepared for fighting. Indeed, it may be "hegemonic," that is, with influence on its neighbors' affairs and with power to defend them as well as itself (1327b5–7). Rule and force will be also needed at home, for the regime must be defended against criminals and rebels (1329a10–12). Accordingly, Aristotle wishes a leisured citizenry spirited as well as intelligent, with a disposition "to command." He recommends gentleman-guardians with the mix of spiritedness and justice that the *Ethics* fosters: "great-souled," but, unlike the *Republic*'s guardians, not "fierce" except to wrongdoers (1328a9–15).

Nevertheless, while there is a place in this politics for commanding souls and for commanding, it is very much a subordinate and instrumental place. Aristotle begins his account of the best regime with an attack on political greatness in the usual sense, that is, on largeness, especially imperial largeness. Empire is not the measure of a good regime (1333b10–25). A city's size should suit its function (*ergon*), which is certainly not to lord it over others despotically (1326a8–13, 1333b30f). War is for peace, and business is for leisure and the noble (1333a8). Greatness of soul reappears in this context, now on the side of leisure. Pride in great accomplishments, such as the Greek triumph over the Persians, may foster the "greatness of soul and virtue" that leads to all kinds of learning. To "seek for utility everywhere" is least of all fitting for those "great-souled and free" (1338b3–4, 1341a28–31).

But leisure is not for great deeds: "reason [*logos*] and intelligence [*nous*] are the end of our nature" (1334b15–16). When Aristotle in this context lists the virtues needed for peace and leisure, it is surely significant that he does not include greatness of soul. He includes temperance, justice, and "philosophy," which is the first mentioned. What is more surprising, he does not include greatness of soul even among the virtues needed for war. These include courage and endurance or fortitude as well as, again, temperance and justice (1334a10–34). From the most rational point of view, it seems, war may be about courageous deeds and endurance, not greatness. In the best politics, in war as well as peace, the great-souled man's desire to be superior should be subordinated to law and shared rule.

At the end of the *Politics* is a famous discussion of music, which includes a remark that bears poignantly on our topic. Music, Aristotle suggests, should be taken seriously as a "pastime" as well as a mode of character education. For it affords a pleasant rest, which is to be encouraged, since "it happens that human beings rarely obtain the end" (cf. 1339b26–30). This is Aristotelian humanity from the heights. It is a humanity not least, I suspect, for the great-souled man. His soul in any political order, even a just order, is unlikely to get the superiority it cannot but crave. He is unlikely, too, to find in philosophy a satisfactory completion. These final thoughts of the *Politics*, Carnes Lord has said, present music, poetry, and other fine arts "as at once the vehicle of civic education and the central component of a kind of leisure that is essential in any decent political order precisely because it serves to moderate the claims of politics."[22]

Given the likelihood of war, the difficulties of preserving any regime, and the extreme rarity of the best regime, there will be opportunities enough for noble deeds, great things, and superiority over others. A great-souled man will have his opportunities; he will be often needed. But such a force, if a blind force, may also harm itself and those whom it would rule, including the most thoughtful. Whatever else Aristotle's *Ethics* and *Politics* may be, whatever the defects, his is surely a model effort to supply comprehensive light to the grandly ambitious and to those who depend on them.

CHAPTER THREE

Imperial Ambition in Free Politics: The Problem of Thucydides' Alcibiades

WHY ALCIBIADES?

WHAT CAN THAT QUESTIONABLE ATHENIAN Alcibiades teach us about grand ambition? To begin with, he shows it in a more unvarnished form. Alcibiades exhibits unbounded ambition, unbounded, at least, by the restraints moral and political of an Aristotelian gentleman-statesman. Then, too, Alcibiades' career is revealing as to the problems such grand ambition poses for free countries. For Xenophon's Cyrus, undermining the Persian republic is just the start; he occupied himself with acquiring an imperial monarchy. Alcibiades may exhibit a rather similar passion—he took Cyrus the great as a model, according to Plato—but he is throughout his tumultuous career one public man in the midst of many. He is never the sole or chief general or king; except for his time as advisor to a Persian satrap, he acts in and among the democratic and oligarchic republics of ancient Greece. Indeed, one big lesson of Thucydides' *History* is the inability of such republics to contain an Alcibiades. It is not merely that he was a conspicuous strategist and general in the culminating war between Athens and Sparta, the topic of the *History*. What stands out is that Alcibiades did such things for every one of the chief antagonists. The simplest sign of the political problem is the most famous. Alcibiades turned traitor to his homeland, democratic Athens, spurred on decisively its oligarchic enemy, Sparta, then aided monarchic Persia against both Athens and Sparta, all before returning to save, albeit temporarily, his homeland.[1]

Yet the question of Alcibiades' effects is not so simple. There is an inherent problem in free politics as well as in Alcibiades. While such a man wants a superiority that threatens a free order, it is also true that a free order may need his superior qualities and yet can hardly tolerate them. Athens needed Alcibiades. But it twice drove him out, each time with disastrous military consequences. The Athenian democracy could not live with Alcibiades, Plutarch said, and it could not live without him.[2] Thucydides' account shows the complications in the political flesh. He shows the indispensability of Alcibiades to Athens (and to Sparta!) on crucial political-military occasions, and also the dangers he posed to any established order and indeed to himself. That Alcibiades was an outstanding general and political strategist is true. That he became a traitor to Athens somehow fits. That he was amazingly reincarnated as Athens's political savior fits too. That he was expelled again by the Athenians, to die at the instigation of the Spartans and the contriving of the Persians (as it seems), unfortunately also fits.

One must add that Alcibiades' ambition is itself not simple. While in him the passion for superiority showed itself plain, strong, and rather unconstrained by law and convention, it was also not limited by the disciplined rationality that shows in Xenophon's Cyrus. Cyrus's discipline, we will see, made him a "cold" king. Alcibiades was not cold. While he exhibits an almost palpable drive to rule the world, a Napoleonic drive, his life exuded excesses of luxury in every way. We get a type of grand ambition less single-minded and in many ways more interesting.

By this I do not mean the nasty despotism or twisted cruelty of some Saddam Hussein or Stalin. Alcibiades seeks something warmer and more splendid than empire and domination, and he seeks it with political and military genius acknowledged by his peers and by a wide variety of writers. With all his genius, it is not at all clear Alcibiades ever wanted to be tyrant or king of Athens, for example. Alcibiades has always had admirers as well as detractors, and indeed one finds ambivalence in the best diagnoses.

Which brings me to the true advantage of Alcibiades as topic and example: the commentators he attracted. As to him and his type, one can obtain first-rate instruction. Similar human comets have often existed in the world, no doubt, but the enterprises of most must have been stillborn, lost in oblivion, or crudely recalled. But by chance, and by his exploits and qualities, the phenomenon of Alcibiades won consideration from such contemporaries as Thucydides and Plato.

This chapter surveys Thucydides' picture of the man and his

political exploits. It focuses on the exploits, on the soul seen in its public effects. The purpose is chiefly to set the stage for Plato's psychological diagnosis, which omits any explicit discussion of the deeds. Still, Thucydides has his own account of the psyche, and I attend to that too.

Why is Thucydides' account especially valuable? Suppose that Thucydides might be "the most politic historiographer that ever writ," as Thomas Hobbes once said. Suppose, too, that Alcibiades was a turning point in a war that revealed the very nature of political things, as Thucydides himself seemed to think. If these two suppositions are true, or might be true, or are even partly true, then the *History*'s account of Alcibiades' doings may be particularly revealing.[3] So competent people in most centuries since have thought. Admittedly, these suppositions of permanent relevance and Alcibiades' importance are controverted, not least by the historical scholarship of the past two centuries. Also, one has to acknowledge doubts about the text we have, especially since the *History* seems unfinished. (It concludes with the twenty-first year of the war's twenty-seven years, although Thucydides upon occasion mentions later events, including the final Athenian defeat.) Still, the scholarly skeptics characteristically focus more on dating textual passages and correcting details of this or that event than on the incisive judgments in the remarkable text we do have. ("Every single word . . . seems to imply choice and arrangement," a sober scholar has said.)[4]

Who was this figure Alcibiades, who became by himself and for himself a major player in the decisive war among the ancient Greeks, who won the serious attention of Socrates, Xenophon, and Aristophanes as well as Plato and Thucydides, and who plays such an extensive role in Thucydides' narrative? Alcibiades, born about 450 BC and killed in 404, lived during the peak both of Athenian power and of Greek philosophy and comedy. He himself was prominent from birth, so to speak. Born to a distinguished aristocratic family, he later was ward of Pericles, the most powerful man in Athens and in Greece, after his father died in battle. Alcibiades soon stood out by himself. He was known from his youth for beauty, spectacular hubris in appearance and in deed, and immense and precocious hunger for enterprise and glory. He enters Thucydides' account rather young (about thirty), with the war half done (thirteen–fourteen years thus far), and immediately excites to actions that decisively affect the second half. First, he rouses up for Athens a democratic alliance among Sparta's neighbors in the Peloponnesus (419–418) and thereby manipulates an end to the armistice of 421 called, after his rival, the peace of Nicias. Three years later Alcibiades, as much as anyone, spurs on the Sicilian expedition (415). But within the year he flees Sicily and Athens, under threat of a rigged trial for impiety, and fatefully turns to aid Athens's deadly enemy, Sparta. His contribution to Sparta's eventual victory was considerable. He more than anyone prods that sluggish city to three of the four crucial measures: pricking up Syracuse to defeat the Sicilian expedition (6.88.10, 6.90–93; 415–414); fortifying Deceleia, which "debarred" Athens from her territory in Attica and obstructed transshipment of supplies from her empire (6.91.7, 7.18.1, 7.19.1, 7.27.3–5, 7.28.1–2, 8.95.2; 414–413); and prosecuting a naval attack on the empire in Ionia, across the Aegean (8.11–14, 8.26). Besides, the Ionian enterprise may have given rise to the fourth measure: in this context Thucydides introduces the Spartan alliance with Persia (8.26.6). Forced to flee monarchic and oligarchic Sparta three years later (412), Alcibiades manipulated his influence with his new Persian master, an influence "in all matters," to check Sparta and win his own restoration to Athens (8.45–47).[5]

Count up the effects. Alcibiades was in turn a cutting edge of Athenian empire, the sharp brain (and one key agent) behind the demise of the empire, and then, as Thucydides intimates and Xenophon's *Hellenica* details, reviver of the Athens that his efforts had helped bring down. Some genius; some versatility. Indeed, he was an equal opportunity manipulator within Athens itself. While he comes to sight as a Theodore Roosevelt, the outsized aristocrat as democratic leader, he turns to a cabal of plotting oligarchs to obtain his recall (8.47.2) before turning, as they became suspicious, to seduce the democratic army and navy (8.81–82, 8.108). If we follow out the story as related by Xenophon and Plutarch, Alcibiades was welcomed home euphorically as virtually a god, and by his generalship he soon and single-handedly revived Athens's military fortunes "everywhere." Then the democratic assembly again took away command, again for no good reason, and forbade him to return.[6] With successors came disaster. Mistakes led quickly and directly to loss of virtually the whole Athenian navy, to the end of Athenian freedom as well as empire, and then to a despotic oligarchy imposed by Sparta. It was a catastrophic defeat (Aegospotami, 405), and it came in the teeth of explicit and voluntary warnings from Alcibiades, despite his exile.

A kind of political genius, yes—but an evil genius, as he has been called? Should one seek instruction from a character so opportunistic, who was self-centered from the start and who seems the cause more of troubles than cures? Alcibiades has always seemed to many a firebrand for disastrous foreign wars and a traitor to all the great parties involved, especially to his democratic homeland. He led the Athenians in restarting the war with Sparta that eventually proved catastrophic. He pressed the disastrous Sicilian expedition that violated Pericles' famous warning to avoid "schemes of fresh conquest" while the Spartan war continued (1.144.1; cf. 6.10.5). He betrayed in turn democratic Athens, oligarchic Sparta, and even the Persian monarch and satrap as well as the few and the many of Athens itself.

Nevertheless, these are not reasons to avert the eyes. Even if Alcibiades was nothing but trouble, he illuminates the potential trouble caused in free politics by such an ambition. That's a useful lesson, especially for those who reserve their worries for states and state systems, irrespective of who is in charge, or who hope for peace and the rule of law from a liberated, transformed, and democratic humanity.

Besides, Alcibiades was not merely trouble. If Thucydides is right, there is a case for Alcibiades, even as perhaps the outstanding general and political intellect of the war. Of the other leading candidates, Pericles died two and one half years into the war, while Demosthenes of Athens, Hermocrates the Syracusan, and Brasidas the Spartan had more limited or subordinate roles. (Thucydides' account does not extend to the brilliant Spartan Lysander, who won the war for Sparta.) Alcibiades stands out at least in this: he was indispensable to both Athens and Sparta. He thus affords useful lessons in leadership and in the occasional dependence of free states upon rare and unconventional figures.

In addition to such general considerations, there is a case, too, for his particular policies. It is true that Alcibiades, in breaking the armistice of 421, broke the fifty years' peace, but it is truer to say he broke a pretend peace. It was a "treacherous armistice," according to Thucydides himself. The war had in fact continued (5.26.1–3). If so, then Alcibiades sheds light, not darkness, on the true situation. If so, then the Argive alliance, which undermined the enemy Sparta in its homeland, shows enlightened vigor, not blind ambition. Argos, long fearful of Sparta, had already been challenging its hegemony in the Peloponnesus (5.28). It was Alcibiades who revealed that the Argives' retreat toward reconciliation rested on a mistaken supposition of Athenian friendliness toward Sparta (5.40, 5.44.1). He awakened Argos, as well as Athens, to its true situation.

As to the great Sicilian expedition of 415, Alcibiades pressed a project that the restless daring of Athens had long envisioned, repeatedly scouted, already attempted, and already determined to attempt again (6.1.1, 6.8.2; cf. 3.46, 3.86, 3.88, 3.115.1, 4.1, 4.65.3, 5.4). Nine years before, in a flush of confidence after Demosthenes' victory at Pylos, the Athenians had punished returning generals who had failed to subdue Sicily (4.65). Might the incoherence have been in Pericles' policy, to graft restraint onto the democratic imperialism he fostered (1.144.1)?[7]

Still, some say that Alcibiades should have tried to stop the people's impulse. One must agree at least in part. He certainly should have taken the trouble to estimate accurately Sicily's strength and the difficulty of an invasion (cf. 6.46 and especially 6.55.1–2). He did not, despite Nicias's truer estimates, and the Athenians paid dearly for such complacent miscalculations (6.46, 6.55.1–2). One sees in miniature a certain Alcibidean intellectual laziness, on which Plato's *Alcibiades I* focuses.

Nevertheless, Alcibiades has an argument against the broad policy of caution, Nicias's policy, which might have been Pericles' policy. Only an active policy will protect the empire, fit the Athenians' restless imperialism, and keep Athens from "wearing

herself out upon herself" through softness and internal strife
(6.18).[8] Caution is almost incompatible with democratic Athens.
More to the point, Alcibiades was probably right on the particular point at issue: the Athenians could have won or at least not lost
disastrously. It is generally agreed that the expedition might well
have succeeded had Alcibiades, rather than the excruciatingly
slow and fearful Nicias, remained as initiating general. With Alcibiades in Sicily there had been quick enterprises of outreach
and then of force and fraud, which won at least a starting point
for the newly arrived allied forces (6.51). At the least, as he had
said, the force under him could return if it could not conquer.
When Demosthenes arrived on the spot in Sicily and came to
think the Athenians could not conquer, he twice counseled return. Nicias refused until it was too late (7.44.4; 7.47, 48.1).

Such particular considerations explain Thucydides' famous,
if qualified, exculpation. He blames not Alcibiades but "the people" (*hoi polloi*), who failed to support the expedition and who
committed "affairs to other hands." Before long, they had ruined
the city (6.15.4, 6.53.2–3; cf. 6.54–59, 6.61.6). Thucydides never
blames Alcibiades' generalship, of this or any expedition. On the
contrary, "his conduct of the war was most excellent" (or "most
powerful": *kratistos*). Indeed, Thucydides never blames Alcibiades' public actions, despite all of the maneuverings and treason-
able changes of sides. But his praise is nevertheless ambiguous.
He does blame the private "license" and "ambition"—for alarm-
ing the Athenians (6.15.4).

Still, given the similarity between Athens's hunger for territory and Alcibiades', one might well wonder whether his ambition is the anomaly his critics assert. Is Alcibiades rather a dis-
tilled expression of the dominant motive of Athens itself? Might
Alcibiades be democratic Athens in microcosm, at the peak of its
power and ambition, at what Steven Forde calls its "Alcibidean
moment"?[9] "Least of all men do the Athenians enjoy what they
have, because they are always seeking more." Admittedly, these
words are the Corinthians', inducing the sluggish Spartans to
prepare for war long before Alcibiades arrived on the scene. But
they seem telling and true. Unlike the Spartans, the Athenians
embrace "innovation," are "daring," "venturesome," "sanguine,"

and "bold"; they "regard untroubled peace as a far greater ca-
lamity than laborious activity" (1.70). Alcibiades' continual striving for more glory and rule, his daring innovations in politics and
war, could seem a culmination of Athens's own imperial striving.
But his case then brings out the dark side of free and enterprising
politics more generally: the risks, the injustice, and even, I will
suggest, the dangerous incoherence. Alcibiades seems a superior
illustration of a political paradox: the indispensability in free politics of a kind of man who unsettles free politics. He exhibits an
imperial tendency within free politics that itself threatens free
politics.

The strife was within the man as well as in his politics. There
had to be an uncivil war between Alcibiades' boundless political
hopes and his disillusionments with a homeland that both celebrated him and exiled him, that could not live without him but
would not live with him. We will see Plato's Socrates make an attempt to lance the boil, the attempt in the two *Alcibiades*. Socrates
would turn Alcibiades away from politics, thus to moderate both
the immense hopes and the awful furies that their frustration
provokes. But any success in turning Alcibiades from politics
could be only around the edges, as Socrates came to know (if he
did not know from the beginning). Thucydides shows us this political man in his chosen arena, although he also shows that no
political arena can fully hold or sustain him.

AMBITION

It is surprising that Thucydides never blames Alcibiades' public
counsel. Still, his reservation is important. The lawlessness and
bodily indulgence in private life, and the vast ambition and the
corresponding designs that the people (*hoi polloi*) could see in
every intrigue—these made them fear tyranny. The political mistake may have been theirs, in putting public affairs in other
hands, such as those of Nicias. Yet the variety of excesses in love
and life, and especially Alcibiades' spectacular ambition, made
their mistake politically inevitable (2.65.11–13, 6.15.1–4).

In clarifying this kind of ambition it helps to set it off from
some contemporary likenesses. Alcibiades loves distinction and

glory. His ambition is certainly not a colorless force, or cool interest, or mere calculated maximization of utility. Neither is his striving caught by the theoretical formulations behind these familiar notions, such as Hobbes's cold passion for power or even Machiavelli's cool seeking of a calculated reputation for the sake of domination and man-made immortality. It is certainly not a desire for mere "recognition" or "dignity" as a person, or the civil servant's anonymous pride in duty fulfilled or a job well done. It is less like these somewhat derivative and semitheoretical modern doctrines, and more like the familiar everyday desire of the politically ambitious for office and reputation. Yet Alcibiades' ambition is, of course, not for everyday honors. He is voracious for spectacular glory and superiority, and voracious too for grand accomplishment. This is not mere vanity or charisma, either. It is not vanity because Alcibiades looks for deeds in war and politics of which he proves capable, and it is not charisma because he announces his superiority frankly while knowingly giving offence. "It is not unjust," he says to a democratic assembly, "that one who has a high opinion of himself should not be on an equality with others" (6.16.4). In short, Alcibiades desires superiority over others, not equal dignity, and honor above others, not mere power. But he desires genuine superiority of worth, not pretend capacity or a merely emotional tie, and he would have a warm and splendid glory, not mere honor or reputation. Alcibiades' glory seeking is not that of the self-interested individual (in the modern enlightened sense), if only because he is "a lover of my city" and wishes most to shine over it and through it (6.92.2–3). This is not pretense. In Sparta he seeks to win Athens over and back (6.92.4), and in Persia he intrigues to restore himself at Athens (8.47.1–2). Alcibiades' ambition is a love for the good opinion of others, not an anxiety moved by merely individual anxiety or a desire for recognition by anybodies. But in his proud estimate of his worth, he can hold himself above the conventional loyalties when they fail him.

Thucydides himself speaks first of Alcibiades' love of victory (*philonikon*), and then of his love of honor (5.43.2). Alcibiades first and foremost loves being first and foremost among others, especially in reputation, but not only reputation. For we are immediately told that it was for wealth as well as name that Alcibiades was "warm" and "eager" to conquer Sicily and beyond (6.15.2). That is, he would be knowingly extravagant as well as knowingly preeminent (6.15.2–3). There was a mixed motive: to be number one in some great accomplishment and to have the prerogatives of the superior, including superior wealth as well as name. And then there is the superior man's almost insolent pride in his superior qualities. Alcibiades' first words in the *History*, to a democratic assembly, affirm his eminence with a Henry Adams–like allusion to forebears: "It belongs to me more than others to rule." There follows un-Adams-like decisiveness: "And I suppose that I am worthy of it" (6.16.1; cf. 5.43.2).

This first speech contains a baroque illustration of how all of these—the glory, the pride, even the wild extravagance—fit together. Alcibiades seeks a spectacular aura to which even his private life contributes, an aura that seems to rise above the distinction between private and public. Remember, he says, the recent Olympic games. He, a private individual, had entered seven chariots, more than any private man ever, and had won first, second, and fourth prizes, that too unprecedented. Cities vied to fete him and celebrate him, Plutarch reports. But the point in Alcibiades' own remarks is this: his grandeur is a public benefit. From "the magnificence of his display" abroad and from the spectacular expenditures at home, Athens's neighbors infer its power (6.16.1–3). Athens can seem still powerful, despite the tribulations of war, because Alcibiades sheds upon the city the light of his own power and glory.

The Alcibidean relation of individual to imperial city is precisely opposite to the model famously set forth in Pericles' Funeral Address. Pericles had related citizen part to political whole. By Athens's glory the citizen is glorified. Athenians should live and die for the empire, "by which their glory survives in everlasting remembrance" (2.43.1–3). Alcibiades, to the contrary, presents himself as the spectacular whole. By him, Athens is glorified. His is the universal ambition, in Forde's words, and he, not the particular country Athens, is the completed spectacle.[10] It should go without saying that Alcibidean ambition is neither that of the executive, leader, or representative who is subordinate or instrumental to a whole, nor that of the authoritarian or dictator, who lacks the desire grandly to shine and to benefit others by the shining.

Still, there are dark sides, not least the anger that is visible when the great passion is frustrated. Thinking himself above everyone, Alcibiades regards anyone's failure to place him first as an insult—a dishonor. In the *Posterior Analytics* Aristotle will illustrate through him one meaning of greatness of soul, that is, intolerance of dishonor.[11] (The other meaning, equanimity as to changes of fortune, is illustrated through Socrates and Lysander, the Spartan who in defeating Athens long subordinated himself to jealous superiors.) Thucydides brings out the same thing in his own way. Every major appearance of Alcibiades in the *History* begins with his protest against being dishonored. He opposed the fifty years' peace on its merits, but also because the negotiators had "in every respect slighted" him (5.43.2–3). He favored the Sicilian expedition on its merits, but only after first defending himself. He "must begin with this because Nicias attacked me" (as a young man filled rashly with "morbid longing for faraway things") (6.16.1, 6.15.2; 6.12.2–6.13.1). Even the great speech upon arrival in Sparta begins similarly. Alcibiades has to explain why he had betrayed a crucial Spartan peace mission. His justification: revenge. The Spartan emissaries had ignored him and his family's Spartan link, thus strengthening his "enemies" and "dishonoring me" (6.89.2–3). Sparta, that is, should have dealt with *him*, this young man just entering public life, as the authoritative Athenian in such matters. Later in the speech he explains to the very patriotic Spartans why he himself has betrayed his native country. Again the explanation involves revenge—getting back at those who injured him. True, his contention is complicated and affirms his patriotism. But this is a paradoxical patriotism. Athens left him, not he it. It left him by treating him unjustly. He now goes against not his own country, but one "no longer mine that I am trying to recover." "The one who rightly loves his country [*philopolis*], is not he who having lost it unjustly, would not be sent against it, but he who so longs for it that he would try by all means to take it back." Alcibiades slips from language about injustice to language about his own passionate longing ("by all means"), a longing to take back his own. Moreover, his "patriotism" involves joining Athens's "bitterest enemies" in their attacks (6.92.2–4). This is a dubious patriotism, one that measures one's country by its exclusion of oneself and would ally with enemies who visit perhaps decisive destruction. Is this love? Or is it self-love with a big dollop of vengeance? Later, after the Spartans too turned on him, Alcibiades "proceeded to damage the Peloponnesian cause as much as he possibly could" (8.45.1–2). Let us allow to Alcibiades real affection for his homeland. Still, the ruling passion in all these circumstances seems inseparable from a passion to get back at those who slighted him, whether Athenian or Spartan.

Empire and Civil War

While fuel for civil war is no doubt always around, especially in the grating enmity of rich and poor, there is no doubt that the great Peloponnesian war exacerbated strife within the Greek cities. Eventually "the whole Hellenic world was convulsed . . . for in war, with an alliance always at the command of either faction for the hurt of their adversaries and their own corresponding advantage, opportunities for bringing in the foreigner were never wanting to the revolutionary parties" (3.82). The classic example is Corcyra, now Kerkira (once Corfu), on an island opposite the heel of Italy, which Thucydides elaborates into a "model" of terrible civil strife.[12] Homegrown class war started it all, with the Corcyran democrats, victorious politically within, being harassed and attacked by oligarchs without. The democrats soon turned for help to democratic and imperial Athens; the oligarchs, to oligarchic Corinth and Sparta. But the warring powers often took the initiative. Corcyra's worst times were caused by a Corinthian shipment of Corcyran oligarchs, primed and bribed to overturn the democratic regime allied with Athens. And if upon occasion the patron powers tried to prevent butchery—at least an Athenian general tried halfheartedly and futilely to mediate between the city's parties (3.75, but cf. 3.81.4)—they had other or bigger fish to fry. The complete and final massacre of the oligarchs occurred when two Athenian generals neglected to save them because other Athenians, who would transport them back to Athens, would have obtained the credit (4.47.2). Thucydides turns laconic. So "the uprising (*stasis*) which unfolded so many events came to an end . . . for of one of the parties there remained nothing worthy of mention." And the Athenians sailed off to Sicily, their first destination, and carried on the war with their allies there (4.48.2–6).

There is another connection between civil strife and the warring powers: war by itself undermines "better sentiments." War confronts men with "imperious necessities" and thus proves "a violent teacher." It imposes scarcity and fear and brings "most men's temper to a level with their fortunes." The Greek cities had been at a peak of power and civilization, but they fell nevertheless to a barbaric excess of savagery liberated from duty, law, and equality. Thucydides' famous description moves from Corcyra to the free cities generally, before recurring to the particulars at Corcyra. Strife between the classes ran from city to city and developed ever more refined "cunning" in men's enterprises and "atrocity in their reprisals" (3.82.2–3). What finally dominated were private greed, vengeance, and hunger for power, which overpowered scruple, trust, kinship, law, and divine law.[13] The leaders of the *demos* might cry for equality, the leaders of the few, for moderate aristocracy, but leaders and followers of both classes came to be for themselves above all. Speaking of courage and loyalty, they meant deceit and audacity for one's party. All aimed at their own riches, power, and revenge.

Although these effects ran through Greece, in like circumstances they could happen anywhere. Thucydides' history is no mere chronicle. He would get to the essentials, which means the nature, of politics and life. "There fell upon the cities on account of civil strife many grievous calamities, such as happen and always will happen while human nature is the same," but which will always differ somewhat with circumstance (3.82.2, cf. 3.84.2). Thucydides calls his book "a possession for all time" (1.22.4). If the great war revealed for him the nature of human things, it revealed not least the necessary precariousness, because the natural precariousness, of decency, justice, and governing itself.

Such a context helps one weigh the indirect effect of an Alcibiades, who becomes the spearhead, for both great protagonists, of expansion, revolution, and war. "Even when he is indifferent," Alcibiades "becomes a catalyst of personal and national upheavals."[14] This is not to charge him with Corcyra-like cruelty. Corcyra was before his time (427), as was Athens's near-slaughter of the Mytileneans; the slaughter of the Melians is not his doing in Thucydides' account (5.84–5.116; Plutarch holds him indirectly responsible).[15] Still, Alcibiades' revolutionary policies had their own effects. Perhaps Thucydides too indicates an indirect responsibility. He inserts the ruthlessness at Melos just after Alcibiades sequesters three hundred pro-Spartan Argive oligarchs (5.84.1) and just prior to the Sicilian expedition (6.1).

Alcibiades was a force for war in Athens and Sparta alike, with obvious and destabilizing consequences. His first coup, the alliance in 420 with Argos and the other rivals of Sparta in the Peloponnesus, put Sparta at mortal risk at home (6.16.6). He personally convinced the anti-Spartan Peloponnesians to take on Sparta in the potentially decisive battle at Mantinea (418) (5.43.2–5.47; 5.54). But Sparta won. It immediately fomented an oligarchic revolution in Argos to reestablish a Spartan alliance. Whereupon the Argive democrats reversed this within a year (417) and then settled their authority by "killing some [opponents] and banishing others" (5.82.2). Alcibiades was often the man on the spot as well as the instigator. He himself seized the three hundred Argive oligarchs who survived, the Athenians settling them offshore on various islands (416) (5.84.1). Thucydides gives no indication that he wished to kill them. But later, precisely in the hysteria connected with the recall of Alcibiades from Sicily and his flight to Sparta, the Athenian democracy gave them up to the Argive *demos* to kill (6.61.3). In another incident Alcibiades' responsibility is more direct. After fleeing to Sparta he exposed the Athenian sympathizers at Messena (in Sicily), who were put to death (6.74.1).

But it was the Ionian campaign that most brought out the revolutionary implications of Alcibiades' genius at war. His influence on Sparta was surely more than "obscure and indirect."[16] Thucydides is emphatic. After orchestrating the decisive Spartan contribution to the catastrophe in Sicily, Alcibiades immediately prodded Sparta to a naval campaign across the Aegean against "the greatest" of Athenian allies, the Ionian island stronghold of Chios (413–412) (8.6.3–4, 8.15.1). The actual expedition ground to a halt owing to the usual (and often ridiculous) Spartan hesitations, superstitions, and timidities. Whereupon Alcibiades turns from director to driving force (8.6.5, 8.12.1), getting himself appointed a leader behind the Spartan leader. Hurrying and bluffing, with un-Spartan agility in deed and negotiation, he gets Chios, Athens's greatest imperial possession, to turn oligarchic and revolt (8.14–8.15.1). That causes more consternation among the Athenians than did the Sicilian disaster. For the first time they tap their ultimate reserve of money. In Ionia the fall of Chios sets off a chain reaction, with Alcibiades as catalyst. Hastening from city to city in Athens's island and coastal empire, often with slight forces, often just ahead of aroused Athenian squadrons, Alcibiades and his new Ionian friends turn a series of Athenian possessions into hostile oligarchies and then defend them against a desperate Athens (8.16–17, 22, 26.3). These revolutions were in addition to the cities in the Hellespont (modern Dardanelles) as well as in Ionia, which other Spartan forces eventually overturned.

To be fair to Alcibiades, one must acknowledge that amidst these adventures in regime change he is not an aggravator of horrors. Indeed, he seems above the malice and private revenges into which civil disputes degenerated and above also the ordinary animosities between rich and poor. We do not see Alcibiades killing out of vengeance, envy, greed, Cleon-like punishing, or Spartan-like brutality. We do see him maneuvering rather impartially between few and many. The judicious Athenian general Phrynichus, who was eventually twisted by his fears of Alcibiades into oligarchic zealotry and treason, warned his fellow oligarchs that Alcibiades "cared no more for an oligarchy than for a democracy." Thucydides agreed (8.48.4, 8.27.5).

There is another mitigating factor: Alcibiades inclined to less bloody ways. He preferred to work by diplomacy and negotiation, not by violence, and indeed his genius tended toward manipulation of appearances and persuasions. Cleon the demagogue was the most violent man in Athens (3.36.6). Alcibiades was not a Cleon, and from reason as well as temper. Cleon won at Pylos by chance and by Demosthenes' foresight and ingenuity, and he lost disastrously at Amphipolis through lack of cunning, foresight, and ingenuity. Under Alcibiades' inventive ministrations things fell together in victories that used a relatively small application of force.[17] He obtained the Argive alliance by ingeniously deceptive management of Argive commissioners, Spartan commissioners, and the Athenian assembly itself. He leveraged the alliance into a decisive threat to the Spartans, even as Athens itself risked relatively little in men and money (5.74.2). Later, for Sparta, he leveraged a minor commitment of Spartan generalship and troops into the Athenian disaster in Sicily. The Ionian campaign, despite all its revolutions, exhibits the same priority of tactics, image, and surprise. Alcibiades seemed to think himself so superior that he could win his way by persuasion and even through admiration. This complicated soul had an optimistic and high view of politics, Forde contended, even "perhaps the highest": "Alcibiades seeks to rule not only for the sake of honor, but by means of honor."[18]

On the other hand, the same Alcibiades mightily exacerbated one great cause of civil strife: rivalry among the ambitious. Indifferent he might be to small gains and the struggles between rich and poor, but he was wholeheartedly engaged in overcoming rivals for leadership. No other character in the *History* begins all his speeches by defending his own claims to command and his worthiness for command. He acknowledged in his decisive speech on Sicily that such claims to superiority give "offence," especially to "equals." But he proceeded to insist that those who resent him would find that their descendents will claim him as their own. Posterity will prefer him to them (6.16.1, 5)! This tactful prediction somehow failed to allay his rivals' hatred and fear, and it was they above all who twice got him exiled by manipulating popular piety and fear.

The upper class had no more love for him. Near the end (411), as he plotted from his Ionian base to restore himself, the Four Hundred at home would throw Athens under Sparta, if need be, to protect themselves. Their rivals, from a similar fear, but thinking to please Alcibiades, both overthrew the Four Hundred and killed the democratic leader who had exiled him.

Nevertheless, in his own governing Alcibiades was not factious or spiteful. He shared credit and induced much cooperation and loyalty. A polarizing figure he was, but one who would if possible manage and even respect the poles, not aggravate them. Apart from the special case of his changes of allegiance, one does not see him block or cause wise action merely out of pride or spite. His attack on the peace of Nicias was wise policy, not merely an attack on Nicias. His reply to Nicias's attacks on him and the expedition to Sicily do not descend to Nicias's level. Alcibiades allays divisions and slanders that Nicias sought to inflame, both the division of old from young and the imprudent slanders of Alcibiades himself, who was already the cogeneral of an expedition virtually inevitable (6.2.2). Alcibiades would unite young and old, and after rebutting the critique of himself he praises the balance which old Nicias will bring as cogeneral.

In Sicily Alcibiades seems to have worked well enough with both of the other generals. Thucydides gives us no reason to think otherwise. He does give us reasons to think Alcibiades coolly and cooperatively rational in such circumstances. Alcibiades in Sparta is masterful in subordinating himself to the Spartan effort. Obtaining finally the chance to get the Ionian enterprise going, he makes it go by appealing to the ambition of Endius, rival to King Agis. When after winning Chios he launches an extension of the enterprise, he does so to win honor for Endius, the Chians, and the other allies as well as for himself (8.17.1–3). Alcibiades can move his fellows by sharing with them. Indeed, he probably feels for them. The desire for his own fame is there, but so is reasonable sharing in the rewards, including the fame. Alcibiades is not domineering. He can be extraordinarily politic as well as insolently impolitic in his frankness. The combination of ambitious innovation with measured sharing is in another league from the slowness and self-absorption common among the Spartans (1.95.1–7, 3.31–34, 93). It differs even more from the parochial jealousy and domineering of a Cleon (3.37–40).

This politic moderation was especially valuable to Athens as it verged on civil war and defeat in 411, the last year treated by Thucydides. Alcibiades proved able to cure strife as well as cause it, and in this case he cured divisions that no one else could have cured. Much of the Athenians' empire across the Mediterranean had fallen to Spartan forces, and then Euboea, the immense adjacent island that was "everything to them" after they were shut out of Attica, threw off the Athenian yoke (8.95.2). In response to these disasters the despotic oligarchy of the Four Hundred managed to take over Athens. A struggle between oligarchs and democrats ensued in the shadows of Spartan superiority and of Alcibiades' efforts to leverage his return from Samos, especially by parading his influence over Persian wealth and power.

Precisely as to these dark maneuverings, Thucydides bestows very high praise. To begin with, Alcibiades showed patriotic and politic restraint. He forbade the sailors at their island base in Ionia to do what they were passionate to do: sail home to Athens to depose the new oligarchy and restore him. That attack would have caused civil war at home, and it would have left undefended, in the face of Spartan power, what was left of the Ionian possessions, on which the Athenians now depended utterly for money and supplies. No one but Alcibiades "would have been able to hold back the crowd [*ochlos*]" at Samos from departing the outposts of empire and invading the homeland. In this action he appeared "first, and more than anyone [else], in being useful to the city" (8.86.4–5).[19]

Alcibiades did more: by ingenious messages home he discouraged a treasonous surrender and led the way to moderate government. He urged the citizens in Athens to hold out against Sparta despite the oligarchs' machinations (8.89.1). "If the city were saved," he wrote, "there were many hopes that they would be reconciled with themselves, but if one of the [parties] were to be overthrown, once and for all, that at Samos, or this one [at Athens], there would no longer be anyone to be reconciled with" (or "to differ from," 8.86.7). The message was impartial and constructive and in these respects deeply humane. It allowed for both parties, and it set on foot a political reconciliation. Alcibiades insisted that the Four Hundred be deposed, as the democrats wanted. Yet he accepted, behind the back of his democratic back-ers, the mildly oligarchic Five Thousand, which had served as the Four Hundred's cover. Moderate oligarchs and democrats fearful of the Four Hundred grasped at the Five Thousand as more moderate but not democratic, or as more moderate and closer to a democracy. Those of the Four Hundred equated such a large group with "outright democracy" and feared it as such. Thucydides himself notes that an assembly of five thousand was bigger than any before (8.92.11).

Nevertheless, the new regime was not simply a democracy. It was better, Thucydides thought, than the simple democracy that the democratic navy no doubt wanted. There was no pay for offices, and there was a small but real property qualification for the assembly (anyone who furnished a suit of armor was eligible) (8.97.1). Such an arrangement seems a mixture of rich and poor, a polity in Aristotle's sense, or perhaps a very moderate oligarchy or democracy. Whatever one names it, Thucydides approved it (as did Aristotle in the *Constitution of Athens*). "For the first time in my [life], the Athenians appeared to be well governed." Strong words from Thucydides, and the key was the mix of classes: "The few and many happened to be intertwined with measure [*metrios*]." The result was good, since the new government "raised up the city for the first time" from its recent disasters (8.97.2). Alcibidean ingenuity and versatility had proven indispensable. However offensive to rich, poor, and his rivals, he helped put back together an Athens at war both with Sparta and itself. This was political impartiality extending to political genius, and it harmonizes with Plutarch's account, five hundred years later, of Alcibiades' actual restoration. He was too magnanimous to take vengeance upon the *demos* most responsible for the accusations against him.[20] Here was an instance of indispensable political contributions from a superior political man.

INDIVIDUAL AND COUNTRY

What made Alcibiades at once quintessentially political and yet eventually antipathetic to every class and ruler? What made him at once the invaluable public man and the traitor to Athens, Sparta, and Persia alike?

To appreciate the problem, one must acknowledge again that Alcibiades was a *political* man, to the extent of actually embodying much of his homeland's political aspirations. What Alcibiades wanted for Athens, his democratic countrymen wanted, too. Alcibiades wanted to take not only Sicily but also Carthage "and thus to serve his private ambition with respect to money and reputation [*doxa*] at the same time" (6.15.2; 6.90.3). The Athenians, too, wanted command and unbounded conquest, and they wanted this in all the combination of patriotic glory with private gain and ambition. They had longed ever more strongly for Sicily (416) (6.1.1; cf. 3.86.1; 4.2). As to the great attempt, the famous Sicilian expedition itself, "everyone fell in love with the enterprise" (lit: "love fell on everyone similarly [with respect to] the sailing away," 6.24.3). One could even say that Alcibidean grandeur suffused the preparations (6.24–6.26, 6.30–6.32), for the armada was famous as much for its boldness and "the utmost splendor of the spectacle" as for its overwhelming force (6.31.6). It appeared "more a display of wealth and power for the rest of the Hellenes than an undertaking against enemies" (6.31.4). But mundane motives were also in play. While elders were sanguine about conquest, the young longed for adventure—"far-off sights and scenes"—and the great multitude itself hoped for pay and a dominion that would be "an inexhaustible source of pay" (6.24.3).

If Athens found in Alcibiades an expression of its hopes for greatness and wealth, Alcibiades himself appreciated the greatness of Athens and the democracy that brought it. Athens's common good, a certain loyalty to his *patria*, is in his soul. More than one might think, the two were made for one another. It is true that the *demos* feared tyranny from him. But their fear was probably misplaced. In the context of the assembly's hysterical recall of Alcibiades from Sicily, Thucydides launches a revealing digression. The people's horror of past tyranny rested on fantasies and falsehoods. They were wrong as to all the important facts: the badness of the tyrant in question, the goodness of his supposed assassins, and even the identity of the tyrant and of the man assassinated (it was the tyrant's brother) (6.54–6.60, cf. 1.20.2). Whatever the popular fears, in any event, there are no reliable signs that Alcibiades wanted to be tyrant or leader of a narrow oligarchy. He does not return from Samos on the bayonets and oars, although such a restoration was pressed upon him. Even as he throws himself upon Sparta he neither eulogizes oligarchy nor disdains the Athenian democracy. He defends his allegiance to moderate democracy as the regime that brought to Athens the "utmost freedom and greatness" (6.89.6). Admittedly, the speech is of a rhetorical complication worthy of Alcibiades' political complications. Also, it proceeds to acknowledge that we all know what "men of judgment" think of democracy, and not least he, who in exile has the most reason to criticize it. But despite these flourishes, Alcibiades' speech does not otherwise attack the Athenian regime, and it does not veer in a decisively oligarchic or tyrannical direction. Alcibiades, if a resentful exile, is not your typical resentful exile. He defends instead his family's leavening participation in the democracy. He and his family worked for the "whole" people, rather than the majority alone, and they would do their part "in preserving the form of government under which the city enjoyed the utmost greatness and freedom, and which we had found existing" (6.89.6). If freedom and greatness are the goals, then a moderated Athenian democracy, moderated by the power of aristocratic families like his, may be the best thing even for Alcibiades.

While Alcibiades' imperialism reflects a general tendency of democratic politics, this is not to say that Thucydides simply favors it. On the contrary: Thucydides speaks well of two rather less ambitious and nonimperialistic cities, oligarchic Chios and oligarchic Sparta. Alone among the cities he knew, these two were able to be "moderate in prosperity, and to order their city the more securely the greater" they grew (8.24.4–5). This is high praise of these nondemocratic cities. It must be taken seriously. Yet Thucydides also shows us the famous necessities that contributed to their restraint. Sparta and Chios had few full citizens and large slave populations (4.80.3, 8.40.2). They were unambitious abroad largely because of an enduring war at home.

The two great democratic cities in the *History* are not so constrained, even if they are also slaveholding. Both, Syracuse as well as Athens, tend to be imperial and glory seeking.

As to Athens, Pericles had been emphatic. Her glory is not the glory of Greece, but the "luster of your name" that comes with "tyranny," not least over the other Greeks. "We have no need of Homer's praises, . . . everywhere we have established eternal monuments of goods and evils" (2.63.2; 2.41.4). Conquest and empire, good for Athens and evil for the conquered, bring to the victor the immortality of glory. Syracuse shows signs of a similar desire, although these are muffled by its defensive posture during most of the war. Should Syracuse defeat the Athenian armada, pronounced Hermocrates (the Syracusan Churchill), she can reap the "name" and the power that Athens has lost (6.33.5). Thucydides himself calls Syracuse's defeat of Athens's invasion the greatest work of the war, and he declares that Syracuse, daring and adventurous, was a more terrible opponent for Athens than the sluggish Spartans (7.87.5, 8.96.5). Prior to the Athenian danger, this powerful Syracuse had already been imperial in its own backyard. In urging union among the Sicilians against the Athenians, Hermocrates had to acknowledge himself a "ruler, furnished with the greatest city and, for that reason, more used to being over others than to defending" (4.64.1).

Can we infer the disturbing truth that the biggest difference among free countries is usually this, empire or submission, whether open as by conquest or hidden beneath the forms of alliance and the wish for peace? Does this suggest the extent of the obstacles in the way of the democratic peace that many in our time hope for? The Syracusan Hermocrates, one of the wisest statesmen in Thucycides' book, never blames the Athenians. He even calls natural their passion for empire: "That the Athenians desire these things and plan for them is excusable, and I do not blame those who desire to rule, but those who are more ready to serve. It is by nature for a human being to rule over all of those who give way and, on the other hand, to resist the one who is over" (4.61.5). This, despite the fact that "all agree that peace is a most excellent thing" (cf. 4.62.2). As to glory and empire, at least, Alcibiades could seem the culmination of free politics or at least of democratic politics.

And yet this surprising conclusion is surely not the whole truth. What of political freedom itself? While Alcibiades seeks glory with Athens, he seeks it primarily for himself, even as superior to Athens. While he loves Athens, he loves it especially as his, that is, as mirror of his (and his family's) superiority. But that points away from political freedom. It points away from any shared rule, whether democratic or oligarchic. Alcibiades sees himself as the great thing that brings glory to Athens. But such a vision makes him above the community, not of it. He endangers free politics, and he is endangered by it. Despite his extraordinary abilities in politics and war, Alcibiades proved indigestible to every Athenian regime, democratic or oligarchic. Pericles, and Hermocrates too, could work with the freedom and energy of their democracies. They could appeal to their strengths and work around their limits and foolishnesses. In that crucial moderation and justice, Alcibiades failed. Alcibiades' lack of seriousness about justice and in general about the limits of politics will prove to be near the core of Plato's own diagnosis.

Still, Thucydides does not blame Alcibiades overmuch, and neither should we. The great Hermocrates was first man in democratic Syracuse, savior of his city and a statesman without Alcibiades' questionable versatility. Yet we last see Hermocrates also exiled by his native democracy and also vulnerable to the Persian empire that his patriotic uprightness had offended (8.78, 8.85.3). Justice, no more than political judgment, assures oneself a just return neither in free politics nor in the clash of empires. Perhaps we can thus comprehend Thucydides' measured tolerance and admiration for Alcibiades.

CHAPTER FOUR

The Soul of Grand Ambition:
Alcibiades Cross-Examined by Socrates

TEXTS AND THE MAN

THIS CHAPTER INQUIRES further into the psychic makeup, the soul, of the Alcibiades type just discussed. The discussion again revolves about Alcibiades himself, now with this excuse: he was examined at length by a very great psychologist, Plato.

Two little dialogues named *Alcibiades*, traditionally attributed to Plato, consider directly and even dramatically the great political soul. We are shown the master-interrogator Socrates twice confronting a masterful man who would rule the world and who did seek to carry out spectacularly imperial designs. The pictures are from two periods, as I remarked before. The first *Alcibiades* examines a promising youth in hope, with gleaming prospects of political success and splendid ease. The slighter, second dialogue portrays a more experienced figure in gloom, occupied with the complications of tyranny and looking to the gods for help in overcoming the obstacles and his scruples. In both dialogues, nevertheless, the governing passion is basically the same. Alcibiades desires to "fill practically all people with his name and power." He would have "everyone" in the world perceive him as "tyrant" (*I* 105c2–3, 124b5–6, *II* 141b5–6).[1] In both dialogues, nevertheless, Alcibiades is drawn to prove that he is in truth superior, that is, that he knows what he is doing and can accordingly give adequate reasons. He cannot. His interrogator shows that his passion to be superior over others conflicts rather unthinkingly with contrary inclinations and opinions, forces he cannot deny or ignore. He exhibits a certain patriotic and familial loyalty, a certain nobility and justice of inclination, a wish to be superior in truth (not merely in popular opinion), a soft luxuriousness, and, eventually, a hope for aid from the gods in overcoming his various difficulties, including his scruples. These two examinations, when supplemented by relevant passages in the *Protago-*

81

ras and *Symposium*, exhibit grand ambition in the mirror of Socratic wisdom about the soul.

Alcibiades is commonly known as a notorious whirlwind of insolence, daring deeds, and ability. He could inspire and direct great acts of war and politics, even from diverse cities and empires. The pages of Xenophon's *Hellenica* as well as Thucydides' *History* come alive with his enterprises, his genius as politician and commander, and the *hubris* public as well as private. Alcibiades enlivened and endangered Athens's decisive war with Sparta, and his final dismissal led to the disastrous naval defeat, which he warned against, that ended it. But the career of great actions is not Plato's story.

Plato inquires of Alcibiades' place not in the public drama of Athenian empire but in the quiet drama of knowing, especially knowing oneself and knowing, accordingly, what a knowing soul truly needs. This is not to deny a plenitude of funny allusions. *Alcibiades I* may play with imperial war, Spartan queens, and Persian empire, and *Alcibiades II* and *Symposium* no doubt allude to the alleged sacrilege that provoked Alcibiades' recall from Sicily for trial. Still, the dialogues focus on the warlike soul, not on the battles and wars; the noble willingness to sacrifice for friends, not particular heroic acts; the ambition for renown, not the empire and the fame; the anger, fear, and despair when thwarted, not the cruel or disdainful actions. The Platonic treatments attend to direction of soul. They bring out especially Alcibiades' clarifying articulations and his refusals to articulate, and they thus exhibit his reasons, both good and bad, and the powerful passions and convictions that help explain the absence of good reasons. The theoretical peak of the first *Alcibiades* suggests that one has to measure any individual soul by a soul with intelligence at work, "one with knowledge and prudence" (*I* 133c1–2). Supposing that this is true, and supposing, too, that a Socratic examination displays intelligence especially active, then the two *Alcibiades* are particularly revealing as to grand ambition itself.

Even for readers who will go along provisionally with the supposition of Plato's discernment, I have to confront one objection at the start: the still-influential opinion that these dialogues are not Plato's. Whatever the Socratic wisdom about ambition, according to this view, it is not to be discovered here. For nearly two centuries scholars have advanced historical and textual arguments that many of the small dialogues, including the two *Alcibiades*, are by imitators and second-raters. Now, however, these arguments have lost their credibility. The alleged evidence is itself discredited. The allegations of primitive librarianship in the keepers and of disparities of style, language, and argument in the texts seem to be more uncritical and unhistorical than the traditional authorities who accepted the dialogues as Plato's. We can again respect the texts that we have.[2]

In any event, as Thomas Pangle has argued, a serious study of the Platonism of such dialogues is reasonable even if the author were not Plato. The author must have been a competent Platonist indeed to command respect from such knowing students of Plato as the Arabic philosopher Alfarabi (c. 870–950). Alfarabi thought both *Alcibiades* to be Plato's and one of them, the first, paradigmatically Platonic. Indeed, a prominent tradition had long accepted for it the subtitle "On Human Nature" or "Of Man" and placed the work as the introduction to the whole Platonic corpus. Proclus, in a fifth-century Neoplatonist commentary, held that the *Alcibiades I* contains the starting point "of all philosophy," which is "knowledge of ourselves" (1–21). Alfarabi himself used an epitome of the dialogue to introduce his whole review of Plato's philosophy. There, he explained, Socrates the philosopher confronts the alternatives to a philosophic life, especially the shining alternative of "being glorified and exalted, ruling over a group or a city in which his command is enforced and which submits to his wish." In short, there are good reasons to suppose that both *Alcibiades* are Plato's, or at least Platonic, and to suppose that the first, at least, is important. There seem not to be good reasons to suppose otherwise.[3]

Actually, the texts themselves have signs enough that these conversations with Alcibiades were important for the Platonic Socrates. Socrates seeks out these conversations; he was not compelled to converse, as in many of the dialogues. The two *Alcibiades* are in fact particularly voluntary on his part, that is, strikingly at his initiative. Socrates gets the conversations going despite Alcibiades' acknowledged disdain in the first and his preoccupation with going to prayer in the second. Actually, the first *Alcibiades* shows a ridiculously eager Socrates. His story is that he watched Alcibiades night and day even from the youth's childhood, watching and waiting until the governing ambition had developed (else he would "converse to no point," *I* 105e7–106a1). Also, Socrates calls himself Alcibiades' first, longest, and indeed "only true lover" (*I* 103a2, 104c5, 119c5, 131e1–4, 10–11). An older Platonic Socrates still says "he loves Alcibiades . . . and philosophy" (*Gorgias* 481d3–5). To Alcibiades alone, it has been said, does the Platonic Socrates ever profess love.[4] Also, Alcibiades is the only person for whom a pair of the surviving Platonic dialogues is named, except for the sophist Hippias. Admittedly, this is a dim sign, since Hippias is rather an ass. But there is a Platonic comparison, a small confrontation between the two in the *Protagoras*, which exhibits Alcibiades' superior promise for certain Socratic purposes.

The context is a Socratic examination of the sophist Protagoras. When the vain Hippias tries to insert his own poetical speechifying, Alcibiades checks him, decisively (*Protagoras* 347b3–7). It is a brusque intervention without a move or word in excess, a striking little mixture of command and intelligence. The intervention is not exceptional. It is revealingly characteristic. There are three such Alcibidean interventions in the *Protagoras*, and the two others are also instrumental in permitting the Socratic examination to proceed. The first challenges the foolish impartiality of a politic moderator, Callias, who was impartial between Socrates' crisp dialectic and Protagoras's poetic obscurantism (*Protagoras* 336b7-d5). The last shamed Protagoras himself, the most famous teacher of Greece, into following through on the dialectical procedure agreed upon (*Protagoras* 348b1–8). What these show, I think, is that the still-young Alcibiades is wiser about justice than his gentlemanly peers and wiser about inquiry, perhaps, than the famous and fancy teachers of Greece. The dramatic date of the *Protagoras* is said to be about a year after that of the first *Alcibiades*.[5] If in the *Alcibiades I* we see Alcibiades superior in "nature of the soul" (*I* 123e5, cf.135e7), we see in the *Protagoras* the promise of such a soul when informed by the Socratic education. So educated, the grandly ambitious Alcibiades proves here, at least for now, to be a guardian of rational inquiry. I shall suggest that this is as much as Socrates attempts, at least by the end of the *Alcibiades I*.

It is also true that the differences between the two men, which give such tension to both *Alcibiades*, are confirmed elsewhere. All is not love and protection between the masterful man and his cross-examiner. Even the *Symposium*, in which Alcibiades alone eulogizes Socrates, reveals a deep antipathy. Alcibiades, who had as a youth promised to attend on Socrates "from this day forth" (*I* 135d9–10), soon "fled." He now makes a point of avoiding Socrates, who is the only man to make this proud soul feel ashamed (*Symposium* 216a6-c3). Pride stands in the way. Even the *Protagoras* had intimated a distance. While Socrates praised Alcibiades' support in the conversation, he attended the colloquy of sophists with an unnamed interlocutor, not with Alcibiades, and it is the interlocutor, not Socrates, who mentions Socrates' love for Alcibiades. Socrates pays Alcibiades no attention in the course of the discussion and proceeds to forget all about him (*Protagoras* 309b7–9). These sophists taught things useful for wealth and fame, and Socrates went to their gathering partly out of concern for the effect they would have on the young narrator. Alcibiades went on his own. The arts of rising are the things he would know. While the young Alcibiades is of a promise that a Socrates can love, he is finally without the seriousness about truth that Socrates can fully love or finally keep.

"It will be impossible for you to accomplish all the things you have in mind without me" (*I* 105d2–4): this is the big hook with which Socrates seeks to attract the attention of the young and proud Alcibiades. It works, and he succeeds. Alcibiades probably hopes to obtain arts of politics, especially arts of obtaining power. He never gets them. But Socrates' meaning is probably less obvious. He will show instead that Alcibiades has more "things" in his mind than he realizes. While Socrates brings out in the first *Alcibiades* the pride and love of fame that bedazzle Alcibiades, there are also conflicting things churning in the young man. Besides, there will arise also a terrible fury at "the many" who eventually stand in his way, and qualms and furies of moral self-hatred that are exacerbated by the gods to which he eventually turns.

These more sober themes govern the second dialogue, in which Socrates waylays an Alcibiades on his way to pray. The two dialogues seem complementary, the second, which addresses an Alcibiades now unequivocally bent on rule, lacking the fundamental struggle over Alcibiades' soul that enlivens a large part of the first.

In what follows I focus in turn on six distinctive desires or convictions. The most obvious are the first two, already familiar from Thucydides' descriptions, a striking pride and an overwhelming desire for honor and power. But there are others less evident and yet important for a full picture of grand ambition. These are Alcibiades' wish to know what he is doing, a certain justice and nobility, an equivocal political horizon, and, finally, an impulse to turn to divine help. Perhaps any such catalogue and any such clarification will be somewhat partial, what with the different kinds even of grand political ambition. But Plato seemed to think that Alcibiades somehow embodied the crucial essentials.

PRIDE AND ITS PROBLEMS

The obvious feature of the young Alcibiades is not his ambition but his pride. In pride he has offended his lovers, and in pride he would conceal his ambition and thus his neediness, even from himself. He thinks himself great and in need of nothing. The first *Alcibiades* is less about ambition as such than about whether his ambition measures up to this opinion. (*Mega phronein*, thinking oneself great, is the characteristic formulation of his pride.)[6] Socrates' opening gambit imputes a question to Alcibiades: he must be wondering at the incongruity between his superiority and the presumption of that nobody Socrates in approaching him. To which Alcibiades hurries to assert that Socrates had "barely beaten me to it" (*I* 104c7-d1). A first little hook catches in Alcibiades' pride.

Alcibiades' pride rests first on advantages of height, looks, distinguished family, and, as Socrates puts it, the "power you have in Pericles," his guardian and the most powerful man in all Greece (104b4). Alcibiades is a man without the scars of neces-

sity. He has the grace and confidence of reassuring advantages.
But there is a more fundamental advantage. Alcibiades "can by
far surpass" the usual Athenian politicians, "thanks to my nature"
(*I* 119b9-c1). Socrates never disagrees with a certain trust in
"your nature" (*I* 135e7). It is this superior power, it seems, that so
attracts him. Alcibiades has an immense desire for the best for
himself, beyond the usual conventions (*I* 104e6–105a7). But
Socrates challenges the young man's contentment with a second-
rate development of this nature. Alcibiades' move to rely on his
nature had been intended to evade an acknowledged contradiction to which Socrates had brought him. In politics he can stand
out by virtue of his gifts, without having to bother himself with
labor and learning (*I* 119b8–9). A certain softness and laziness
accompany the pride of this one who has been given so much.

Socrates directs most of his efforts to cracking the ambitious
youth's pride, that is, his opinion of his self-sufficiency. For why
should Alcibiades trouble himself to learn about politics and a serious life if he thinks it unimportant that he is ignorant? Four Socratic attacks shape the dialogue and inform my discussions.
First, Socrates offers a proof that Alcibiades cannot know justice,
which is assumed to be the core of the politics he claims to know.
After Alcibiades denies the importance of justice in politics, second, there is a proof that he contradicts himself—that he nevertheless affirms justice by a noble willingness to sacrifice himself
for his comrades in battle. After Alcibiades denies the need in
Athenian politics of confronting contradictions and in general of
wisdom, third, Socrates supplies a genially absurd proof from authority—from the alleged counsel of Spartan and Persian royalty
to take trouble and seek wisdom (*I* 123d2–3). And fourth, after
Alcibiades affirms the priority of taking care of one's country,
there is a demonstration that politics as Alcibiades understands it,
politics in the sense of shared community, is self-contradictory.
Alcibiades understands politics as friendship, but this cannot provide for what he regards as just, the individual's care of his own affairs, to say nothing of the superior place and activity he thinks he
deserves (*I* 127b5-d8). Shared politics cannot satisfy him.

This last strikes a decisive blow to Alcibiades' conviction of
his self-sufficiency. It had been prepared by the earlier stages. Al-

cibiades had been made "strange" (*I* 116e3) to himself by his contradictions as to justice; by authority of the royals he was made
docile to the point that Socrates treated "the two of us" as comrades (*I* 124d2–3). But it is his realization of the inadequacy of
political superiority for his own superiority that shakes to the
core Alcibiades' supposition of superiority. "I myself don't know
what I am saying, and I've probably been in the most disgraceful
way for a long time without noticing it" (*I* 127d6–8). It is a remarkable admission showing remarkable strength of soul. From
this point docile pupil follows didactic teacher in a compressed
dialogic journey, up to what it is to take care of the self, down
again into taking care of others. From proudest of the masterful
proud at the start, Alcibiades becomes at the end a willing "slave"
of Socrates (*I* 135c8-d10). It seems an extraordinary conversion.

The *Alcibiades II* presents a different picture from the start. Our
hero is in need and gloom, not pride and hope, and Socrates is
eventually concerned to restore a certain pride. The old *hubris* of
the *naif* is gone. There is a certain similarity to Alcibiades' condition at the end of the first dialogue. The cause is not awareness of
his ignorance, however, but anxiety about his knowledge, his
knowledge of obstacles on his way to "tyranny."[7] Nor is it lack of
pride in his superiority. But now he seeks a political superiority
above shared politics, not a just politics. And although he does not
seek wisdom as such, he does seek knowledge of how to avoid the
terrible things connected with tyranny, or, rather, he seeks help
from the gods. The young Alcibiades had thought to rely on accla-
mation from *hoi polloi* as well as on his natural superiority. Now he
disdains the people generally as "mad," and now he sees that his
natural powers cannot be enough. Ahead of him could lie doubtful
deeds of violence and horror, and we see him here turning to supernatural powers. But he evades telling Socrates why he turns to
prayer, and he himself did not turn to Socrates. A certain pride remains, although it is undermined by his dependence on the gods.

In this second dialogue, indeed, Socrates restores something
of Alcibiades' pride in himself. More precisely, he restores pride
in his rational powers. By dialogue's end Alcibiades is moved to
more reasonable prayers and especially to more of his own inquiry as to what to pray for. This late and more reasonable Alci-

biades is rather bemused by the gods, and he awaits with parallel amusement a mysterious teacher in lieu of the gods to whom he was to appeal. He wreathes Socrates (as he also does in the *Symposium*), instead of the gods, and he puts off his worship, which he now calls "conventional" (*II* 151b2). While Alcibiades perhaps remains somewhat dependent upon the gods, he is now conscious of his ignorance, perhaps his necessary ignorance, of their will. He is much less dependent. Moved by the joint authority of a reasonable Socrates and the more reasonable gods that Socrates has exhibited (who honor outstanding human beings, especially the knowing ones), he displays something of the urbane Socratic *hubris* on which he himself remarks in the *Symposium* (215b7). We see something of the Platonic enlightenment, as Nasser Behnegar has called it.

The first *Alcibiades* considers the great soul in its youthful but also more rational pride, the second, in a barer feeling of great capacity. In the first, the term characteristically used for Alcibiades' pride is to think oneself great (or thinking greatly of oneself) (*mega phronein* or *megalophronein, I* 103b4–5; 104c1). This phrase does not appear in the second dialogue. In the second, the corresponding word is "greatness of soul" (*megalopsuchia, II* 140c9, 150c8). This does not appear in the first. Perhaps the difference marks the power of grand desire governing this older Alcibiades, rather than the authority of thinking with which Socrates experiments upon a more intellectually open and susceptible youth. In the second dialogue *megalopsuchia* is first called a form of imprudence (*II* 140c5) and then, with respect to Alcibiades, the "noblest of the names, at least, of imprudence" (*II* 150c8–9).

From the standpoint of Socrates, the second dialogue is addressed to a fundamentally imprudent man who is not to be cured, even if he may be guided somewhat through the noble names that prevail in his world. The dialogue describes as almost natural the unthinking desires for tyranny and generalship as well as for children (*II* 141d1–142d3). People will seek these things, Socrates acknowledges, despite the evils that may follow. Alcibiades will, too. From the true point of view he is one of the people (*hoi polloi*).

Still, while Socrates encourages a healthy dollop of theological deference among people generally, he fosters in Alcibiades a more thinking doubt and a more thinking deference. If Alcibiades' passion to distinguish himself does not permit a philosophic independence, it also does not permit an unthinking deference (*II* 150c2-d2). If Alcibiades as he develops will not be philosophic, he might be, with the right education, somewhat philosophic. We find at dialogue's end a more attractive, amusing, and urbane Alcibiades, one more independent of Athenian religious names and custom, one who takes a corresponding pride in his reasonableness.

It may very well be that this mixture of command and urbanity could be a guardian of philosophy, if not a philosopher. While at the end of the first *Alcibiades* Socrates talks of love and of sharing in pursuit or care of wisdom, at the end of the second he merely hopes for a victory over Alcibiades' lovers. Those lovers seem to include not only the people, who can be mad about the gods, but also the orators and the poets—the teachers of sophists and orators—who are much discussed in the second dialogue. An Alcibiades respectful of philosophy might be what the *Protagoras* displays. He is protector of Socratic inquiry from ordinary politic men and from sophists who rely on poetic accounts.[8]

But this particular mixture of pride and respect for philosophy is an unstable mixture, with the second much the weaker element. To the Alcibiades of the *Symposium* Socrates causes "shame" and is hence particularly painful. "Many is the time" that he would "with pleasure" see Socrates dead. To relieve his pain he would see Socrates dead. One sees the dangers to wise counselors, especially to philosophic types, of such natures. And yet "should this happen," Alcibiades would be "much more greatly distressed." Even a partial Socratic persuasion of such a nature, so armored in pride, is no small victory (*Symposium* 216a4-c4).

AMBITION ITSELF

What most moves Alcibiades is what his pride keeps him from proclaiming, but what he tacitly admits and in the second dialogue more or less acknowledges: the passion for ever-increasing fame and power. The first *Alcibiades* may focus a little more on the fame. Alcibiades intends to prove to the Athenians that he "is more deserving of being honored by the Athenians" than Pericles or anyone else, ever. Your love for renown, Socrates pronounces grandly, is a love as "no one has ever loved anything else" (*I* 105b, 124b5–6). The young Alcibiades, more moved to *think* himself great, is more moved accordingly to wish that others *think* him best. Still, there is also a desire for "power" (*dunamis*). And if power is first presented as a means to fame, it almost immediately reappears as a separate aim. He aims to obtain "very great power" first among the Greeks, then in Europe generally, and then in Asia. You could not live, Socrates says, "without being able to fill with your name and your power all mankind" (*I* 105b2-c4). Accordingly, Alcibiades thinks the only human beings worth mentioning are Cyrus, the conqueror who founded the Persian empire, and Xerxes, the Persian emperor who was would-be conqueror of Greece (105c5).

For the more hard-bitten Alcibiades of the second dialogue the priority of words has receded, and hence, too, both the "deserving" of rule by consent and the talk of love. Alcibiades wants to be "tyrant" over Athens, not a part or leader of Athens, and so over Europe and more.[9] Nevertheless, even his admission of all this remains couched in popular authority of a kind: "anyone else" would want such a tyranny. And the aim remains a certain soul-presence in all humanity: "that all men perceive that Alcibiades son of Cleinias was tyrant" (*II* 141b4–5). This is not exactly fame, in words, but it is at least a "perception" (the word is *aisthesesthai*) by all. Is this more glory than fame? So it seems. It is not merely power, but it seems to involve less of speech, less of reputation, than of a visible shining.

Plutarch supplies a wonderful word-portrait of Alcibidean glory seeking, a portrait in Technicolor, so to speak. Alcibiades would return from exile, Plutarch says, only after orchestrating a series of spectacular victories over the Spartans. That is, Alcibiades would return only in triumph. Plutarch downplays others' reports of purple sails, rhythmic rowing to a famous flutist, and rhythmic calling to a famous actor. But he includes those reports, and he allows that Alcibiades' ships were certainly adorned all around with innumerable shields, hundreds of figureheads from the enemy's ships, and immense spoils of war. His would be the glory of great victory. While Alcibiades wished again to see Athens, "he wished more to be seen by his fellows now that he had conquered their enemies so many times."[10] Generalship and war fitted Alcibiades' ambition. He would author spectacles of accomplishment. Lawgiving, such as Washington's, seems comparatively drab.

One might usefully compare this effulgent Alcibidean ambition with Socrates' thematic account of ambition, in the *Symposium*, which is much more austere. Socrates' speech there does interpret grand ambition as an erotic engendering. But it focuses on immortality, which doesn't quite catch the warm and "aesthetic" splendor that Alcibiades was after. According to Socrates, or at least his prophetess-instructress Diotima, statesmen and poets are like men seeking intercourse. In their mortal particularity they desire the immortality promised through children or by an undying name (*Symposium* 207e7–209e4). But this is a rather high account of ambition,[11] and of intercourse too. It doesn't speak of generalship and glorious victories. The two *Alcibiades*, which do, don't dwell on fame undying. It is true that if Alcibiades would fill practically all people with his name and power (105c3–4), those to come are also included. And it is also true that in the first *Alcibiades* Socrates exaggerates in the direction of immortality: Alcibiades' "love of renown" is stronger than any other love, "ever" (*I* 124b2–6). (How could he know?) Still, whatever these intimations of limitless bounds, Alcibiades for his part wants *now* to be perceived as ruling in the flesh. He never speaks of wishing an immortal reputation through such austere and enduring measures as lawgiving. Even as filled with animus against the people (*II* 139c, 145e–146c; cf. *I* 110e–111a, 114b–c, 119b–c), Alcibiades wishes above all to be *perceived* as tyrant by "everyone" (*II* 141b4–5). Alcibiades loved the visual effects. Hence he is more concerned with war, with superiority that can be seen and gloried in. He would live, and live it up, now. Socrates' high interpretations of the *Symposium* are followed immediately by the arrival of a drunken Alcibiades basking in wine, women, and song.

KNOWING

But Alcibiades is moved by his opinions and intelligence as well as by pride and ambition, and indeed his pride and ambition involve his opinions of himself and of what he should seek. Otherwise, Socrates' interrogations would not have shaken him much and changed him considerably. In both dialogues he wishes means to his ends; in both, he finds himself reconsidering his ends. He had supposed that he knew broadly what he is about, and he supposed especially that what he wanted is worthy of himself. These are two crucial suppositions, and when they become questionable, the doubts in his mind shake his pride and shake even the priority of his ambition. He does not "know what" he is saying as to the noble and just; he does not "know what" he means as to whether politics is about sharing or freedom; he is in a "shameful" condition (*I* 116e2–3, 127d6–8). Deposed from his self-sufficiency, doubting now that his politics will adequately serve his wish to be superior, he can be led to consider what it is truly to provide for himself. That enables Socrates to set forth the priority of the soul, and the priority of the intelligence that harbors "the virtue of the soul, wisdom" (*I* 133b9–10). The now-tamed Alcibiades follows, agrees, and subordinates himself to become a pupil (*I* 135d7–10).

This is a radical effect, and it brings out the radical mirror Plato had set before the Alcibiades type, the mirror of the knower. The question put to the youth is whether he truly understands what he is doing, that is, understands what he is and what accordingly he should be doing. Plato puts a Socrates front and center. Thucydides had shown us political comparisons, albeit differing in judiciousness. Xenophon in the *Education of Cyrus* shows us at most political approximations of Socrates, such as Tigranes, except for the occasional ironic glance at the real thing. But Plato's Alcibiades has to measure himself by Socrates, which seems laughable, proved to be profoundly painful, and led to a conversion.

Nevertheless, one lesson of Plato's dialogues is that any such conversion of an Alcibiades will be short-lived. The Alcibiades of the second dialogue is bent on tyranny, not inquiry. This, interestingly enough, leads to a kind of reversal of the mirror. When in that dialogue Alcibiades attacks ignorance, Socrates defends ignorance (*II* 143b6ff.). More knowledge may not be a good thing if it is an instrument of tyrannical ambition. Enlightenment is bad for some people; the mirror of the knowing soul shows many not concerned with knowing and who will misuse the weaponry it gives. Still, even in that dialogue Alcibiades listens deferentially from the start, and by the end he is more knowing, if not of what to live for, then at least of what to pray for.

To grasp the intellectual side of Alcibiades one must see that his ambition is not simply some dominating passion to which his thoughts are but instrumental. Alcibiades is not the merely calculating Augustus of Shakespeare's *Julius Caesar*, the cold, cold Antonio of *The Tempest*, or Machiavelli's thematically ruthless Cesare Borgia. His ambition is accompanied by a certain intellectual openness. Socrates plays on his "wonder" (*thaumazein, I* 103a1–d4). He plays on Alcibiades' respect for what is just, including his *patria* and its customs, and for what is noble, especially courage. As a young man Alcibiades understands the charms of music in terms of the divine muses (*I* 108c11–12), and he can later speak of Socrates as that "daemonic and amazing being" who deserves the greatest "wonder" (*Symposium* 221c3).

Nor is this awe merely some unthinking or aesthetic amazement of mind. Alcibiades exhibits impressive dialectical powers. He follows much of the political and moral argument, most of it, anyway, and he can rise to manly admission of error or to pungent refutation of a crucial Socratic allegation (*I* 110e1–112a3). If at times the *Alcibiades I* seems indeed a précis of Plato's teachings as to the best life, it is one provoked by a fresh, spirited, and confident opponent. Paul Friedländer went so far as to say that the first *Alcibiades* exhibits "a tension unequalled in Plato."[12] One sees a master wrestler trying his holds upon a powerful young athlete who contends for the world title passionately, as if by nature, but who also learns from the superior technique of his victorious opponent.

Which is not to say that Socrates provides us some model of pure deduction. These two dialogues exhibit the sometimes foolish suppositions almost natural to an intelligent lover of the greatest honor. Socrates starts with what Alcibiades thinks, repeatedly, whatever the tacit contradictions and foolishnesses, and he himself relies on a variety of irrational appeals, partly to win Alcibiades' attention and partly to discipline his evasiveness under strain. At the start of *Alcibiades I* Socrates flatters Alcibiades and insinuates himself. At the start of *Alcibiades II* he has to make Alcibiades less impassioned. He has to make him acknowledge, for example, that those politically or morally repulsive to him may be not "mad," but of mistaken opinions that cause their errors (*II* 138c6–139d4). At times he has to overcome evasive silences and insist that Alcibiades "answer with the truth" rather than with slippery pretence (*I* 110a3–4). He uses ridicule—"You are insolent [*hubristes*]), Socrates"—to shake the young man's complacency in the face of contradictions (*I* 109d6, 114d7, cf. 116e2–4). And each dialogue contains long and absurd appeals to imaginary Foreign Authority, whether royalty or gods, thus to undermine Alcibiades' contentment with mediocre politicians and misguided deities.

In short, Socrates wields the arts of prosecutor, poet, and cross-examiner as well as his extraordinary dialectical and deductive power. Only by resorting to all these is he able to move such a youth toward more reasonable and limited expectations from politics, the gods, and his enemies. They produce in particular Alcibiades' two political-intellectual crises, together with the challenge to popular authority that prepares them.

The first arguments of the first *Alcibiades* play on the youth's pride and make him wonder about the cocoon of his country's justice that he has taken for granted. Socrates leads Alcibiades to claim that he could know about justice only if he himself inquired about it or learned it from others, and that he would do these things only if he knew himself ignorant (*I* 106d1-e9). When Alcibiades under pressure claims he knows what justice is and insists he "always knew," Socrates can show he had never believed himself ignorant and therefore never could have inquired. Alcibiades is man enough to admit his error. But from this first admission of insufficiency he moves easily to a complacent reliance on the people's sufficiency. Like "everybody else," he learned about justice from "the people" (the many, or the majority: *hoi polloi, I* 110e1). To Socrates' pregnant objection, that these are not very serious teachers, Alcibiades manages his pungent reply: they taught me a serious subject, Greek, didn't they?

That reply compels a more pregnant Socratic questioning of popular authority in knowing. The people may be good teachers of language, but are they of justice? They can teach Greek, since they don't differ with one another as to what sort of thing, say, a piece of stone or wood is. A fundamental point is intimated. Socratic knowing, the flexible and questioning dialectic, begins with a certain trust in what we see and say, about things such as stone and wood as we select and name them. But things such as justice are not so simply presented, and about justice the people contradict themselves. Can one say that a teacher who contradicts himself is good, any more than is a general or a horse trainer who issues contradictory instructions? Alcibiades agrees with this standard of noncontradiction. He also agrees, and with an oath, that the people disagree most of all "with themselves or with one another concerning just and unjust men and affairs" (*I* 111e11–112a3). This superior man has his own doubts about everyman. QED. The people don't know about justice, and Alcibiades, having this incompetent *people* as teacher, does not know either.

Socrates sharpens the point so it cuts not merely into everyman. He applies this criticism of "the people" to the characters in the *Odyssey* and *Iliad*, to the Greeks in their wars, and to Alcibiades' own father, who died fighting for Athens. All differed with one another, and none of them, then, knew what they were doing. This is a dagger into Alcibiades' proud fealty to the heroes, the Greeks, and his family. There arises a quick, intense rebellion against cross-examination as well as an attempt to overthrow justice as the standard of politics. But this step has shaken the certainties that mist his mind. It prepares the two later crises, already summarized, in which Alcibiades faces up to his contradictions and is shaken by them.

The first crisis arises from Alcibiades' dismissal of justice as being important to politics, at least to Greek foreign policies. Alcibiades is forced shortly to admit that the separation of justice from advantage is contrary to his devotion to a "justice-like courage" (as Christopher Bruell calls it): "I wouldn't choose to live if I were a coward" (*I* 115d7).[13] The final crisis arises from his supposition that to take care of the community is to care for himself. Alcibiades is forced to admit that politics as he understands it, as community or friendship, does not necessarily provide for justice as he fundamentally understands it, as enabling people to do their own things, especially ruling. These difficulties in his presuppositions make him doubt himself. It is no longer Socrates who seems strange to him in his pride, but he who is now "strange" and even "disgraceful" to himself (*I* 116e3, 127d8). This acknowledgment of ignorance earns Socrates' comradeship (all need to take trouble over themselves, but "most particularly the two of us," *I* 124d2–3) and finally even Socrates' encouragement ("take heart"; if you had waited until a midlife crisis to undergo this, it might have been too late, *I* 127d9-e3). Alcibiades is moved. He is changed. From then on in this dialogue, and throughout the second dialogue, an intellectually docile Alcibiades exhibits only mild recalcitrance at even Socrates' more alien moves (see especially *II* 147e1–2, 150b5–7).

With Alcibiades cowed by his ignorance, Socrates proceeds to outline the priority of knowing. The point is more than the need for awareness of ignorance. We get an account of man (not merely of stone or wood). Socrates sketches an account in particular of the soul at its best or true state, the knowing soul.[14] By arguments not always airtight he suggests that the true self is the soul and that true care of the self is care of the "region," intelligence, of the virtue of the soul, "wisdom." This seems a crucial outline, although but a sketch and rather one-sided.

I will try to state the argument. That the soul and not the body is the self, Socrates proves from agency (*I* 129b4–131c10). One uses a tool, and one uses one's body as a tool. To this Alcibiades mostly agrees easily, up to a point. Is it not a contention to which the ambitious man must agree? He lives for a name, not for his body, up to a point. And yet there are the pleasures of the body, which the actual Alcibiades was famous for indulging. Socrates just at this point in the argument hints at a more austere kind of love: soul love rather than body love. He proclaims himself Alcibiades' true and indeed only lover, since only he is a lover of Alcibiades' soul (*I* 131c11–131e11). There are exaggerations here, perhaps the exaggerations befitting the topic of ambition and above all the supposition that knowing is truly the best thing.

That wisdom is indeed *the* virtue of the soul gets a conspicuous proof here that satisfies Alcibiades, which does not make it fully satisfactory. Socrates "proves" his famous thesis in three steps: from an oracle, an analogy, and an assertion. First, he recollects an oracular pronouncement, "Know Thyself." Then, he illustrates from an analogy (another's eye as mirror of one's eye and thus as the way to see vision, "by which we see"). Finally, he asserts that the soul knows itself by looking at "the region in it in which the virtue of the soul, wisdom, comes to exist" (*I* 132d1–133b6). This key assertion then receives a corroborating question—"can we say anything is more divine" than "knowing" (discerning: *eidenai*) and "prudence" (*phronesis*)? (133c1–2). And following all of this quickstepping is a corroborating compound assertion that gets us farther into divinity. This region of the soul, later called intelligence, "resembles" the god, and one who knows "all that is divine" ("god and prudence") would come to know himself also (*I* 133c4–6; 134e8, 135a5, *II* 146a9, c12). (Further such assertions follow, according to some later commentators, but they are not in the manuscripts.)[15] Alcibiades agrees to these steps but only qualifiedly: "it seems to me, at least" and "it appears so."

Caution is justified. The Socratic conclusion fits only by analogy with our experience of vision, and the fit, I will show, is not very good. Accordingly, the conclusion that intelligence is the highest thing in us finally rests only upon Socratic assertion—insofar as it does not rest upon an oracle or "resemblances" to a more ineffable "god" or "divine." The account actually moves toward identifying (the unnamed) intelligence with such resemblances, so that it becomes hard to tell whether "the divine" resembles the intelligence in the soul, or the intelligence in the soul resembles "the god." In short, a first look finds the crucial "proof" dubious and finds too a muddying of the relation between the virtue wisdom first named and the divinity subsequently suggested.

Nevertheless, the big point here is that the young Alcibiades is persuaded of the superiority of the life pursuing knowledge, and the older man of the world Alcibiades, he of the *Symposium*, remained persuaded. He remained "incapable of contradicting" the argument that "I neglect myself and handle instead the affairs of the Athenians" (*Symposium* 216a5–6, b3). While fleeing the arguer he retained a painful dependence on the argument as to his true self.

Why is he so persuaded? Perhaps it is partly due to the muddied form of the argument that tends to persuade one with respect for the divine. He might also be moved by some vague experience of an eye of the mind; the analogy works to that extent. But I suspect that his persuasion is due less to the proofs just chronicled, to which his acquiescence is languid, and more to the preceding and dialectical refutation of the alternative life. Indeed, the authority of such reasonings is even hinted at in the proofs, especially in the argument from analogy. Contrary to Socrates' assertion, one who gazes into the eye of another does not see a reflection of one's vision as such. One sees only an image of one's eye, that is, of the bodily organ of vision.[16] Similarly, in examining the intelligence of another, one does not see one's own intelligence as such. Rather, one hears the opinions expressed and one sees the intelligence of oneself (and the other) by examining their adequacy to the phenomena and their consistency one with another. Examining others' opinions, and one's own, is what dialectical reasoning is. Dialectics is what unsettled Alcibiades. To be knowing, Alcibiades needs a knowing examiner of opinions. This, provoked by the examiner Socrates, is his own conclusion in both dialogues.

Whatever the cause of Alcibiades' conversion, the conversion does not last. At the start of the second dialogue Alcibiades is set not on knowing but on praying, probably for the tyranny he wants without the bad fortune or divine punishments that he fears. What we see in the second dialogue is a Socratic attempt to restore knowing to authority, albeit now within the context of Alcibiades' political and religious priorities.

Basically, the second *Alcibiades* encourages him to think again. Alcibiades is bent on evasion, this time of the evils he knows are likely to follow on what he seeks. Socrates shows that he should not think the gods will help him be evasive. The means again is a dialectical examination, this time of what Alcibiades wants from the gods. Alcibiades is finally led toward reconsidering what he thinks good, that is, what he would pray for. But this progress is limited, more or less, to a correction of his hopes from the gods. From the start the theme is: be careful what you pray for because you may get it. Still, since tyranny seems so obviously good to Alcibiades, Socrates has also to remind of the murders, assassinations, and sins likely to follow. It is when Alcibiades wants to know supernatural ways to avoid such necessities that Socrates wheels to what surprises Alcibiades: a defense of ignorance.

Socrates' is a distinctly qualified recommendation of ignorance: ignorance "of some things and for some people and people in a certain state" (*II* 144c9–10). The relevant people prove to be those knowledgeable of specialties, such as war and oratory, but "without knowledge of the best [*beltistos*]" (*II* 144a45, 146e1). These people are eventually equated with those who trust in "opinion without intelligence" (*II* 146a9, c11–13), that is, with those whose opinions, of what is good, are not moderated by intelligent weighing of which good or goods are best. They may know this or that art or skill, as generals or diviners may do. But they do not understand the limitation of their particular expertness, and they try to dominate their country through that art in which they are best and honored. It follows that a wise concealment of certain arts may be prudent (*II* 147c6–d8). Probably this explains the two dialogues' silence, in the context of what Alcibiades wants, as to the arts of war and power.

Caution in invoking the gods is especially needed if they too have the specialist's defect. They do, Socrates hints. In a passage quoted from Homer the gods appear as knowing only particular arts, not as comprehending what is truly best.[17] The first *Alcibiades* had criticized the arts as partial; the second applies the criticism to people and things religious (*I* 124e–125c). Accordingly, Socrates recommends a deferential acknowledgment of ignorance in some people, and he engages in theological reform. Popular deference paves a way for deference to what the gods bestow, rather than what one wants, and also to what the wise understand the gods to be.

But Alcibiades is too great of soul for any such deference to what the fates bestow, and he accordingly needs some theological wisdom of his own. He is not content with Socrates' reformed and rather resigned prayer, that the gods give the "noble things as well as good ones," whatever the worshiper might ask for (148c2–4). Alcibiades wants what he wants, not what any god might give. Perhaps contradictorily, he wants especially to avoid what he fears when he prays for what he wants. Hence he wants to know the art of propitiating and winning over the gods. For such a man, reforms must go deeper. The gods themselves must be reformed. Socrates' improved theology holds that the gods, like intelligent men, favor especially "intelligent men," that is, "those who know what one should do and say both to gods and to men" (150a6–b1).

I discuss later such reforms. It is enough to say here that all these steps, in the two dialogues combined, do lead to an Alcibiades more knowing, even in matters religious. At the end of the second dialogue he postpones his prayer and will wait upon some teacher for knowledge of what to pray for. He becomes again more an inquirer.

Yet this Alcibiades is by no means chiefly an inquirer. If the intellectual tension of the first *Alcibiades* is largely absent from the second, it is because the issue of what life to lead is not in play. Alcibiades, more docile, is less open and interesting, and Socrates, more the exhorter and speechifier, is less the intellectual friend and coach. By dialogue's end, nevertheless, the political Alcibiades has become more philosophic, perhaps especially more philosophical (in the loose sense) about things religious. As he may be more patient and understanding as to his many enemies, he is less wild and irrational in his divine models of righteousness and punishment. Perhaps only for the moment, we find an urbane Alcibiades, one who resembles some charmingly ironic member of Socrates' philosophic circle (consider *Menexenus* 234a1–236d3).

JUSTICE AND THE NOBLE

While Alcibiades is moved by Socratic argument, the crucial premises of argument originate in his scruples. One must not

miss the moral in such a man, who is moved by a certain justice
and a certain nobility as well as by pride and ambition. He always
knew what justice meant (*I* 109e9–110c11); he "would not
choose even to live as a coward" (*I* 115d7); he feels a sacred horror at even speaking the possibility of matricide ("Hush, by Zeus,
Socrates" *II* 142d2). Nor are such scruples mere names, sym-
bolic, without influence. Alcibiades is not *uno solo* without restraints of scruple, even if his passionate wish for his own fame
and power, like Cyrus's, presses somewhat in that (Machiavellian)
direction. It is the young Alcibiades' devotion to father and fatherland, to a certain justice, that makes him rebel against the inference that their justice may be unexamined foolishness. It is his
concern for nobility that makes him first acknowledge his devotion to justice and then, at the first crisis of confidence, acknowledge his confusion. It is his concern for an elemental justice, a
right to take care of one's own affairs, that makes him question
whether political life can provide the superiority he wants. And it
is his moral horror to which Socrates appeals in the second dialogue, warning against bad things that one might mistake for
good. Alcibiades' scruples are the toehold for Socrates' development in him of a truer understanding.

Correction is needed, for in both dialogues we see Alcibiades
may go wrong through his scruples as well as right. His notions of
right may lead him to go wrong. The second dialogue shows
souls going spectacularly wrong through an unexamined righteousness. Oedipus and other legendary tragic heroes, according
to Socrates, went wrong accordingly.

Admittedly, the Alcibiades we first see is not exactly an icon of
moral seriousness. He certainly finds it hard to grasp Socrates'
initial suggestion that justice is what politics is about. His head is
full of vast plans, with the conquests of Cyrus and Xerxes wan-
dering around as imagined models, and his characteristic means,
after election by the people, will be war. He is finally brought to
acknowledge that when we go to war we claim to have suffered
some injustice, and he even asserts that this "makes all the difference" (*I* 108b1–109c8). But this is a momentary effusion. While
Alcibiades is unwilling to say that Athens may war against the
"just," even saying that such an assertion is "terrible," it is only

because such action is not "lawful" or customary. He will not agree with Socrates that it is ignoble.[18]

Still, his doubts about justice are accompanied by certainties, and the doubts in crucial cases prove to rest upon the certainties. Alcibiades had been confident that the assembly would give him the superiority he deserves (*I* 105a7–b2), that justice is obtaining what he deserves, that leadership in war and peace will provide what he deserves, and that the people will give due deference to his rule. It is doubt of these underlying certainties that finally shakes Alcibiades. Their root seems chiefly his intense love for what is best for himself as superior, together with his opinion that a political life will provide it. He always knew that those who took what belonged to him were "unjust" (*I* 110c1–2). But this view of justice, as the superiority he deserves, proves to be in contradiction with another of his convictions about justice, as what free governments such as Athens uphold. He does not understand the disparity between himself and the political whole. Socrates' first probings at what politics is about unearth a faith in political justice.

We see this faith in Alcibiades' violent reaction to Socrates' tacit questioning of Greek justice. If those who disagree about justice cannot be knowledgeable of it, to repeat, then the quarreling Homeric heroes, the warring Greek cities, and Alcibiades' father, who died on behalf of Athens, did not know what they were doing. That implication Alcibiades cannot stand. His agreements turn tentative ("it seems," "it is likely") and then stop (*I* 112d10). On the authority of what the Greeks do in practice he discredits justice in favor of "the advantageous," then discredits inquiry as the way to test knowledge of the advantageous, and finally refuses to participate in any inquiry as to whether justice can be separated from the advantageous.

We see in sullen microcosm the ever-present antipathy between political loyalty and clear thinking. For the sake of a justice-like common good and justice-like models of heroism, Alcibiades inaugurates before our eyes a political rebellion against Socrates. Socrates quells it but only by exhibiting public-spiritedness, that is, a kind of justice. That is, he holds up the prospect of proving that "what's just is also advantageous," a prospect Alcibiades expressly welcomes (*I* 114e7–9). Perhaps Alcibiades' fears, of justice and of philosophy both, have a similar cause. Either may be bad both for his country and for himself. The Alcibidean type can lead a political attack upon Socratic philosophy, not only from private jealousy, but also from self-denying righteousness and from right-denying expediency.

The Socratic response is an appeal first to a self-denying higher morals, noble courage, and then to a right-denying higher politics, luxurious royalty. The higher morals shows Alcibiades' nobler side. While he would separate what is good in politics from justice, he himself thinks good a willingness to sacrifice himself, in battle, for a comrade or friend. He would sacrifice for others because cowardice, he thinks, is "the ultimate bad thing" (*I* 115d8–9). Still, even such a spirited type cannot rest content with such high-minded spiritedness. A man can get himself wounded or killed while so aiding a comrade (*I* 115b1–4). Alcibiades' doubts about just actions prove to involve the question whether justice is bad and whether, then, disgraceful acts, such as fleeing danger, are good.

At this turn, Socrates himself moves to defend sacrifice and courage. Socrates, the philosopher who takes morals and politics seriously, would bolster Alcibiades' noble inclinations. But his argument evades the cost of nobility. His defense relies strangely upon a separation of the goodness of courage, its nobility, from the bad consequences that are possible, such as wounds and death. Socrates separates the danger of death from the nobility of courage, a doubtful step that Alcibiades (with hesitations) nevertheless accepts (*I* 115e9–116a).

Why does Alcibiades accept this utopian or idealistic version of courage (and justice)? What in him (and us) leads in this higher but paradoxical direction? It is, I suspect, his concealed justice. Supposing that what's good for Athens is good, he is willing to agree that nothing shameful can be just and that everything just is also noble and hence good (*I* 115a6–10). But this paean to justice neglects the existence of bad laws, bad customs, and bad rulers as well as one's own danger. One might be fighting for a bad cause (or an evil comrade). In itself, therefore, Alcibiades' political loyalty itself implies the separation of just or noble things from bad things, the separation on which Socrates plays. Yes, Socrates fosters noble ambition in Alcibiades, as Plutarch emphasizes (*Lives*, vii, 3). But he does so only by pointing above both politics as it is and expediency as we know it. Socrates develops an idealistic tendency within men's belief in justice and within honorable political ambition. Alcibiades, despite signs of doubt, accepts the argument.

He might well doubt. Whatever its salutary political effects, such a distinction, when examined, undermines nobility as we know it. A courageous act consists in standing firm against the dangers, say, of death in battle. Without the possibility of death, that is, of sacrificing oneself, it would not be a standing firm. The need for strength of soul, that is, for courage, would disappear. Courage disappears into mere doing what should be done, or mere knowing what should be done. Alternatively, if such action were only good or advantageous, there would be no need to sacrifice. The courage, the nobility of the action, again disappears. A defense of justice and nobility as good, as what Alcibiades supposes, tacitly elevates what is good over what is just and noble. It dissipates devotion to justice and nobility as such.

Indeed, after this passage at arms, the "noble," with its connotations of sacrifice, more or less disappears as a topic in the *Alcibiades I*. The exceptions are perfunctory (quick mentions near the end, of Alcibiades as noble and of how ["nobly"] to speak with due regard to god [*I* 135d3–6]). And justice too largely disappears as a topic, until its reappearance as advantage. It reappears not as law and noble sacrifice, but in Alcibiades' supposition that men are just when they do their own business (*I* 127c5–7). This self-regarding understanding of justice resembles Alcibiades' elemental view, that justice is protection of his own (*I* 110b1–c5). But now it is simply his own, without the admixture of family, city, or Greekness. It receives a final Socratic development in the *Alcibiades I*: justice is an approximation, a "resemblance," to the primacy of wisdom or intelligence. Justice so understood does not involve noble sacrifice. But it also does not essentially involve one's own domination or superiority. The thinking through of justice has yielded a separation not only from nobility but also from grand ambition.

Accordingly, the first *Alcibiades* more or less concludes with a rather preachy exhortation to duty. The public man should foster virtue, not wealth, walls, and harbors, and should act according to "justice and moderation," not according to "personal license and rule for oneself" (*I* 134c10–11). One's own superiority is not the object of either leader or country. Thus one acts according to the "light" rather than the "dark," and the "divine" rather than the "godless," that is, according to resemblances of intelligence (consider the progression in 134d1–135b5). Socrates clarifies political morals with a view to the true peak of human nature.

But will Alcibiades, or any country, for that matter, ever follow such a self-denying path of light? It is doubtful, certainly as to Alcibiades. Socrates is explicit. It is "likely" that Alcibiades will "act unjustly," looking in his "ignorance" to what is "godless and dark" (*I* 134e4–6). Socrates anticipates here the Alcibiades we find in the second dialogue. For how can justice be so separated from what men, including Alcibiades, mostly want and think they deserve?

Actually, the first *Alcibiades* supplies a picture of what would consume Alcibiades in the absence of either the grand politics to which he tends or the philosophic life of a Socrates: luxuriousness. Absent grand and serious activities, Alcibiades is likely to indulge the lower and lighter, albeit on a spectacular scale. We are given a comic paean to the court life of Persian and Spartan queens, a fluffy caricature in the first dialogue that complements the second's heavy doses of the darkly tragic. It bowls Alcibiades over, this picture of royal descent, royal wealth, and royal luxury. Perhaps an image of the trappings of despotism is where one is led by a wish for nobility without sacrifice and for superiority without sacrifice. Nothing is said here as to kingly ruling or kingly battles. Only queens speak, and they speak mostly of common things on a very royal scale. Good family, but via a line of kings. Wealth, but in Persian excess. Luxury, but in "fine and good" territories devoted to supplying the queen's undies (*I* 125b5–c2). Our young Alcibiades takes all this as a sign of superior authorities.

What then of his great ambition? While Alcibiades wishes power and a grand name, what would he do with this power over others, and reputation from others, without justice or philosophy within? If he did not continue conquering, as did Xenophon's Cyrus, he would pamper himself, perhaps seeking a splendid name even in that. He would especially pamper his body with luxuries. In the *Symposium* Alcibiades enters in what seems success. He enters drunk, surrounded by attendants and flute girls, and, if he comes to wreathe his friend the poet, he thinks the fit celebration to be a drinking bout. Startled to find Socrates, he accuses him of another "ambush" (*Symposium* 213b9-c1).

In the second *Alcibiades*, by contrast, we see the terrible side of grand ambition, the dark side that Socrates quietly predicted for him in the first. The topic is not nobility, justice, or comedic vices, but evil deeds and evilly harsh retributions. No cotton candy royalty here; the examples are mostly tragic figures limned by tragic poets. They are Oedipus, Orestes, Alcmaeon, and Alcibiades himself (Socrates' addition), and tyrants who rose and fell by assassination. Oedipus killed his father, married his mother, and in remorse tore out his eyes. His eyes! What a reversal of Socrates' analogy between vision and intelligence (*I* 132d1-133c17). He also cursed his sons—consider what you pray for—and lived to see them kill one another. Dark thoughts and dark acts. Orestes and Alcmaeon killed their mothers in revenge for involvement in murder of their fathers and were pursued in turn by the avenging furies (*erinyes*). This, like Xenophon's dark prince, reminds of the other side, hardly to be called grand, of grand ambition.

Then there is the startling example of what the ambitious Alcibiades himself might do. Socrates offers the supposition, purely hypothetical, of course, that this seeker after tyranny might wish to murder "your own guardian and friend, Pericles" (*II* 143e9-144a2). At the possibility of killing his mother, another possibility that doctor Socrates brought to the surface, Alcibiades recoiled in revulsion. At the possibility of murdering Pericles, who has the rule that Alcibiades wants, there is no outburst.

If we turn from the evil possibilities to the Socratic prescription, one thing stands out: an absence of moral strictures. Socrates focuses on knowing what is truly good, but he leaves out anything resembling exhortations to justice or common decency. His theme is not "moderation," as might have been expected from the first *Alcibiades*, but rather intelligence in selecting what is good for oneself, especially the comprehensive good (cf. *I* 133c21–23). Still, is this intelligible? Even in the first dialogue moderation had been derived from the primacy of wisdom; it consisted in ranking accordingly what belongs to oneself and others. The theme guiding the second is similar. While the ostensible theme is the need to take care as to what one prays for, the particular care finally commended is "knowledge of the best," or "knowledge and insight as to the best" (*II* 145c2, e8–9, 146e1). Besides, the "moderation" of the first dialogue led to the unrealistic exhortations to a justice without regard to one's wants or one's good.

Nevertheless, the absence of moral exhortation is strange. Base things are called "terrible," but that does not lead Socrates to celebrate noble and just conduct. He may evoke a horrified "Hush" from Alcibiades, but he never encourages simple obedience to righteous morals or sacred laws, even as politic. Why this abstraction from moral prescription?

The reason seems to be the impolitic and imprudent excesses that can go with moral prescription, especially in so powerfully volatile a man as Alcibiades. The demands of noble vengeance or sacred righteousness may lead to indignant despotism or irrational severity. Judging from the examples, the danger is greatest as to relations with mother and father, especially of son with mother. An Alcibiades may do terrible things, in extremes of self-revulsion, guilt, and indignation, should the crimes involve his father and especially his mother. Such a type should think about the good of what he does, not about vengeance or retribution as such.

The first step is to be able to think about what in such circumstances a man should do. Socrates begins by correcting Alcibiades' impulsive characterization of Oedipus: he was a "madman" (*II* 138c6). No, Socrates asserts with laughable calmness: Oedipus was imprudent in his opinions. Alcibiades also thinks the Athenian people "mad" (*II* 139c8–9). What revenge might such an impassioned man wreak upon the religiously hysterical people by whom he was in fact eventually exiled, deprived of his property, and sentenced to death? What might he wreak upon himself for killing a Pericles? The people, and Alcibiades himself, are less mad than ignorant. They act according to their opinion of what is good, and need to be treated less in indignant rage than with knowing judiciousness.[19]

What all this finally amounts to, nevertheless, is moderation of Alcibidean morals, not replacement. Socrates eventually allows some encouragement to those who pray for noble victories and superiority. For example, he recommends the prayer that "a prudent poet" provided to imprudent friends: "King Zeus, give us the noble things, whether we pray or do not pray"; also, ward off the terrible things, even when we pray for them. (Noble is *esthlos* here: that is, things that are conventionally noble, as good family, victories, and other things commonly admired, *II* 143a1– 3.) Later Socrates recommends a Spartan prayer asking that the gods give "the noble things [*kalos*] in addition to the good things" (*II* 148c2).

Still, these prayers for things noble make a point of slighting one's own wants or wishes, and by dialogue's end Socrates' final reforms go much farther in this direction. The wisest gods favor or should favor piety, justice, and prudence, he says. One is to look up to the dutifulness with which the first *Alcibiades* closed. It is true that Socrates closes by counseling that Alcibiades needs some teacher to "apply the things through which you are going to recognize bad on the one hand and noble [*esthlos*] on the other" (*II* 150e2–3). This, however, involves the primacy of a suitable teacher, and it involves the noble and bad only as these names are put in the true light.

Socrates thus points beyond "resemblances" to the wisdom to be applied in such political, moral, and religious matters. The wisest gods, he finally says, favor "those who know what one needs [*dei*] to do and say regarding gods and human beings" (*II* 150b2–3). Looking for divine help, as well as for noble and just things, is to be guided by the knowing man.

These two dialogues exhibit knowing guidance in the flesh, so to speak. The special topic of the second dialogue is moral-theological therapy, to which my concluding section recurs. But first I reconsider briefly the fragility and errors of political justice, taken by itself and without divine help.

POLITICS AS THE ANSWER

Alcibiades' most powerful conviction is about politics, not nobility, justice as such, or the gods. He supposes that politics will bring him the superiority he so ardently desires. Socrates' efforts at moderation depend upon making him doubt this very powerful and very familiar opinion. He means to relieve Alcibiades of excessive expectations from Athenian democracy in particular, from free politics in general, and even from rational politics simply.

Even at the start of the first dialogue Alcibiades seemed at once of the Athenian democracy and above the Athenian democracy. He will present himself before the assembly, but with a view to greater honors than those obtained by Pericles or by anyone else who has ever lived. He would have "the greatest power" in the city, although it is the assembly that selects him. Socrates draws out the contradictions. It is not that he encourages tyranny beyond Athenian law. The first *Alcibiades* closes by warning against mere "licentiousness" and "tyranny" and exhorting to moderation, justice, virtue, and respect for law (*I* 134b9–135c7). The point is rather the inadequacy of any politics, including Athenian politics, for the superiority Alcibiades seeks. Alcibiades prides himself on his learning and inquiry, but he obtained his knowledge of justice from the people (*I* 100e1). He prides himself on superior knowledge, but he depends on those whom he acknowledges to be mediocre judges in difficult matters. We have touched the most revealing incongruities: devotion to fatherland and forbears leads him in turn to disavow justice, nobility, and finally serious inquiry. For Socrates the decisive effect is the last: Alcibiades will content himself with the intellectual level of Athenian politicians. He is like the sharp pol on his turf who puts a familiar arm around a would-be reformer. "Let us consider it in common, Socrates": you and I know that the other pols are "uneducated," but that I can surpass them "thanks to my nature." So why "train and bother oneself with learning?" (*I* 119b1–c1).

It is this response that leads to the one Socratic crisis of either dialogue. "How unworthy." " I lament for you and for my love" (119c2–3, 5). This is not an Alcibidean crisis. Alcibiades is revealingly surprised at Socrates' disdain and rebuke. But it is a Socratic crisis, for Alcibiades' politic complacency with the second-rate shakes Socrates' estimate and his love, perhaps decisively.[20] It leads also to a change of tactics. Socrates turns from demonstration of intellectual confusion to shaming, and then to a visionary political speech.

The new Socratic approach accepts Alcibiades' political ambition but raises his political sights. The appeals are to aristocratic prejudice and then to the supranoble royal authorities. How could a noble Alcibiades be content to compete with some vulgar tradesman? Is not his true competition world-class, with Spartan and Persian royalty rather than mere Athenian democrats? Alcibiades thinks he has all the advantages. Socrates appeals from that prejudice to Spartan and Persian advantages, especially on a kingly or, rather, queenly scale. In the longest speech of the dialogue Socrates manages to call upon Spartan and Persian queens to attest that anyone with the minor wealth and family of Alcibiades had better turn to "care [*epimeleia*] and wisdom [*sophia*], for these are the only noteworthy things among the Greeks" (*I* 123d2–4). If Alcibiades inclines above free politics, we noted, it could be to a rather effeminate despotism.

It was in the face of this all too likely possibility that Socrates pricks up Alcibiades' noble ambition in a long exhortation that concludes with the bravura rendition of Alcibiades' quest for fame—"something you seem to me to love as no one has ever loved anything else" (*I* 124b5–6). The effect of these many comical exaggerations is all Socrates might wish: "How must I take care of myself, then, Socrates? Can you explain it? For you really seem like one who's spoken the truth" (*I* 124b7–9). Socrates moderates Alcibiades' devotion to Athens by appealing to superiority far above what free Athens can bestow.

Still, the decisive discussion is the ensuing dialogue touched on before. Socrates provokes the now-docile Alcibiades to say what taking care of himself is. Alcibiades makes the political move: it is taking care to be a good ruler. What then should a good ruler promote? Well, what does politics most need? The hopeful young Alcibiades thinks that shared friendship or concord is the crucial thing. (It is Socrates who equates "concord" with Alcibiades' more hopeful "friendship.") But the thought of men sharing women's spinning, and women sharing men's battles, makes Alcibiades think again. He faces the contradiction between friendship as involving shared views, as citizens, and friendship as involving respect for each in his or her own qualities, as, say, man and woman. "By the gods, Socrates, I myself don't know what I'm saying" (*I* 127d6–7). Alcibiades does not know himself. He now doubts the political presupposition by which he lives. The acknowledgment is devastating, and this passage at argument is the serious peak of the dialectical battle of wits.

In the hopefulness of youth Alcibiades had thought of the Athenians cheering him on and of politics in general as voluntary sharing or voluntary minding of one's own business. But such a community "neither needs nor can admit a ruler."[21] Alcibiades was foolish in thinking that free politics works without constraint or could provide adequate room for him; he was naïve in expecting the assembly to defer to his power.

The famously political Alcibiades has to learn from Socrates the essential importance of the regime, that is, of the pervasive effects of a ruling class and its ethos. Those sharing in community are not free to mind their own business, but the business defined by the rulers who share, and those minding their own business will not necessarily share it with the community. Besides, those so sharing want a share, not subjection to a superior; those so minding mind their own business, not that of a superior. This revelation of inner contradictions had been prepared by the doubts Socrates had raised about Alcibiades' own Athens. It is succeeded by the doubts Socrates proceeds to raise about a truly rational politics.

Intelligent rule demands that the ruler encourage human being at its best, which is, as Socrates argues, intelligence. This means that a statesman and his city live by what is right, that is, what is right for the ruled. One must forbear "personal license and rule" for oneself or even for one's city. All are to be guided by the correct; they are to practice "justice and moderation" (*I* 134c9–11). Accordingly, Alcibiades the statesman should be occupied as little as possible with "walls or warships" and as much as possible with giving "the citizens a share of virtue" (*I* 134b7–c5). But for this "you must first acquire virtue yourself" (*I* 134c5). This seems to persuade Alcibiades. In subjecting himself to Socrates at dialogue's end he promises to "take trouble over justice" (*I* 135e4–5).

But what then of what so concerns him, himself? The problem arises within the argument. Justice, this virtue of ruling, is here derived by way of "moderation," which turns from the priority of the thinking self to measure the things that should belong to oneself. But a turn to belongings is to secondary things, Socrates has repeatedly argued. These may be complicated things, like being a statesman, which leave little for oneself per se. (Compare the requirements for doctor and helmsman with those for "all rule and exercise of personal authority" [*I* 134e10–135b1].) Then what of oneself per se?

This makes precarious the conversion of Alcibiades to justice. A turn to concern for others is very dimly related to his desire for more of the best for himself. It should be no surprise that in these preachments Socrates looks for divine help. He swears by Zeus, and he urges that "if both you and the city act justly and moderately, you will act in a way dear to the gods" (*I* 134d1–2). Is it the profound awareness of the fragility of political justice that makes Socrates so serious about the gods and theology?

It is also true that the difficulties of any "Alcibiades the Just" are exacerbated by the Socratic bath he has taken. Alcibiades has lost much of his native patriotism. He has lost much of his faith in the people and in free politics. Indeed, the very premise of his new docility is reverence for the spectacular trappings of (Spartan and Persian) monarchy. It is hard to say how this goes with his new seriousness about the state of his soul and about justice especially. It is easy to say that license and seriousness don't go together easily. It is also easy to say that his ambition would have led to such discordances anyway, and wildly.[22]

Something is indicated by Alcibiades' state at the start of the second *Alcibiades*. He is angry with the people, who now seem his enemies—"mad," "imprudent," and perhaps bent on killing, confiscating, and exiling (*II* 139c10–d4, 145b4–10). He is unashamedly in search of tyranny and is bent on evading by divine help the troubles one might expect from such a quest. In his loneliness among political men he has not turned for light and counsel to the philosopher Socrates, even if he is surprisingly docile when they chance to meet (135e6–8). Alcibiades is on his way to pray, and he is gloomy and looking down rather than confident and looking up.

Aid and Absolution from Above: Reformed Theology

The second *Alcibiades* addresses chiefly the wish for divine help to avoid facing up to the bad consequences of tyrannical desire. That evasion of thinking is what Socrates discourages, with the indirect effect of moderating the desire itself. By dialogue's end preoccupied gloom and the turn to prayer have been replaced by a bemused awareness of ignorance, at least as to what the gods wish, and a turn to some wise man who can instruct him. This is a more reasonable and attractive Alcibiades than the docile pupil at the end of the first dialogue. This second Socratic dose is necessary, if still no complete cure.

All the occupation with divinity in the second *Alcibiades* may seem surprising to modern readers, and even the Alcibiades of the first had been languid on the topic. He had exhibited only rather typical Athenian beliefs. He knows of Homer's epics, of course. He also acknowledges a sphere for diviners, traces his ancestry to Zeus, and, when he came to doubt himself, swears "by the gods" and "by Zeus" (*I* 107a4, 112a3, 116e2, 121a1–2, 127d6, 130c7, 133d4). But his heart was not in these things. His bent had been to rely on himself, his advantages, and his city, and, when convinced of the confusion among his opinions, to turn toward the thinker Socrates. He had thought Socrates "joking" in his talk of a *daimon* (124d1), and he had to be reminded to speak "nobly" as to god's will, rather than Socrates' will, when finally subordinating himself to Socrates' tutelage.

It is Socrates who there seems pious. He begins as if "a god" were questioning, defers to his *daimon* (*I* 105a2, 105c7–8, 103a5, e5, 7), trusts his own divination (*I* 127e6–7), and reminds Alcibiades that noble speaking calls for placing responsibility with the god. Is there a rhetorical-educative pattern? Perhaps he shows Alcibiades the political theology of public speaking. Socrates' remarks move from the gods to the divinity within, and then, for noble speaking, back again. He himself does not swear by Zeus, as he does twice in the less philosophic second *Alcibiades*, or by any personal god. He does account as "most divine" and "resembling the god" the thinking and prudence that manifest the region in which "the virtue of the soul, wisdom," exists (*I* 133b7–c4). He later names this region "intellect" (*nous, I* 134e8–9, 135a6). The intellect is what can appear to be most divine. In this dialogue, Socrates' *daimon* prohibits what Socrates' reasoning determines to be imprudent (*I* 105e5–106a1). Theological reform is under way, it seems, although by no means atheistic reform. Socrates is moderating Alcibiades' pictures of Zeus, Achilles, and the rest with a view to intelligent reasoning, while also reminding Alcibiades that it is fitting to credit not the intelligence of man but a god. Alcibiades of the second dialogue gets the point at the end, including the urbane rhetorical point. It would not "be seemly for me to vote against the god" (*II* 150b6–7).

If all this is true, then the second *Alcibiades* is a continuation of Socrates' moderation of religion, although now with the urgency obvious. A tyrannical Alcibiades seeks help and absolution from the gods. One might think the theme less political-philosophic than political-theological. In the second dialogue Socrates defends knowing, but the context is mostly a defense of ignorance. Knowledge has to be measured (up to a point) for its goodness or badness, and to that extent it has to be subordinate. Alcibiades' great project is no longer in question, and Socrates never presses dialectically for a fundamental conversion. One sees much more of didactic lectures, interspersed with the occasional perfunctory request for student participation: "I would wish to learn from you, too, whatever you have in mind regarding these matters" (*II* 150b3–4, cf. 143a5).

The second dialogue no doubt involves Alcibiades' own good, but it involves also and more the removal of such a type from the ranks of philosophy's enemies. The first dialogue ends with an apprehension that the city will overcome "both me and you" (*I* 135e8). The second ends with Socrates wishing to become "a noble victor over your lovers." These lovers are related to religion. Socrates explains. For "I" am at the mercy of a "wave" like that which the blind prophet Teiresias forced upon the wise King Creon (*II* 151c1–3). In Euripides' *Phoenician Women* the prophet Teiresias prophesies that Creon, husband of Oedipus's daughter, must sacrifice his son to save his city from pollution.[23] This kind of divine counselor would lead an Alcibiades to sacrifice potential philosophers and philosophy itself as well as his own better judgment. If the first *Alcibiades* shows Socrates triumphing over the city, in a competition with the people for the most promising youth, the second shows a certain triumph over the city's gods, in a competition with the poets for a hero. Alcibiades, it becomes clear, looks up to dubious models of gods and heroes and is himself the heroic type to the poets—the theologians of the ancient Greeks—who dramatize the gods and heroes. Socrates would win him away from such models and modelers. How does he succeed?

The opening wedge is the argument for wary thoughtfulness when praying. Be prudent in what you pray for because you may get it. This is the broad argument at beginning and end; it can work because its premise is Alcibiades' supposition that the god gives some people what they wish for. But the calming that eventually ensues comes chiefly from three other considerations, political-moral, prudential, and theological. In the face of Alcibiades' ambition, Socrates reminds of terrible things tyrants may suffer and do while supposing they pursue what is good. In the face of Alcibiades' now passionate desire for knowledge of how to avoid the bad while getting the good, Socrates surprises him with a qualified defense of ignorance. Alcibiades, seeking prophecy and absolution, should be modestly skeptical of his knowledge of what the gods want and correspondingly deferential to the wise who know. Finally, to meet Alcibiades' expectations of help from compliant gods, Socrates develops a reformed theology. He shows how to improve upon the poets, and he improves especially their descriptions of jealous and vengeful gods who help those who give rich offerings and punish horribly those who disobey their decrees. Consider what you pray for, face up to the harsh deeds that tyranny requires, be aware of one's ignorance as to the gods and their wishes, follow a theology that fosters reasonable justice and rational knowing—these are four Socratic lessons taught more or less in turn. Cumulatively, they help bring about an ironic reasonableness in even an Alcibiades. I conclude by saying more about each.

Socrates' first step resembles that in the first dialogue: he gets Alcibiades to consider how best to do what he is passionate to do. Given that his gods may give what he prays for, he can hardly avoid agreeing that he should be prudent in what he asks for. And given that the ordinary Athenian does not beat and strike him, as madmen would, he cannot avoid the conclusion that the people may be imprudent but they are not mad (*II* 139c1–d6). This is the prefatory inducement, to thoughtfulness about friends and enemies, that a residual respect for Socrates permits.

Still, even this intimates the problem posed by the divine legends carried on by the poets. It was the awful tale of Oedipus's cursing of his sons that Socrates uses to prove that imprudent prayers can yield bad things. It is Oedipus, not the people, whom Alcibiades first explains away as "mad" (*II* 138c6–7). Yet Oedipus, murderer of his father and husband to his mother, had been himself victim of "curses" and of a divinely fated punishment ("heaven's device," Teiresias called it). His father, King Laius, conceived him in drink and desire and thus violated a prohibition, in a prophecy, against intercourse.[24] Oedipus's line was accordingly demon-possessed from an original sin. Might Alcibiades be susceptible to such possibilities? Could he too be so "mad" as to suffer such remorse and do horrible things while thinking them good? He had not been horrified at the prospect of murdering Pericles. But in reaction might he and his heirs lash out in righteous horrors?

Then, second, Socrates elaborates the problem of mistaken prayers with more political and calculable examples, especially with the "tyranny" Alcibiades (as he here acknowledges) would no doubt pray for. He moves from legendary figures to Alcibiades, and from "madness" to the imprudence of praying for an apparently good thing without observing the bad consequences. Does not tyranny put one in danger of assassination, even from a lover? Socrates proceeds to reason similarly as to generalship, since the Athenians have killed, exiled, and pestered their generals, and even as to children, since people pray for children and then have to deal with wicked ones and with misfortunes to the good ones (*II* 141a–142d). Socrates' obvious strategy is to bring to mind the evils that can accompany things that seem obviously good and are prayed for. For even if the evils are only occasional, those who pray need to take into account the possibility that evil, not good, may come from their prayer. But this argument also intimates the natural root of these desires and thus their inevitability. If tyranny as well as generalship is like the desire for children, then the prospect of possible evils will not end Alcibiades' overpowering desire for tyranny. Might such a sober prospect at least moderate the desire, however? But what of gods who can provide against the evils?

It seems to be the natural power of self-serving ambition that provokes Socrates' first effort in *Alcibiades II* to reform prayer. He quotes a "prudent poet," who may be his mouthpiece (neither prayer nor poet is otherwise known). The poet's prayer asked that, whatever it is we pray for, Zeus give the "noble" and avert the "terrible" (*II* 142e1–143a2). This deference to what the gods think good rather than to what he thinks good Alcibiades rejects out of hand. He wants what (he thinks) is "best for himself." Yet the argument has caught in him, and he is now worried. What if he prays for what brings the "worst," which would "be more a curse than a prayer"? "The worst" seems to involve especially "curses." Perhaps thinking of an Oedipus, he wants to avert such a fate by knowing what is to come (*II* 143a8–b5). He wants prophecy. It is Alcibiades' aroused wish for prophecy that leads to Socrates' third step, a defense of ignorance as to things theological.

A Socratic defense of ignorance? This takes Alcibiades aback. Why should he not learn what he needs to know? Whereupon Socrates proceeds to show knowledge that is bad for him. Alcibiades is even more taken aback by the example. A certain knowledge might make him kill his mother, as Orestes and Alcmaeon had killed theirs. (Alcibiades was of the Alcmaeonidae, descendents of the legendary Alcmaeon). "Hush (keep reverent speech), by Zeus, O Socrates" (*II* 143d2). Surprised that knowledge is sometimes bad, he nevertheless shies, as from a violation of sacred law, from bad knowledge, from knowledge about murdering his mother. But Socrates probes on, toward the ignorance that might have made old Alcmaeon himself more reasonable. He emerges with an odd kind of ignorance. It would have been better for Alcmaeon, given his state of mind, not to recognize his mother. Such ignorance, of the identity of his mother, Socrates defends. Similarly, should Alcibiades think it best to kill Pericles, better that he were "ignorant that it was he" (*II* 144a9–b1).

Why these strange examples of failure to recognize one's own mother or father? I'll venture two possibilities. The examples may point, first, to the danger of confusing one's mother or father with sacred and avenging figures. Or they may point, second, to the related danger that those unguided by knowledge of the best will often mistake the quality, the goodness or badness, of the particular objects they seek. They may see not a father but rather an obstacle to their tyranny. Or they may see not a mother but the killer of their father, whom they must avenge as a sacred duty. Alcmaeon and Orestes killed their mothers in retribution—Alcmaeon, as commanded by his father. For their matricides both went mad and were pursued by divine furies (*erinyes*).[25] Is the question of mistaken identity really the question of not mistaking the Greek gods and heroes for models of reasonable human conduct?

This possibility seems confirmed by Socrates' procedure here. His own accounts of Oedipus, Orestes, and Alcmaeon abstract from the legendary sins, furies, and fated revenges. They dwell instead on the unreasonableness of the acts themselves. One would hardly recognize the characters by his descriptions; it might seem a case of mistaken identity. That Alcmaeon and Orestes killed their mothers in retribution for murder of their fathers, Socrates leaves unmentioned. That Oedipus's terrible acts were in response to incest with his mother and murder of his father also goes unmentioned. We do learn that Oedipus "in a rage" was imprudent in cursing his sons and that Orestes was ignorant of "what was best for him" (*II* 141a1–2, 143d8). Socrates leads Alcibiades to what is wise in the circumstances (killings are not excluded), as opposed to paying back or punishment per se. Consider: might Oedipus and his Thebes have been better off if the prophet Teiresias had not blabbed out the truth about Oedipus's wife and father? Oedipus had been a good king, and although he had killed his father and married his mother, his violations had been utterly inadvertent. They were, so to speak, cases of mistaken identity.

The final arguments for ignorance are clearly political. Even when in this context Socrates recurs here to things religious and the poets, his focus is on the poets as legislators of customs. What is the political case for "awareness of ignorance"? Why does this argument in particular persuade Alcibiades?

The point seems to be that the common claims to rule, on account of numbers, say, or wealth, are doubtful on their face, at least to competing claimants. Socrates' example is of men who may know how to confiscate or exile; without guidance by knowledge of what is "the best," they may do great harm (*II* 145b8–c3). Alcibiades, no stranger to such democratic stings, leaps to agree. He agrees also to the more general point: the case for a certain doubting hesitancy in such seekers of rule. Whereupon Socrates raises the problem of judging among all claimants who in any country compete for control. The argument is against narrow specialists. Warriors and musicians, athletes and artisans, those expert at warring and killing, mingle with orators "blowing a political wind" (*II* 145e7). But none of these have "knowledge and discernment [*eidenai*] of the best." Each trusts his "opinion," even if "without intelligence," and wishes honor for his particular art (*II* 146a3–9). These people would be better off if aware of their ignorance about what is best.

The necessary qualifications are made *sotto voce*. Socrates acknowledges the need for particular knowledge, and he qualifies his big recommendation. Self-doubt as to what is best is only for those whose doings for the most part harm themselves and others (*II* 146d2–5).

The thing conspicuously encouraged, nevertheless, is self-doubt about the big questions, doubt in people generally as to their competence to judge of the whole or the best life. This majority includes an Alcibiades. For "the many are imprudent," and those great of soul, such as Alcibiades, will be great among the imprudent (II 150c7–9). It is correspondingly important to reach an Alcibiades. A certain intellectual modesty, a corresponding deference to the knowing, is for most men the secret of good life and good politics. In order to be safe, the soul and the city alike should "cling" to such a modest hesitancy. Else the soul gets "puffed up" over wealth or power or handsomeness or any of the things the young Alcibiades, and citizens generally, get puffed up over (II 146e4–147a4). Here is a political argument for humility before the knowing as to ultimate matters.

Having established the case for awareness of ignorance on political grounds, Socrates makes it bite higher, much higher. He applies it to those who pride themselves on learning and then to the gods who seem highest of all. If the many are to defer to the knowing, it should be to the truly knowing. We get a critique of pretenders, such as the learned (*polymathes*) and multiskilled (*polytechnes*). Such specialists may be multispecialized, but they lack knowledge of the best and will founder on the seas of life. Learning or skill is not wisdom. Quietly, by no more than a phrase quoted from Homer, Socrates includes in this criticism the gods.[26] Are Zeus and the other gods unknowing as to what is in general best? Are they, too, puffed up and erring in particulars, as, perhaps, in their command of sexual abstinence to Laius and their punishment of Oedipus? The problem of the political whole persists in the divine whole, which poets elaborate and to which political men look up and pray.

Socrates applies his cautionary note especially to the architectonic poets. Perhaps these are the polymaths and multiskilled he has particularly in mind. His concluding argument for the people's deference proceeds openly to correct the opinions of Homer, the prince of ancient poets (II 147c6–d8). Socrates gets Homer to affirm the crucial thing Socrates knows, that knowing itself is the measure of human being. The effort involves some charmingly labored philological acrobatics. A Homeric quotation appeared to maintain that a character (Marmites) knew many things, but badly. What Homer meant, Socrates informs us, was that the character knew many things, but it was bad for him to know them. For the "most wise and divine poet" would surely know that "it is impossible to know badly" (*II* 147c6–d8). That is, Homer would know what the *Alcibiades I* shows (*I* 133b7–e2). In short, while Socrates defers to the knowing arts of a wise and divine Homer, he also, enigmatically, corrects him, thus to make more rational the horizon of opinions. The poetic suits this esoteric task, for it is "altogether enigmatic and unknowable to just any man," especially when the poet wishes not "to reveal but rather to hide from us as much as possible his own wisdom" (*II* 147b9–c4).

This whole passage is probably a lesson principally for poets and philosophic interpreters of poets. At least it flies high over the head of an Alcibiades (*II* 147b5–6). This is not to deny what the *Symposium* says: good poets are like lawgivers who leave behind immortal marks of their virtue (*Symposium* 209a6–7, d1–e3). But actual poets need correction in their actual work. This is true especially of the Greek poets and their tragic legends of punishing gods avenging hubristic violations of the city's laws.[27] We see how Socrates informs poetic legends with wisdom more respectful of the politic and the wise. Perhaps we also are given a hint as to why Plato's philosophic dialogues are so enigmatic, poetic, and difficult to understand.

Whatever the subtleties here revealed, the whole argument for ignorance, even with the authority of a reconstructed Homer, leaves Alcibiades rather cold. He is decisively unpersuaded. "Persuaded" he is in a sense, but he remains of two minds and one powerful want. He still wants to know, "by the gods," when he might be "praying for bad things" while "holding the opinion" that they are good. Perhaps he is even more anxious. What might appear as a wish for truth and good is now vitiated by another opinion: that the gods can put things right even if he is mistaken and wrong. Still worried about an inadvert ent prayer for bad things while seeking what he thinks good, he now wants the chance for a second prayer that the first one "be taken back" (*II* 148a8–b4). A worried Alcibiades wants more than prophecy; he wants absolution. Even if the later prayer contradicts the first, he wants the gods to correct the first. The gods too should contradict themselves and their actions. A willful Alcibiades, increasingly impressed with his ignorance of divine power, wants willful gods beyond the restraints of human rationality.

Socrates' fourth big step in this little dialogue is to reform theology. It is not enough for an Alcibiades to be aware that evils can accompany what he wants and to be aware too of some ignorance as to the gods. For he expects the gods to provide against the evils, thanks to his prayers, and to overcome his prayers for evils, even if he should be so ignorant as to make them. Socrates moves to provide a more reasonable understanding of the gods themselves. This involves gods not so rigorous and vengeful in what they demand of human beings, the exclusion of gods who condone and make good bad human choices, and gods who look up to wise men.

When in the second *Alcibiades* Socrates speaks of the traditional legends, of Oedipus, say, he omits not only much of the harshness and vengeance but also the supervision by harsh and punishing gods. We do hear of Oedipus's curses upon his sons, for example, but we do not hear of a divine curse, fated punishment, or vengeful furies. Socrates revises the tragedians' divinities. In Aeschylus's *Seven Against Thebes* the chorus had chanted ominously of "the all true, evil-boding furies [*erinyes*]," which consummate Oedipus's wrathful curses. A son of Oedipus, Eteocles, had lamented "the mighty *erinyes* of my sire" (719–21, 69–71; cf. 95–183, 693–95). Nor does Socrates speak of some original sin or "pollution" brought upon Oedipus's descendents, as does Eteocles in Euripides' *The Phoenician Women* (800–817; cf. 767) and in Sophocles' *Oedipus Rex* (1288–1305, 1350ff, 1357, 1370, 1420–31). Similarly, he never mentions either a need for "expiation" (*Phoenician Women* 681–88) or an ancient curse or a doom from the oracle at Delphi (*Oedipus Rex*, 785–95). It is the same with his brief accounts of Orestes and Alcmaeon: silence as to the furies who visit fated retribution for violation of sacred law.

The Socratic theology focuses instead on beneficial gods and especially on gods who benefit those who deserve it. His divinities are said to bestow on us the noble and good things; they ward off bad things; they honor pious, just, prudent, and knowing human beings (*II* 143a1–4, 148b5–7, 150a6–b2). Theological reform in this respect mirrors the moral reform he encourages: the measurement of conduct by a measure appropriate to men, that is, to reasonable guidance of men, not one that fosters warring heroes and the passions of vengeance and indignation.

The most conspicuous of Socratic reforms, however, is the exclusion of gods who can be bought, that is, gods who change their mind because of human offerings, especially expensive ones. The traditional gods, like Alcibiades himself, were tempted to contradiction and evil by their desires for great honors and wealth. They were models for tyrants and for injustice by the powerful. This Socratic reform occurs in the midst of an expanded lesson for poets and their instructors.

The secret of successful theological reform, it seems, is appeal to higher authorities. Socrates proceeds to motor through three: political-religious (a Spartan prayer), theological (the chief Egyptian god Ammon, identified by the Greeks with Zeus), and literary (the much-abused Homer). This is a quietly hilarious account, and it corresponds to the first dialogue's more raucous caricature, of Persian and Spartan royalty. That had raised Alcibiades' political sights, while exhibiting the silliness of his noble prejudices. This makes more reasonable his expectations from the gods, while indicting the silliness of his religious opinions.

The beginning of this section is an appeal to Socrates' unnamed poet, who now merely recommends that one pray to ward off terrible things (he drops his earlier appeals to Zeus and for noble things). Then we are led to the powerful Spartans, who are said to have a like prayer (which fails to mention warding off the terrible things, reinstates the request for both good things and noble things, but still omits Zeus). However, even this prudent prayer, with the king of the gods omitted, makes the Spartans only "no less lucky than any others" (*II* 148c5–6). Alcibiades could reasonably wonder as to the point of prayer. He has reason to become bemused.

Another step in ironic enlightenment arrives with a political-religious appeal to a foreign god, told with the respectable authority of "Athenian elders." The Athenians, indignant at losing to the Spartans, had sought some stronger charm. They sent away to the Egyptian god Ammon. Why do the Spartans win, despite miserable sacrifices, while the Athenians lose, despite "the richest and most august processions to the gods"? (*II* 148e7–8). A prophet replies for Ammon: the god praises the "Lacedaemonian reverent speech" more than all the Greek sacrifices put together.[28]

At this point Socrates steps forward to equate "reverent speech" with his Spartan prayer. Accordingly, one need take much care as to what one must say and not say, since the gods think rich sacrifices to be blasphemous. The wealthy Alcibiades can't buy his way out. Indeed, by trying he risks certain evil, that is, offense to the gods. This godly disdain for riches is then confirmed by a passage from the divine Homer. The passage is absent from all the manuscripts of Homer and contradicts plenty of passages that are present. One can infer that the wise Socrates has again stepped in for the divine Homer as well as for "the god and the prophet of gods."

The argument finally turns from divine authorities to explicit Socratic criticism of divine authorities. It would be "terrible" if the gods look to expensive gifts and sacrifices, since these can be performed precisely by the rich and powerful, who err "greatly against gods and greatly against human beings." The Socratic intervention is against gods who condone the injustice of the rich and powerful, whether personal or political.

According to the new Socratic theology, on the other hand, "it is probable" that both gods and human beings with "intelligence" honor most the pious, just, and prudent. These turn out to be—surprise!—none other than those "who know what one needs to do and say regarding gods and human beings" (*II* 150a6–b3, 150b2–3). A paean to decent men, and finally to knowing men who act and speak wisely about gods as well as men, completes the philosopher's reformation of worship.

As for Alcibiades, it is possible once again that he approves but is not convinced. He is, Socrates acknowledges, too "great souled" to accept any such deferential prayer. Still, progress has been made even in his commanding soul. The whole argument has convinced Alcibiades of one thing: that he should put off his worship. He agrees that it is not safe for him to pray and sacrifice, since these might not be accepted, might be offensive as blasphemy, or might get "by chance" something in addition. He will delay his turn to the gods until he reconsiders his plans, until he learns, that is, "how to be disposed toward gods and human beings" (*II* 150d1–2).

This is a tall order. It requires more than mere delay and is more than a negative accomplishment. If indeed Alcibiades needs "to recognize bad on the one hand and noble [*esthlos*] on the other" (*II* 150e2), he will have to consider whether the victories and reputation he seeks are not intertwined with bad things and are therefore not so good. He may be less preoccupied with what he thought good and more moderate in pursuing it. He has already become less preoccupied with fear of the gods, more ironic, and more ready for theological reconsiderations. A certain openness to Socratic philosophy, to inquiry as to what he is doing, moderates considerably the passion to rule the world.

CHAPTER FIVE

Imperial Grandeur and Imperial Hollowness: Xenophon's Cyrus the Great

I believe that there is nothing more unequal among human beings
than thinking the bad and the good to deserve equal things.

— CYRUS, in *The Education of Cyrus*

XENOPHON'S CYRUS

XENOPHON'S *Education of Cyrus* examines a legendary political general whose imperial quest, unlike Alcibiades',
proceeded without failures or mistakes, strategic or otherwise. The Cyrus in question is Cyrus the Great, who founded
the Persian empire in the middle of the sixth century BC (about a
hundred and fifty years before Xenophon composed his work).
But Xenophon's account is surely less history than model. It
treats Cyrus's achievement as politically paradigmatic and revamps the story accordingly. It shows that a certain enduring
rule is possible and in particular one superior man's enduring
rule over very many people, cities, and nations. Xenophon had
doubted such a possibility, he tells us at the start. Rebellions and
revolutions overturn democracies, oligarchies, and monarchies; a
tyrant can win admiration if he manages merely to retain his rule,
not to speak of expanding it. Indeed, disorder seems inherent to
politics. People generally unite most of all against those "whom
they perceive attempting to rule them" (1.1.1.), and most rulers
are content if they can manage to control their own country.
Cyrus's achievement is then worthy of "wonder" (or admiration
or amazement, 1.1.6).[1] It is wonder, a scientific or contemplative
reaction, that sets Xenophon's inquiry in motion. Perhaps politics is not a dangerous and unpredictable madhouse. The example of Cyrus shows the possibility of great political achievement,
great individual supremacy, and political science itself. What is

not clear from Xenophon's beginning is whether this greatness and this art are also good, either for the community or for the individual. His book weighs that issue.

In the two Platonic dialogues just considered, Socrates tries to show an ambitious Alcibiades that he cannot get the happiness he wishes from the imperial rule he seeks. Xenophon, the other leading student of Socrates, may lead us toward a similar lesson in his *Education of Cyrus*—so I shall argue—but if so, his method is paradoxically different. He spells out a grandly successful imperial enterprise. His Cyrus's quest to rule the world could seem a great adventure, and the *Education* is one of the greatest adventure stories ever written. Unlike the two *Alcibiades*, it lets the attractions of great politics shine forth. Politics and war shine forth. Indeed, in the light reflected from Cyrus we get to compare and measure a panoply of other political types, some very attractive indeed, some not so devoted to imperial politics. We see the wise old republican statesman (Cambyses), a thoughtful and ardent young prince (Tigranes), an exemplar of noble courage (Abradatas), and a luxuriously clever ruler (Croesus). We also see a tyrant who seems a paradigm of evil (the younger Assyrian king). Some of these, in some respects, outshine Cyrus. In this way, as in others, the *Education* investigates the shadows about Cyrus as well as his gleaming accomplishments, and all the more powerfully since his could seem the most gleaming of political accomplishments.[2] Xenophon's Cyrus is at once a conspicuous model and a model questioned inconspicuously.

I first contend that the *Education of Cyrus* is not a history but a consideration of great political ambition at its most rational. Then I try to clarify both Cyrus's genuine superiority of soul and the dilution nevertheless of some of his best qualities by his overarching ambition. In the last sections of the chapter I examine more closely this passion for mastery, especially the extent to which the greatest mastery actually brings him the happiness he so forcefully wants.

But why should one take this imperial kind of ambition, of an Alexander or Napoleon, as gleaming, that is, as a model? It may be grand, but is it admirable? Very doubtful. Many thoughtful people will deny it and will shudder at such conquerors, if only because they harmed so many. Napoleon's incursion into Russia alone cost over five hundred thousand lives in his own forces, not to mention the wounded, and for his whole imperial quest the estimates range from nine hundred thousand dead to two million. For all combatants the toll was three million lives, or even five million.[3]

Still, one must face the fact that such rulers *are* widely admired, in their time and later too. Their fame lives on in what they built, in legend, and even in hero worship. It lives on among those who harbor like ambitions, no doubt, but also among others who do not. One must look the phenomenon in the eye. Many in France still venerate Napoleon as a hero. Nor can this be dismissed as merely the foolishness of the undiscriminating. It suffices to mention the novelist and psychologist Stendhal, who admired Napoleon to a point, the point at which greatness of soul expanded into ambition without limit.[4] And any discriminating historian can admire the extraordinary political generalship of a Caesar or an Alcibiades, at least by contrast with the instability and blundering of many of the monarchies, oligarchies, and democracies that tend to populate the political world—and who kill so many. Think of the sluggish and hopeful democracies that failed to squelch Hitler in his nest. Napoleon, after all, is hardly the best example of vast ambition. He pressed on into Russia despite the enemy's withdrawal, which foiled his plan for quick victory, and this irrational hubris, in his chosen field of war, caused the worst losses and his fall.[5]

On the surface the *Education* seems mostly a how-to book for an imperial quest perfectly rational in its choice of means. It investigates how imperial rule may be achieved and especially the ways and arts of the human being that can do it. First Xenophon speaks briefly of Cyrus's birth, nature, and education, then, at length, of Cyrus's modes of acquiring and then ruling. If one were fond of contemporary formulations, one might call the *Education* a text of management on a world scale. It shows how to gain empire by building an ever-increasing army of willing followers and by overcoming one's enemies through force, fraud, and the promise of benefits. I shall venture the estimate that the

Education is the greatest such text of the leader's art, at least in the philosophic tradition.

This will seem a strange claim. What, to take the obvious alternative, of *The Prince?* The *Education*, I suggest, is a rational account in a fuller sense than is Machiavelli's masterful handbook. The victory of *The Prince* over the *Education*, which has developed over four centuries of Enlightenment, may not be deserved. For the *Education* considers not only the most efficacious form of acquiring, as did the ruthless *Prince*, but also the most just, noble, and beneficial form. We get continual quiet contrasts between the rational Cyrus and a viciously irrational counterpart, the young prince (and eventual king) of the Assyrians. Xenophon does not make Machiavelli's fateful attempt to reduce truth to effective truth, truth realizable in the world (*Prince*, ch. 15). Accordingly, he does not systematically exclude claims of justice or nobility simply because they are often violated in practice. *Honestum* is not pruned from the most knowing hearts, and we are given a more real realism, truer light, a full spectrum of the colors, as to grand ambition in particular. While Xenophon's Cyrus is a great military man, he prefers to acquire by benefiting rather than harming. He prides himself on his justice, nobility of soul, and friendship. It is true that Cyrus's quest leads to much sacrifice of these things. But the reader of Xenophon, unlike the reader of *The Prince*, can see and feel the cost as well as the benefit. That is the point. The reader can appreciate the tragedy and the evil as well as the triumph. This is one way Xenophon measures the goodness of his Cyrus's enterprise. *The Education of Cyrus* is said to have originated that genre called the mirror of princes, and Machiavelli himself saw the *Education* as *the* literary predecessor and philosophic rival to his *Prince* (ch. 14). But Xenophon's mirror shows more seriously the price as well as the benefit of princedom, and for Cyrus himself as well as for those ruled by him.

There is no doubt, however, that Xenophon begins with the benefits and the grandeur, and this corresponds to a reader's broad impression that Xenophon's Cyrus is of virtue without defect. This is a distinctive literary characterization. It differs sharply, for example, from Herodotus's account, in which the historical Cyrus is presented as visibly unjust and cruel as well as much less farsighted and ingenious. Herodotus's Cyrus begins his imperial quest by throwing off the Medean empire of his grandfather Astyages (I.46).[6] Xenophon's Cyrus, on the contrary, commands an army sent to defend Medea, an army requested by the son and heir of Astyages and sent by Persian authorities. Herodotus's Cyrus orders a group of captives stoned to death, burns his captive Croesus on a pyre (until moved to compassion by a storm from the gods and by Croesus's lament), pillages Sardis until Croesus suggests the shortsightedness of such a policy, and attacks head-on except when Croesus (now a counselor) devises a deception (I.84, 86–88). Xenophon's version is by contrast a paradigm of reason. He restrains even his allies from pillaging Sardis, discusses urbanely with the captured Croesus how to obtain its riches without looting, corrects Croesus's tactical suggestion, is a master of deceptions in war and peace, avoids direct battle where possible, obtains in every battle the advantage in strategy and maneuver, and prefers to win followers by persuasion and benevolence. Herodotus's Cyrus wastes months draining a river to avenge the drowning of a sacred horse (I.189). Xenophon's Cyrus himself interprets prophecy and divine signs, never consults a priest or augurer, and never has to do or desist because of auguries alone.

Generally speaking, Herodotus gives a memorable chronicle of vicious irrationality, itself no doubt largely fictional, and this tenor extends beyond Cyrus in particular. After a dream of bad omen, Herodotus's King Astyages had ordered his infant grandson Cyrus killed; the plot failing, he roasted the son of the minister who failed and then served up the body parts to the father at dinner (I.107–19). The death of Herodotus's Cyrus brings out the implicit and antityrannical lesson: a would-be conqueror to the last, he is defeated by a queen who reproaches him for crookedness and plunges his severed head into a container of gore: "Now I give you your fill of blood" (1.214). Memorable, indeed. So much for a Napoleon.

Xenophon would instill different memories. His Cyrus is a darling of his grandfather, who, if an absolute and dissolute despot, is wary of war, affectionate to Cyrus, and admiring of his courage and daring. Nothing nasty is advertised as to Cyrus's relatives, despite quick indications of Uncle Cyaxares' savagery and mean cunning (2.4.15–16; 4.5.9, 19). Cyrus's mother defends Persian justice under law against her father Astyages' despotic power in Medea. Cyrus's father, a constitutional monarch and a rather Socratic counselor, defends the Persian republic against the inroads of his own son. It is true that Xenophon eventually tells of very nasty things, such as the murder of Gobryas's son and the castration of Gadatas. But these are perpetrated by Cyrus's great enemy, the prince (later king) of the Assyrians, who goes unnamed as if to be left in the dark. It is significant that this dark prince is Cyrus's enemy and dramatic foil, from first skirmish to final victory. To that extent, light and dark, good and evil, rationality and passion frame the political drama of Cyrus's artful rise. Indeed, Cyrus seems in victory the vehicle of just retribution. Evil is left in the shadows, a dark prince who proves the darkest of several foils in bringing out Cyrus's luminous rationality. Xenophon's Cyrus dies in his bed, at the peak of his power, after pronouncing himself happy and satisfied (8.7).

It all might seem perfect were it not for a famously incongruous concluding chapter (8.8), which is well known, and troubling if inconspicuous indications all along, which are less noted. The final chapter announces the empire's factional divisions and soft corruption upon Cyrus's death. This final pronouncement by Xenophon, if I may call it that, contrasts strikingly with Cyrus's final expression of happiness. The contrast is prefigured, notably in Cyrus's increasingly oppressive and narrow rule. Even at the start there are disconcerting references to rule by intimidation (as well as by satisfaction) and to peoples as "herds" ruled by and for a shepherd (1.1.2, 5). Near the end, the conquests having reached their limits, Cyrus's activities seem the more vapid as his rule becomes the more completely self-centered (8.6.21–22). So I shall argue.

In short, Cyrus manifests the promise and the defects of the political life par excellence, that is, at both its most extreme and its most rational. Cyrus rules in a sense the world, and he does it as rationally as a man might. The *Education* thus shows the essentials of rule itself, that is, unqualified rule over all or as many as possible. Such a project appeals above all to the adventurous young, especially to the few of great ambition, like Cyrus, or like Plato's Alcibiades, who took the legendary Cyrus as a model. This class of human beings seems the book's most important audience, and Xenophon presents the most rational ways to the object of their desires. But for others, the more philosophic and the fair-minded young, Xenophon shows not only the arts and the underlying motives, but also the shallowness and the danger.

Still, one might wonder why he does not warn more against dangers. Even if Xenophon has such a mixture of audiences in mind, why does he not make the imperial quest less attractive than he does? Why is Xenophon not the John Locke of the *Second Treatise on Civil Government?* Here, as one ponders Xenophon's broad intention, one should keep in mind his Socratic measuring of different kinds of lives and his own appreciation of the political life in particular.

In the *Memorabilia* Xenophon presents recollections of Socrates that are from start to finish a defense of Socrates' way of life. But the defense is somewhat exaggerated. At one point a certain difference of priority shows itself between the characters Socrates and Xenophon, a difference as to the (nonphilosophic) pleasures of beauty and sex.[7] It is reminiscent of another Xenophontic disagreement with Socrates, as to the attractiveness of a political expedition led by a later Cyrus.[8] Xenophon resolved to join the expedition, despite Socrates' doubts, just as he retained some affection for kissing, despite Socrates' doubts. The *Memorabilia* closes by inviting the skeptic to compare "the character of others" with the virtues attributed to Socrates.[9] Perhaps the *Education of Cyrus* is part of such a comparison. Cyrus the Great is the type with ambition and lordship so unlimited that he is stopped only when nature itself, in the form of heat, cold, sea, and desert, put boundaries to his acquiring (8.6.21). Xenophon's intent is not unlike that weighing of political lordship that Alfarabi attributed to Plato's first *Alcibiades.*

Although Xenophon describes other political models, this one stands out for combining such unbounded ambition with such rationality. The others are either not so ambitious, not so rational, or both. King Agesilaus, a Spartan general much praised by Xenophon, obeyed the Ephors' order to give up his command and return home. Hiero the tyrant, in the *Hiero*, was beyond obedience to shared rule but hardly grand: he was consumed by fear and by longing for love. There is, of course, the example of Xenophon himself as general in the *Anabasis*. But he became a general only out of necessity and would not impose his project of founding a city when the men under his command proved unwilling. Still, both Xenophon and his Cyrus are alike in cool foresight and in mastery of ingenious and deceptive tactics. Agesilaus, by contrast, inclined foolishly and dangerously to head-on battle, and the other Cyrus, of the *Anabasis*, with a battle nearly won and monarchy at hand, died in a foolishly impassioned attack upon his hated brother.

In short, the *Education of Cyrus* considers the political way of life at its most extreme and rational, perhaps finally in light of another extreme and rational life exemplified by Socrates. But the book presents no explicit comparison. Socrates does not appear. One puzzle of the *Education* is that it is not much about education; it presents the political life with its own claims and, indeed, as in itself incompatible with a life of self-examination. But that must mean that Cyrus's life, the fullest political life, is in some ways foolish. Perhaps that explains the work's many tacit comparisons with political types that are less thoroughly political, some, like Cambyses, Croesus, and Tigranes, with rather Socratic features. I will argue that Cyrus displays a superiority that seeks true accomplishments, not merely superiority in domination, but that his quest involves him somewhat thoughtlessly in domination above all.

Cyrus's Soul

Who then is this Cyrus, who was the object of song and legend when barely sixteen and whose uncle Cyaxares, heir to the Medean throne, said prophetically, after the boy's first hunt, that he looked to be "now our king" (1.4.9, 25)? His allies tended to become devoted friends awed by "the strength of his soul" and not least by his justice and nobility (4.2.14; cf. 5.4.11; 1.4.23–25; 6.4.7). One will not grasp the problem of a Cyrus if one does not grasp his grandeur, that is, what makes him stand out from boyhood as admirable and attractive as well as able and intimidating (3.3.3). Napoleon and Caesar too were inspiring to their followers.

Throughout the *Education* Cyrus displays an extraordinary and winning mixture of charm, force, and alertness. In court circles Cyrus was completely winning; in war his manly qualities evoked wonder to the point of astonishment. Cyrus thrust himself to the fore in his very first battle, won an unprecedented victory for the Medeans, and in the process overturned the desultory customs of border warfare. The old despot Astyages was "astonished" at the youth's innovations and daring (1.4.23–25). Later, the grown-up Cyrus draws admiration from those around him, and not from mere flatterers. The noblest characters in the book are the beautiful Panthea and her shining husband, Abradatas. They sacrifice themselves in Cyrus's service, all to repay Cyrus's protective generosity to the wife (6.4.7). A barbarian cavalryman and potential ally of Cyrus "wondered at the strength of [Cyrus's] soul" (4.2.14); his addition of forces had been greeted warily despite an ongoing offensive against great odds. The new ally Gadatas came "to contemplate you again, how you appear in sight, you who have such a soul" (5.4.11); he had been rescued unexpectedly by an extraordinary forced march. More to the point, Cyrus himself shows a corresponding self-awareness. When he urges his army to the aid of Gadatas, it is because of what is just and noble as well as what is advantageous (5.3.31). He visibly prides himself on piety, justice, and truth and in general on an outlook above small calculations and low conduct. The exemplary case involves another new ally, Gobryas, who, having put himself and his fortress in Cyrus's power, offers Cyrus even more than he had promised. Cyrus refuses. But he proclaims gratitude nevertheless. For Gobryas has "made it clear to all human beings that I would not be willingly impious where hospitality is required, unjust for the sake of wealth, or voluntarily false in agreements" (5.2.10–11). At another point Cyrus disdains a gift of gold in addition to what he has agreed to obtain: "You will not make me . . . do good deeds for a wage" (3.3.3).

To begin to appreciate the enlightened or rational character of Cyrus's ambition, consider Xenophon's presentation of a counterpart, the prince of the Assyrians. This prince's plundering expedition occasioned Cyrus's youthful victory under Astyages; his defeat and death as king brought Cyrus the empire. Between these bookends we hear of terrible deeds moved by terrible passions, but we only once hear this prince speak. He asserts to Gobryas his lack of regret for killing Gobryas's son, his regret that he had not killed Gobryas too, and his wish to delay battle (5.3.6). The words show nothing fair, noble, or direct. They bespeak malice and a complete absence of compunction as well as a calculating wariness. We never learn this prince's name, nor do we ever see him direct a major battle. He remains in the shadows, as if his impulses are unspeakable. His impulses are not moderated by the light of decency, consideration, or even prudence. But such types exist, and various incidents show what unbridled passion in power does. On a hunting expedition this prince twice missed, while his companion—Gobryas's son, who was to marry the prince's sister—twice hit and exclaimed at his accuracy. At first the prince "held his envy down in darkness"; then (out of envy, Xenophon repeats), he plunged his spear into the breast of his companion (4.6.4, 9, 5.2.7). When at another time the prince's mistress chanced to remark on Gadatas's attractiveness, the prince had Gadatas castrated (5.2.28). Cyrus safeguarded Panthea for her husband. The Assyrian had sought to get her from her husband (6.1.45).

This dark prince wishes superiority without any scruple of justice or nobility, or at least without the light of intelligence to look up to. He is, Gadatas says to a very attentive Cyrus, full of "hatred not when someone does him an injustice, but if he suspects that someone is better than he is." Whatever intelligence may be present is that of the ambitious intriguer, servant of his overpowering envy: "always contriving until he takes the one who is better than he" (5.4.35–36). Cyrus, interestingly, seems less indignant than Gadatas as to this phenomenon of evil, perhaps because very familiar with his own passion for superiority. He is content to call him "unusually arrogant" (5.2.27). But he is also more knowing about how a certain twisted justice and reason exist in even such a prince. He corrects Gadatas. The Assyrian will hate his former allies but not Cyrus, precisely for their "injustice," that is, for their rebellion from the duties owed to his superiority as king (5.2.24). As a man, the prince too cannot but think of what is due to him and others, including what is due by custom. Precisely this misdirected rationality will make his vengeance particularly perverse, especially against affronts to his unbounded estimates as to what is due him (cf. 3.1.11–12). He is the dark type, we may surmise, who enjoys showing his superiority by exquisite tortures.

Cyrus wants true superiority as a ruler, not mere subordination forced on those around him or mere lawful superiority at the head of things established. His bent is more generous, more grand. This is most clearly exhibited in his hunts and battles as a young man under an indulgent grandfather in Medea, when his dispositions were not yet concealed under his stratagems or suppressed by Persian republican customs. The big point is this: the youthful Cyrus seeks true victories in genuine competition, unlike his dramatic counterpart. When the Assyrian invited Gobryas's son to the fatal hunt, it was in confidence that he himself was "by far superior" in horsemanship (4.6.3). Cyrus, on the other hand, challenged his age-mates only when "he knew quite well that he himself was inferior" (1.4.4). Although Cyrus had been no horseman, being from mountainous Persia, in Medea he threw himself into riding and weaponry. Xenophon dwells on the point: the boy did not take "refuge" in avoiding that in which he was inferior. Laughing at himself in defeat, Cyrus "immersed himself in trying to do better the next time." The result was improvement and indeed superiority. He quickly equaled and surpassed his age-mates (1.4.5). Similarly, he rejected a privileged place during a hunt: let each compete "as well as he is able" (1.4.14). It is an impressive example of concern for his friends, or rather of delight in the activity and therefore in true accomplishment. The old king was delighted to see young Cyrus teasing and praising the others in their efforts, "not being envious in any way whatsoever" (1.4.15).

Nevertheless, it is a later conversation with his father that reveals more fully Cyrus's self-understanding of true superiority. This is a compelled revelation. His father, perhaps concerned about Cyrus's intentions as he departs from Persia with an army, accompanies him to the border and amidst other advice cautions him as to the difficulty of ruling well. Cyrus is provoked to justify his (underlying) passion for rule. He admits that when he examines "rule itself," ruling well seems a "very great work." But when he considers the many mediocrities that have succeeded, it is "shameful to be intimidated before such and not to be willing to go in contention against them" (1.6.8). It is a crucial passage, reminding of a similar response by Plato's Alcibiades to a Socratic cross-examination (*Alcibiades I* 119b–c). Both would evade a consideration of what ruling requires of a ruler—and therefore of both duties to the ruled and pains to the ruler. While Cyrus does not want the shame of voluntary inferiority, he is content to measure a superior life against the political types he observes. I will return to the point.

Yet he does stand out in comparing himself with a view to his virtue, and in particular to his rationality and capacity to apply himself. Most rulers, he says, are content with more elaborate meals, more gold, more sleep, and less labor. But "forethought" and "love of labor" should distinguish the ruler, not "easy living," and a superior ruler would be disgraced if he did not contend against such inferiors. Cyrus understands himself to be superior in reason and its application to life. It is this conviction, together with his ruling passion for ruling, that makes Cyrus contend for rule and not merely defend Persia and Medea.

Consider the contrast in rationality with his rival, which shows from their first military initiatives as young princes. We first see the Assyrian when he impulsively turns a hunting expedition into a plundering expedition, having happened upon a surplus of Assyrian troops at the Medean border. There is a rationale: such an exploit would make a more "brilliant" deed and provide more cattle for sacrifices to celebrate his impending marriage (1.4.17, 20–24). The dark prince also wants to shine, but according to convention, on impulse, simply by stealing from foreigners at a private occasion and without considering justice or the advantage to the

Assyrian empire he will inherit. His gambit is smashed by the alertness and ruthless intensity of the novice Cyrus, tagging along that day with grandfather Astyages' Medean forces. Later, Cyrus himself disguised his first battle and first attack as a hunt. But it was a disguise planned from the start, and the plan had a just cause, a big prize, and an ingenious stratagem. He invaded Armenia on behalf of his ally Medea, was correcting a treaty violation, and was under necessity, since he and Cyaxares needed Armenian money and troops to defend against an Assyrian invasion. Besides, Cyrus's hunt camouflaged an agile entrapment that avoided long sieges, many casualties, and a hardening of enmity. He obtained the men due Cyaxares and double the money. He got also money and mercenaries for his own army and got not one but two nations, who were subjected so ingeniously that they were pleased to be allies. Cyrus led like a man above boys.

But is superior forethought and industry alone the sort of superiority that justifies one's rule? What, to raise the obvious question, of justice and the common good? Cyrus says nothing to his father about what is due the ruled, or even about the public purposes of rule. He will indeed prove to be of marvelous forethought and concentration in providing for his army and allies. But he provides for them as instruments of his superiority. He in fact will eventually overturn all the rulers, tribes, and nations that he can reach throughout Asia, including his uncle's Medea, his friend Tigranes' Armenia, and the free republic of his Persian fatherland and his father. He rules for "his own special advantage," as his father Cambyses says at their next meeting, after Cyrus has conquered an empire and parked an ominous army on Persia's frontier (8.5.24). Cyrus proves to disdain republican justice— and for that he has an argument. He will prove averse to noble sacrifice—and for that he has a mixture of argument and a certain willful aversion. But in addition to both of these dispositions, there is an immense ambition he hardly articulates—and as to this one finds a complicated mix of passion and wish, not an argument. When I come to consider at length this passion, I will argue that Cyrus's ambition for his own superiority fails to do justice to his desire for true superiority. He pursues his advantage, but the advantage he seeks proves hollow. Foresighted and concentrated to an extreme in pursuing what he seeks, Cyrus does not seem wise in what he seeks. Cyrus pays a price for evading the question of the difficulties in "ruling itself."

JUSTICE

I outline first the case for what Cyrus rejects, the shared authority under law of the Persian republic, and then Cyrus's own understanding of justice. That understanding, complicated as it is, affects the shape of his ambition. Wanting to benefit people, he wishes to provide them what is their due. Cyrus is proud of his justice, which he parades. Nevertheless, his justice amounts to a distribution of secondary things (such as wealth) in a manner that enables him to get for himself his primary thing, imperial rule. Cyrus's justice goes with much injustice in primary things; he overturns some rather good rulers as well as the independence of his impressive fatherland, the republic of Persia. Nevertheless, as the world goes, Cyrus's rational empire proves to be in some ways a haven for much fair treatment, at least by comparison with the other empires contending for domination. Fairness proves to be complicated, in practice and in theory.

To begin with, Cyrus's passion for superiority cannot willingly accept his fatherland's shared authority. Xenophon presents Persia as a republic public-spirited to an extreme; the Persian king, Cambyses, is a monarch under law with limited authority extending only to war and worship. This is completely unlike the situation in Medea. There Astyages is "the master of everything," as Cyrus's mother puts it while urging Cyrus, unsuccessfully, to return for a Persian education in justice. In Persia "to have what is equal is believed to be just," and Cambyses is leader in this. He is "first both to do what has been ordered by the city and to accept what has been ordered, and not his soul but the law is his measure" (1.3.18). But Cyrus refuses, and he has an argument against republican justice to which neither his mother nor his father, so far as I can discern, fields an adequate reply.

Equal rights under the law are not necessarily good for the parties concerned, and if not good, do they give to the parties

their due? If not, is equal justice under law just? Cyrus's example
is one of the best-known passages of the *Education*. As a boy he
was confronted by his Persian teacher with this problem: how to
judge fairly between the big boy with a little coat and the little
boy with a big coat. Cyrus would exchange the coats. For this answer he was immediately beaten. The question, the teacher reminded him, is not of the fitting but of the just (1.3.16–17), and
justice protects those in possession equally under the law: "the
lawful is just, and the unlawful violent." If the rule of law protects
things unfitting or bad, however, is it to that extent bad? Eventually, in Cyrus's new army and new order, he shows a fairer or better way. He disposes of spoils and honors according to merit and
to what fits the individual. In the army rewards go not to all
equally but are distributed to "the superior" after "examining the
deeds of each person" (2.2.18–21). Cyrus decides the fitting reward. In the empire one who wishes to acquire and bestow gives
up his estate to one who wants the pleasure of possessing (8.3.46–
48). In the face of Cyrus's lighthearted insistence that he already
knows Persian justice and thus can remain in Medea, Cyrus's
mother could only resort to threats. If Cyrus learns "not the
kingly [way] but the tyrannical," he will be "beaten to death"
when he returns home (1.13.18). A republic will enforce its justice, truly just or not. But the young Cyrus proves chameleon
enough to conform at home and superior enough to be vested
with an army, and the older Cyrus himself proves threatening
enough when he has the rule that he thinks fitting. If a free government resorts to force to make its justice stick, Cyrus will have
more force on behalf of his own superiority.

Cyrus's father has no better luck in arguing against the ambition for empire: he cautions the departing Cyrus but offers no argument sufficient to dissuade him. Cambyses does not even try
the arguments from justice: that it is unjust to turn one's country's
army into a means of one's own empire, and that it is unjust too to
rule foreign peoples despotically and to take away their self-government. Why this restraint? It is not as if Cambyses could be ignorant of Cyrus's intention. If he had not known of his son's ambition from his behavior in Medea and from his winning over the
officer corps to his enterprise (1.5.7–10), he would know it from

this conversation. Cyrus is ashamed at the prospect of subordination to less worthy rulers, which seems to him unjust or at least ignoble and shameful. He is restless to acquire followers and to "contend against *his* enemies as soon as possible" (1.6.8, 11, 22, 24, 26, emphasis added). His enemies are whoever keeps him from rule. Faced with such motives, Cambyses must think that arguments from injustice will have little effect. Indeed, any arguments from him against tyrannical rule have to be cautiously put, and this is itself a lesson in the weakness of his republican justice and the force of Cyrus's superiority. Cyrus is now head of a big army on the road to Medea and his enterprise. He had invited neither the father's presence nor his comments. These are at the father's initiative (1.6.1–2). Nor could Cambyses have negatived Cyrus's appointment as general, given the Medean king Cyaxares' request for Cyrus, the ties with Medea that the assiduous young Cyrus had cultivated, his status as heir to Cambyses' throne and its generalship, and, above all, Cyrus's superiority in war.

Cambyses, I have noted, does advance a crucial argument that could go far on the road to justice: the difficulty of so presiding over "others" that they will have provisions and "will all be as they must" (1.6.7). He brings out the ruler's duties and their difficulties and thus opens up the questions of whether ruling is necessarily for others and of whether it truly provides what a man by himself deserves. But Cyrus evades the argument and any such questions, moved as he is by his desire for rule and his opinion that ruling befits the superiority he deserves. No wonder Cambyses contents himself with cautions as to the harsh necessities that the hopeful Cyrus has not confronted (1.6.9, 16, 19, 21, 24, 27, 35–36). Still, he shows his worry in the final cautions, which are broader than military. He warns against unexpected and unanticipated dangers that can arise from great ambition. What of the dangers from launching war, from men and cities whom you elevate to power, from friends treated as slaves rather than equals, from being ruler over all, and, finally, from acquiring great riches? Still, the argument is inconclusive, especially for one who dares to think himself superior. At the end, the republican Cambyses in effect gives up his attempt at just and reasonable counsel and urges obedience to authority, just as his wife had turned from her appeal for justice to threats. He cautions altogether against following human wisdom, which "no more knows how to choose what is best" than someone "casting lots" (1.6.45–46). He urges deference to the gods. But Cyrus thinks himself superior to the rulers he knows, thinks himself wise enough to get great goods without misfortunes, and is impassioned to try.

There is little doubt that the law-abiding republican Cambyses was more fearful of Cyrus's enterprises than he here lets on. We should not think he agreed with the Persian authorities who eventually sent another army when Cyrus promised them "the rule of Asia, and its fruits" (4.5.16; 5.5.3–4). Those Persians would give up their small city in favor of the great gains of empire, or they suppose they can have it both ways. Cambyses seemed to have doubts. If a later and admittedly jocular remark is accurate, he had ordered Cyrus to return just as Cyrus was orchestrating the imperial turn (6.1.4–5; cf. 5.5. 44–48). Later still, Cambyses does counsel the Persians to try to have it both ways (8.5.22–26). But he is responding to a fait accompli, the imperial army being at the border. He seeks not to have it both ways but to retain some independence for a republic in the new circumstance of universal empire. He counsels that Cyrus respect and defend Persian laws and Cambyses' kingship (Cyrus inheriting after Cambyses' death), and that the Persians accept and defend the new empire and Cyrus's rule. Cyrus and the Persian authorities agree. There are signs that Cambyses sees more than he says. It is "just" that he "say openly" only "as many things as I think I know to be good for both of you," not necessarily all that he thinks he knows. He obtains what justice he can from the dangerous situation he sees.

Despite all that has been said, however, it is also true that Cyrus himself is in his own way devoted to justice. The problem is to understand whether his way is genuinely just. Still, the obvious point is his many professions. He can tell his soldiers to be "unjust" to none of the unarmed Armenians they come across (2.4.32), and he cautions allies: if you are "unjust, we shall side with those suffering injustice" (3.2.22). Even in his imperial rule he has a maxim of justice: if "he should show that it was very important to him not to be unjust to friend or ally, and if he should watch justice intensely, others would abstain from shameful gains and be willing to make their way by the just course" (8.1.26). Justice seems to involve abiding by the law, agreements, others' possessions, what others deserve by their merits, what oneself deserves. It differs from the noble, which goes beyond what duty or desert requires. "What is more just than defending ourselves, or more noble than aiding friends?" (1.5.13). We do what is noble by aiding Gadatas, a benefactor, he urged the army; we do "what is just by paying back his favor." Cyrus would live up to his opinion of what is right or admirable. Should we neglect Gadatas for one reason or another, "how could we dare to approve of ourselves?" (5.3.31, 33).

Still, I am forced to return to my thesis: Cyrus's ways of justice subordinate justice to his imperial enterprise. Justice becomes a means of rule. His talk of justice is mostly as to his friends and allies, not for people generally or his enemies, and it does seem that all humanity he does not control is an actual or potential enemy. As he sets out to defend Medea he can say to his officers, the Persian peers, that "the appearance of unjustly desiring what belongs to others is far from impeding us" (1.5.13). But he has already persuaded the same peers to turn from defending their city to gaining for themselves (1.5.6–10). While Cyrus may tell Gobryas of his pride in showing justice, he begins with talk of being true and not false, moves to his aversion from impiety, injustice, and faithlessness as to contracts, and concludes as to steadfastness with respect to friends and enemies (5.2.9–12). Justice and truth too come to be subordinated to benefiting friends and harming enemies. Justice has especially to do with providing for friends understood as allies, such as the Armenians and Chaldeans or his own officers and men, and the populations they govern.

But when his uncle Cyaxares, who is a friend of sorts, reproaches Cyrus bitterly for taking away his real power over his country, he accuses Cyrus of "injustice." In this very revealing little exchange variants of "justice" appear more than a dozen times (5.5.10–36).[10] Cyrus never adequately replies to the accusation. He can allege benefits given, but he cannot deny he took

Cyaxares' "entire power." Finally Cyrus buys off Cyaxares, as he does so many of his political subordinates, by enormous gifts coupled with the trappings of honor (5.5.37–40; cf. 8.1.37–40; 8.2 *passim*). But he has taken over the power of Medea without regard to the justice of the takeover. That he is superior and would be ashamed to serve under Cyaxares may be admitted. But he never claims that his overturn of Medean rule is just.

How then to understand what is certainly true, that Cyrus takes pride in his justice? Cyrus thinks happy not those who possess and guard the most, but those who "acquire the most while in keeping with what is just and . . . use the most while in keeping with what is noble." So he tells Croesus (8.2.23). But the acquiring and using seem primary, and they, especially the acquiring of rule, rather limit the rest. Is that why Xenophon immediately adds: so "Cyrus openly acted." What moved Cyrus to his open acts was not necessarily itself open. It comes to light from the shadows, as he thanks Gobryas earlier (5.2.9–11; cf. 8.4.7–8). He praises the opportunity to *show* his justice to all mankind. That is, pride in justice is secondary to love of honor on an imperial scale. Precisely in speaking of his pride in justice Cyrus restricts justice to matters of money and promises, and this after mentioning "tyranny" among the powers that a man may have (5.2.9,10) and that he now has with respect to Gobryas. He does indeed take pride in obeying agreements and keeping his promises. But these concern things secondary to him, things such as gold and riches, women, music, lovers, and so forth. As to the thing primary, he overturns in effect his uncle's rule in Medea and the republican rule of his native Persia as well as rulers good as well as bad throughout Asia. We do not see him discriminate carefully between rulers soft and first-rate.

Croesus was not a bad ruler. Was Croesus justly dispossessed of Sardis? True, he was inferior to Cyrus in war and battles. Is that the cash value in Cyrus's eyes of his own superiority? Cyrus once speaks of an "eternal law among all human beings." It prescribes the right of the conqueror: "When a city is captured by a people at war, both the bodies of those in the city and their riches belong to those who take it" (7.5.73). I have confirmed again the main point: Cyrus may share his gains with his friends, but the sharing does not extend to the most important gain, his conquest of political supremacy. But this in his mind controls all the rest. Cyrus's justice is diluted for himself by the primacy of gain and diluted for others by the primacy of gaining followers.

Still, this reformulation of justice into a means of gain for Cyrus and his followers proves to be itself a useful instrument of empire. It has a powerful appeal, and not merely to Cyrus. For many can thus gain, albeit not the preeminent place. Even the privileged aristocracy at the core of the Persian republic finds it irresistible. This ruling class had a public upbringing in justice and military training as well as a very public life together in the public square, on military expeditions, and in public office. Xenophon's Persia seems to be a just version of the famously austere and warlike Spartan republic.[11] Nevertheless, this model of Spartan public-spiritedness went against the grain. The peers themselves eagerly give up citizen virtue in favor of great gains. As Cyrus begins his persuasion he replaces the sacredness of the ancestors' ways with the "I" of his own judgment, and he probes to the core. "What good they acquired" by practicing the old virtues, "either for the community of the Persians or for themselves, I cannot see" (1.5.8). The worth of virtue as such is questionable, not only the worth of civic virtue. Those who abstain from "pleasures at hand" do so only to obtain "much more enjoyment in the future." Then to the crucial point: "those who practice military affairs" do so to acquire "much wealth, much happiness, and great honors both for themselves and for their city" (1.5.9). Under Cyrus the privileged Persians may consider their virtue and their army as instruments of gain, not defenders of the republic.

This overturn of public-spiritedness, that is, of the priority of law and common good, is followed by a redistribution of power that in effect overturns the preeminence of the aristocracy. While Cyrus introduces justice into the army, it is a justice that serves its power rather than the peers' rule. This is to be an equal opportunity army (except for the most important opportunity). Ordinary soldiers are supplied the same arms as the peers, thus to expand the number of heavy-armed for hand-to-hand fighting. Rewards are distributed according to performance in the field, not superiority of class. Cyrus does the judging. This inclines each to fight, encourages his belief that the others will fight, and encourages him to fight for Cyrus. A considerable democratization is thus mixed with a considerable increase in the general's authority. Considerable democratization is not democracy. While the commoner Pheraulus may say to his fellow commoners that "the educated" will be caught in "a democratic struggle," the commoners in fact lack military training and practice and will remain at a decisive disadvantage (2.3.15; cf. 18).[12] Within the microcosm of the army, which is a quarter of the citizens, Cyrus thus undermines and democratizes the old aristocratic power. Yet the result is not some mixed order but a disciplined, fit, agile force on the march. It mixes personal initiative and friendly teamwork with complete discipline and complete subordination to Cyrus. This is a community fit for acquiring and at its core moved by the prospect. Cyrus's justice seems to everyone's advantage while being especially to his advantage.

There is one thematic discussion of justice in the *Education*, and it clarifies precisely the dependence of justice on the ruler's advantage. By his surprise attack under cover of a hunt, Cyrus had managed to tree the Armenian king and then to put him on "trial" (3.1.6). This has to be one of the more charming political trials in the literature of criminality. The discourse is so reasonable; it so departs from the spirit of prosecution and retribution.

The two features are connected. This trial is like a Socratic dialogue on the priority of the ruler's advantage, well understood, to just punishment, well understood. Cyrus quickly acknowledges that it may well be "noble" for a ruler such as the Armenian king to recover his freedom. But there is a corresponding freedom of rulers to enforce their authority against rebels. The Armenian has to acknowledge in turn that he would punish a rebel with death and confiscation: "So this is your justice, Armenian" (3.1.13).

At this point, with its unpleasant implications for the Armenian and his relatives, his educated son Tigranes comes to his defense with a consideration of *Cyrus's* advantage. Why kill the king just when he is most valuable to you (3.1.16)? To kill or depose

the Armenian (or "us") is to destroy those best at raising the
armies and money Cyrus wants. Tigranes extends the argument
to the dynasty he is to inherit, that is, to his advantage. Who then
will provide settled authority? Who will be more moderate than
those now overcome by fear? Who more grateful to Cyrus
than those saved from losing everything? Besides, and Tigranes
rushes an assurance in face of Cyrus's objection, you can fortify
camps and take strong places: "Our wrongs offer excuses for you
to distrust us" (3.1.26). We may return reasonably to the subject
of wrong when we look at it from a ruler's right, that is, from the
primacy that goes with superior power. In Tigranes' argument,
justice come to sight as a way to enforce a mutually advantageous
agreement that acknowledges and strengthens Cyrus's authority.
Acknowledging political necessity, Tigranes also shows Cyrus his
necessities and how a moderate taking from the Armenians serves
them. Cyrus accepts and then takes pride in his justice in not taking more.

Still, however qualified his justice, however instrumental to
his imperial ambition, there is something to be said for Cyrus,
precisely for the sake of the common advantage. Cyrus's reasonableness in grasping his necessities and others' promotes much
justice. This is a sobering theme, a practical theme that deserves
anyone's attention. Justice needs powerful support beyond itself.
Justice is dependent upon rulers. From this sober point of view
Cyrus in his reasonableness is even a patron of justice. Consider
the alternatives. The alternative to Cyrus's Persian empire was an
Assyrian empire. One empire or the other was inevitable. The
first Assyrian, the good old Assyrian admired by Gobryas and
killed in the first great battle, had himself sought to "rule over all
those in the area" (1.5.2). Even if a nonimperial republic such as
Persia existed, together with plenty of nonimperial monarchies
such as Medea or the little feudalities of Gobryas and Gadatas,
independence was precarious. But for Cyrus's extraordinary generalship, Persia and Medea together would have been at the
mercy of the invading Assyrians (2.1.6; cf. 2.1.8). Cyaxares was no
general to fear. He was no paragon of justice, either. He stays at
home for luxury, show, and women, is feared as "savage" by his

own subordinates, and is a cruel if foolish intriguer who would enforce a treaty of aid by threats to the ally's children (2.4.15). The alternative to Cyrus's empire, in short, is probably an Assyrian empire with the dark prince next in line for the throne.

If only for that reason, one must appreciate the reasonableness with which Cyrus first defends and then treats his allied nations and rulers. The allied nations—Gobryas, Gadatas, and the rest—almost all followed Cyrus willingly. The worst punishment for them was exclusion from his army (7.2.5–7). They begged him to go on to attack Assyria again, thus to gain, to protect themselves, or to take vengeance upon their old imperial master. Cyrus is a liberator, up to a point. Besides, there is a defensive case even for the offensive that led to the overturn of Assyrian rule—at least after Cyrus's annihilating pursuit that concluded the first battle. The Assyrian coalition launched a second great attempt on Cyrus's coalition, and its general, Croesus, meant himself to be "the greatest of human beings" (6.1.26; 7.2.23).

In the world of competitors for empire, in short, Cyrus stands out in treating his allies with a judicious and even benevolent touch. He ruled in good part by restraining his own wish for wealth and pleasure and by benefiting his allies, often in ways they could never benefit themselves. He pacified border wars, as with arrangements between the Armenians and Chaldeans ("still even now they remain just so," 3.2.24), and he obtained for the Hyrcanians and Sacians a fortress crucial for defending against the Assyrians (5.3.21–23). Which is not to deny that Cyrus "expunged" from his Persian army all slackers, or that he ordered the annihilation of the routed Assyrian host, or that he encircled his camp with Persian troops and killed on sight deserters sneaking out with bits of the spoils (2.2.23–27; 4.2.21–26; 4.5.5–6). But these were measures taken for Cyrus's fundamental military strength and advantage and to strengthen the alliance. I am arguing that considerable justice, considerable general advantage, accompanied his reasonable pursuit of his own advantage.

Alternatively, Xenophon repeatedly shows us the weakness of justice when separated from power or from an understanding of one's advantage. Gadatas had been castrated through no fault of his own, indeed because of his very handsomeness (5.2.28). The dark prince did it, and he had the power to get away with it. Gadatas weeps because he had said or done nothing "unjust or shameful" to justify his suffering (5.4.30–31). He is too hopeful, for he thinks the just will be treated justly or that justice will lead to one's good. For connected reasons, he is also foolish and weak: he does not provide for his own advantage. Moved to take vengeance, that is, moved by desire for justice, he forgets the vulnerability of his own fortress to the Assyrian's superior forces. In his weakness some of his own forces rebel. Gobryas, a fellow sufferer, showed a better way. When he sought vengeance he dealt from a position of strength. In exchange for providing his own forces and fortress to Cyrus (5.2.2, 4.6.2), he got protection, vengeance, and prominence, among other things. But for Gobryas as well as Gadatas, who are both decent political types, Cyrus is the sole hope for security and justice in a world otherwise dominated by the sinister Assyrian.

Cyrus supplies more than justice, and thus more than equal justice under law would supply. He provides something good to replace the sons they lost or cannot have and thus something of honor and perpetuity. He provides for his followers' advantage. Cyrus finds the high-ranking husband Gobryas has wished for his daughter (Gobryas's daughter had been destined for the dark prince, the future king, as his son for the prince's sister [4.6.3; 4.6.9, 5.2.7, 8.4.13–18, 24–26]). To Gadatas he promises friends, friends who will try to support him as "would children of your own, if you possessed them" (5.3.19). Cyrus proves himself such a friend. He will rescue Gadatas, gather him and his mother into the campaign, and install him as majordomo of the imperial household and of the eunuchs who made up his personal guard (7.5.65). Gadatas is even his sole dinner companion when other guests are not present (8.4.2). One must admit that all of this, from the rescue to the headship of the household, is to Cyrus's advantage. By rescuing Gadatas Cyrus showed potential friends and enemies that he, better than the enemy, could help friends and hurt enemies (5.3.31–32). In raising Gadatas he put the most grateful and loyal of eunuchs in charge of the eunuchs, whom he had selected precisely for their gratitude and loyalty (7.5.60–65).

Still, Cyrus does not see himself as devoted merely to the advantageous. And there is a grandeur about his understanding of how to pursue his advantage. For both reasons he can to a considerable extent be a patron of justice.

OF LOVE OF THE NOBLE, AND OF LOVE

> Being disposed to you as you know me to be, I nevertheless swear to you on my friendship and yours, that I would wish to be put under the earth in common with you, when you have been a good man, rather than live on, a woman in shame with a man in shame: so worthy of what is most noble have I deemed both you and myself.
>
> — PANTHEA TO ABRADATAS (6.4.6)

But what of nobility? In particular, what of the grand and almost selfless deeds in which human virtue seems to shine most? The words of Panthea to the husband she so loves bring to mind the shining moment of the *Education*. That moment is not Cyrus's. Abradatas, honor-bound as he thinks to repay Cyrus for protecting his wife and gleaming with gold and bronze above even Cyrus, leads a spectacular chariot charge on the center of the enemy's line—and is killed. The book contains no other incident of such noble pathos. It shows the grandeur of nobility—and a certain foolishness. I consider this event at length, partly for the light and the shadows thus cast on Cyrus's rather cool pursuit of his advantage. Cyrus's advancement of himself may make him "world famous," admired by many, and even admired by friends who know him. But is he noble in the precise sense, in the sense of one whose actions involve sacrifice of things important to him for something admirable? Does Cyrus's focus on his own advantage make him disinclined to sacrifice—and thus not noble and even ignoble?

This last suggestion flies in the face of Cyrus's acts of generosity and his estimation of himself as noble. Cyrus certainly has some sense of conduct admirable in itself—conduct not merely instrumental to his advantage. I insist on that. But Xenophon shows, I think, that his admirable conduct, like his just conduct, tends to dissolve into actions for his advantage.

This tendency is somehow related to Cyrus's attitude toward

love of beauty, whether in things or in people. Our attention is occasionally called to the relationship. The luxurious Croesus, for example, loves beautiful things. But he also nobly offers up "every beautiful possession" in the city in order to save his city and its families, not least to save his own daughters, whom he would seclude from Cyrus's notice (7.2.12–13, 26; note the references to "everything beautiful and good" as well as "every beautiful possession"). Croesus's love of things good as well as beautiful extends to admirable exertions on behalf of his daughters, his wife, and his city. Cyrus, on the other hand, shows little care for beautiful things or people (2.4.1, 6) or for a beloved city, a beloved child, or a beloved.

Nevertheless, Cyrus's outlook cannot be reduced simply to the instrumental. He makes a point of distinguishing "something noble" not only from what is just, in paying someone back, but also from what is advantageous, in winning friends and intimidating enemies (5.3.31–32). And he prides himself on his nobility as on his justice. He prides himself in acting on his own motion and on an inclination above the common expectation of reward. "You will not make me go around and do good deeds for a wage," he replies in refusing a gift of gold from members of the Armenian royal family (3.3.2–3). He can seem nobly generous. Let the queen not rebury that gold but use it to equip splendidly Tigranes' army—to "send him off as nobly as possible"—and to see that the royal family lives adorned and pleasantly. Admittedly, the greatest such tribute to Cyrus's grandeur, from Xenophon, involves the extraordinary army being readied: "As a man who was intending to do nothing minor, Cyrus prepared for the war in a magnificent manner." On the eve of its decisive battle Cyrus's army flashes with bronze and is brilliant with purple (6.2.4; 6.4.1). But there are also impressive tributes to Cyrus's soul from characters who know the man firsthand. After Gadatas's rescue, as noted before, he approaches Cyrus to look on the man's nobility itself. He comes "to contemplate you again, how you appear in sight, you who have such a soul" (5.4.11; cf. 33.4, 25).

If one examines the deeds that win such praise, however, not one is exactly an act of noble sacrifice, and if one considers the words of the Armenian royalty and Gadatas, neither actually discerns Cyrus's motives. The rescue of Gadatas was not without benefit to Cyrus "personally," contrary to Gadatas's description. It was to the army's advantage, as Cyrus told his troops, and the army was very much to Cyrus's advantage. Besides, whatever Gadatas might see with his eye, he missed much with the mind's eye. He missed Cyrus's imperial concern for his reputation among potential allies and enemies, that is, among all people everywhere in Asia. Gadatas praises Cyrus for helping friends. Cyrus's exhortation to his troops mentions "friends" but focuses on "benefactors" (5.3.30–33). The Armenians' praise was even less considered. The queen's gold would help an army that had become in effect Cyrus's army, and what was used up in royal equipment and royal adornment would not be available to the dynasty and its independence.

It is significant that no praise for Cyrus's noble outlook issues from the most thoughtful of the royal family, Tigranes, general of the departing Armenian army and heir to the dynasty. This, although Tigranes and his wife had reason to be grateful (the dynasty continued). But they had more reason to be doubtful, and to be quiet too. Cyrus's generosity to the dynasty came after he had established control of Armenia, the future kingdom of Tigranes, and he preferred followers out of "good will and friendship," not "out of necessity" (3.1.28). No wonder, then, that Xenophon's own comments on Cyrus's grandeur relate to preparation of his army. The remark is brief, and Xenophon's description of the army's sheen about as brief. For Cyrus, and for Xenophon too, splendor of things may be fitting, but it is minor compared to readiness. To readiness Cyrus attends at length and continually. Xenophon discusses it at length and more than once. But as to nobility in particular, Xenophon's little remark on Cyrus is completely overshadowed by the big account of Abradatas, which is telling as to bad judgment and disastrous consequences as well as magnificent in its tragedy.

The scenes of Panthea and Abradatas comprise a spectacular picture. These two exemplify nobility even in their love. While they are certainly husband and wife in love ("she loved him intensely" 6.1.32), they love one another for their worthiness, and they sacrifice their love accordingly. When Abradatas rejoined his wife in Cyrus's camp they first "embraced, as was to be expected," and then, immediately, Panthea speaks of Cyrus's virtues and how accordingly Abradatas should not only do but also be. Try "to be for him as he was for you" (6.1.47; cf. 45). Panthea abstracts from the special relation of husband and wife, or she puts honor of her husband above love for him. She would "honor her husband more than her own soul" (6.4.5). Compare the reaction of Tigranes' wife in a somewhat similar situation. She was reunited with her husband after he had offered to sacrifice "his own soul" for his love. This wife disdains talk of Cyrus, despite his magnanimity. She has eyes only for Tigranes. Then, "as was to be expected, after such [words and events], they went to rest with each other" (3.1.41).

Abradatas is cut of Panthea's high-minded stuff. He too wishes most of all to prove himself worthy. Setting off to battle he prays he "might come to light as a husband worthy of Panthea, and friend worthy of Cyrus who has honored us" (6.4.9). In short, the two share a love that seems more selflessly noble than loving. They sacrifice themselves accordingly for what is noble, or at least for what appears noble (there is a movement in Panthea's thoughts from "noble" to "honor" and to how Abradatas would "appear" to others, 6.4.3). The two seem peculiarly selfless (except for their regard for others' opinions), peculiarly disposed to give without limit. In return for Cyrus's honorable conduct Abradatas says, "I give myself to you as a friend, as an attendant, and as an ally" (6.1.48). In exhorting Abradatas to duty Panthea would die "when you have been a good man, rather than live on, a woman in shame with a man in shame" (6.4.6).

The culmination is twofold: a shining deed of courage that crowns what seems a festival of noble sacrifice and a suicide that is, well, less noble than pathetic. Abradatas volunteers for an attack on the center of the enemy's line and obtains this position by lot after the other generals refuse, as "not noble," his assumption of the greatest danger (6.3.35–36). There follows an event reminiscent of the preparation of a religious sacrifice. The scene begins with Cyrus offering sacrifices for the army, which glows as if with divine light. We see Abradatas arming, accompanied by Panthea's tearful aid and exhortation. Panthea, "said to have been certainly the most beautiful woman in Asia" (4.6.11), seems too beautiful to be "begotten nor born of mortal parents" (5.1.8). Abradatas wishes to "come to light" as a worthy husband. The chariot and horse are armored in shining bronze, and Abradatas's armor gleams with the gold melted by Panthea from her jewels. Not able to touch him as he departs, she kisses his chariot until he orders her back. It seems a tableau of goddess and god, less of Aphrodite and Mars than of Hera and Zeus. Perhaps it is not coincidence that "fate" put Abradatas at the fore, that both husband and wife swear by Zeus in this last encounter, that Cyrus's watchword in this battle is "Zeus, savior and leader" (7.1.10). Still, Xenophon's account is of admirable lady and noble gentleman, not of gods, to say nothing of the gamier versions of Zeus and Hera. Abradatas seems human nature in noblest form, as Panthea seemed most beautiful woman. Since he was "a sight worth looking at even before he was clad in this armor, he appeared most handsome and most free, since his nature was already such" (6.4.4).

Yet we can be too moved by the sights. We would miss what is intimated in Xenophon's words: the blindness and shortsightedness of these two, and especially of Panthea. In all their attention to looks and the glowing deed, the crucial thing they do not examine: their conviction that the deed is called for and useful. This presupposition is wrong, or at least much exaggerated. They are blind as to Cyrus's true motives, as blind as Gadatas, and they overestimate their duty in return. Panthea speaks of Cyrus's "piety, moderation, pity" in not possessing her, and she promises him aid in return for the departure of Araspas (who desired her and finally used threats). But Cyrus had sought something "opportune" from protecting this potentially valuable item, had permitted Araspas to take her if it could be done without violence, and had turned the discredited Araspas to account as a spy. Piety, pity, and moderation were not his point (5.1.17). Panthea owes less to Cyrus than she thinks. She should be like Tigranes' wife and think more of the admirable husband she knows and loves. Similarly, Abradatas owes less to Cyrus and more to Panthea than he, relying on her opinions, perceived. That the two owed Cyrus gratitude is true, for he did not take Panthea for himself, and he forbade violence from others. But they owe limited gratitude, for Cyrus held Panthea captive, just as Tigranes in captive Armenia owed only limited gratitude for protection of his family. Although Abradatas had something but not everything at stake, he volunteered everything, and Panthea, as she thought, lost everything. Panthea had volunteered to invite Abradatas to replace the departed Araspas, an act of unthinkingly excessive gratitude. Abradatas leapt similarly to "give" himself to Cyrus, and not only as ally but as "friend." In leaping to the noble deed they were governed by mistaken opinions as to their situation, conventional opinions as to what was "honorable," and subordination in effect to the defining authority in their situation, the opinions of Cyrus.

The two abstracted in particular from bodily life and its necessities. Abradatas rigged for himself a chariot with four poles, a design difficult to turn and almost impossible to turn around. He charged straight into the squares of stalwart Egyptian infantry, the other charioteers veering off, except for his closest companions. At this point Xenophon's narrative turns to the merely bodily. There ensued an "indescribable confusion" in which "heaps of all sorts of things" caused the men to fall from the chariots. The consequence for nobility is stark: "These men who had been good were here cut down and killed" (7.1.32). The picture of formless bodily piles is unusual in the *Education*, its only (and lesser) rival being the description of Cyrus in danger in the same battle, his horse stabbed in the belly (7.1.37–38). Even when the young Cyrus had gloated over bodies struck down in his skirmish in Medea (1.4.24), he looks at them as conquered bodies, not as body parts. But Panthea after the battle is found holding Abradatas's body in parts, as if she refuses to believe and accept the body's fragility and end. When a hand comes off in Cyrus's hand, she would reattach it (7.3.9). Caught up in the nobility of her husband, Panthea had not faced up to the importance of the whole man whom she loved. Gadatas had forgot the vulnerability of his fortress to the Assyrian king; Panthea forgot the preciousness and vulnerability of Abradatas's life. Gadatas forgot in his passion for justice. Panthea and Abradatas sacrificed in nobility, aware of their dependence and for the sake of nobly benefiting a good man and friend. Now, unprepared for her loss, Panthea blames herself for her husband's suffering and blames Cyrus too. One sees something of the blaming and self-blaming of the noble soul, angry that a noble deed has come to a bad end and lamenting a sacrifice made willingly and knowingly, but not fully knowingly. We first come across Panthea in lament for her husband (5.1.5–6). We last see her in lament for her husband. Perhaps these problems are inherent to nobility of soul and to love, too. Still, highminded as Panthea is, she is finally incapable of taking pleasure from Abradatas's nobility.

In all this we can discern something of Cyrus's nobility and of its limits. There is no doubt Cyrus is moved by the sacrifices of these two. When after victory he hears of Abradatas's death and Panthea's grief, he strikes his thigh, leaps on his horse, and orders adornment for this "dear and good man" (7.3.6–7). He "wept for some time in silence" (7.3.11). This is not merely the customary and salutary show of compassion when his followers suffer. He had shown spontaneous affection when Abradatas volunteered for the forlorn hope (6.3.35–36), and, after Abradatas's death, Cyrus promises Panthea sacrifices and a memorial mound as well as an escort for her wherever she may wish to go. He frees her.

It remains a question how much Cyrus is moved. He praises Abradatas not as noble, for his willingness to sacrifice, but as "good," which seems to mean a man who contends for superiority. To Panthea Cyrus says that Abradatas "has obtained the noblest end, for he has died victorious" (7.3.9–11). Victory is the good that makes sacrifice noble. But victory was not the point of Panthea's exhortations or Abradatas's sacrifice. Abradatas was to do the noble thing for its own sake, or for a repayment of goodness, or as honorable. Also, and perhaps more to the point, the victory was Cyrus's, not Abradatas's. Panthea herself had looked up to the honor bestowed on noble deeds, and Cyrus encourages her to take solace in a monument that perpetuates Abradatas's memory. But Abradatas's fame is not the Abradatas that Panthea loved, whatever her earlier focus on his unstained honor. Besides, fame is fleeting. Over the years this monument came to be called after three eunuchs, who followed her suicide with their own. Cyrus himself never mentions the incident again. In short, the story of Panthea and Abradatas may somehow be exemplary of the noblest strivings in war and politics. But Xenophon surrounds it with reminders of the limits of such strivings, and especially the limits in the mind of a Cyrus and, to some extent, of a Xenophon too.

Cyrus's own sense of the noble, like his justice, seems governed by the rational limits that accord with his quest for superiority. As his final soliloquy puts it, he has enjoyed at each stage of his life the "fruits" of "what is believed to be noble" (8.7.6; Ambler says that the Greek could be translated such that the fruits are the belief itself). Cyrus's attention to results, and the distance implied in "belief," shows some distance from an Abradatas. Cyrus does not shine in a suprahuman golden glow (his armor, not golden, "shone like a mirror," as if, perhaps, to reflect the human level [7.1.2]). His opinion of the gods led him never "to think thoughts higher than a human being should" as to his good fortune (8.7.3). The mature Cyrus is never carried away by noble action, just as he is never carried away by love. He begins the decisive battle by attacking where the enemy is weakest, and he stops the Egyptians' advance by attacking from behind. In both cases he leads courageously, putting himself at the forefront of the crucial stratagems. But in both cases also he acts only as the greatest stakes require. And he is victorious.

There are two incidents especially revealing of Cyrus's prudent nobility and of its benefits to others as well as himself. Both occur just prior to the account of Panthea and the dead Abradatas; they show Cyrus's alternative ways. Both involve enemies no longer threatening, the Egyptian infantry and Croesus. Both turn enemies into allies. In the decisive battle the Egyptians alone of the enemy had continued to persevere, although their suffering became terrible. "Admiring and pitying them because they were good men and were being destroyed," Cyrus works out a deal (7.1.41). In exchange for their going over to his side he saves them, promising also a higher wage and, when peace arrives, "land, cities, women, and servants" (7.1.43). Also, the Egyptians can keep their honor by not turning traitor; they need not fight against their former general, Croesus. The honorable Egyptians accept. Cyrus honorably keeps his promises. Here is noble admiration and pity for an enemy, pruned by a fundamental consideration of his advantage and theirs, and unhindered by indignation.

A similar equanimity from strength governs Cyrus's treatment of Croesus, conquered ruler of Sardis and defeated general of the combined forces in the decisive battle. We see a most urbane conversation. One reason is the "good spirits" of Croesus, whose versatile ingenuity enables him to change with his "fortune." He greets Cyrus as "master," while Cyrus, for his part, greets Croesus with understanding and without lording it over him, "since we are both human beings, at least" (7.2.9–10). A bigger reason is that Cyrus has big fish to fry and wishes to fry them most easily as well as pleasantly. He opens with a question: how might he obtain riches for his troops and thus prevent them from sacking the city? The threat is there. Yet Cyrus inquires. We see no recriminations, despite the death of many of Cyrus's troops, Abradatas included, and no passion for vengeance. Croesus, grasping at an opportunity, assures of a voluntary acquiescence and proves his assurances by immediately opening his own treasuries. Bowing to necessity, but bowing with prudent spirit, Croesus angles to save what he can of his life, his family (especially his daughters), the families of his city, and the beauties of his city. He succeeds considerably. Cyrus then urbanely explores whether Croesus, who had relied famously on an oracle, is still ambitious to be "the greatest of human beings" (7.1.23). Croesus confesses that he had misinterpreted the oracle and overestimated his competence "to become greatest" (7.1.23). Pitying Croesus, Cyrus allows him his life and family, but no "battles and wars" (7.1.26). Cyrus shows what we might call a noble moderation toward enemies of grand ambition, whom he treats not as killers or warmongers but as men understandably pursuing what they think to be their advantage. This is a big point in Cyrus's favor. Still, it is a guarded moderation. His is generosity of a sort that does not endanger his quest. He proceeds to seek assurance beyond words, just as he had with the Armenian king. Cyrus holds on to this volatile Croesus, not in a prison, indeed, but as one more part of a swelling imperial entourage (7.1.29).

What Does Cyrus Want?

Cyrus is prudent enough not to say what he wants, with a few crucial exceptions. He had told the Persian aristocrats, the core of his army, that the fruit of military virtue can be "much wealth, much happiness, and great honors both for themselves and for their city" (1.5.9). Wealth and honor seem clear enough. He gets them, in spades. What is unclear here is how "happiness" is related to these, which of the three is most important, and whether all three are chiefly for the self or for the Persian city. In the ensuing conversation with his father there are answers: not to contend against the mediocre rulers out there would be shameful in light of his superiority (1.6.8). His own superiority takes priority, not only over some common good but also over wealth, if not honor. It is true that shame, which is a kind of fear of dishonor, makes him revolt against subordination to his inferiors; Cyrus will prove to be much attuned to honor from others. But it is also true that he conceives of himself as superior and deserving of place and honor accordingly. These objects, honor and deserved superiority, and to a lesser degree wealth, make up Cyrus's understanding of happiness.

All this intimated at the start is clarified in a backhanded way at the end, in his soliloquy when facing death (8.7.6–7). Cyrus orders his hearers to say and do about him as about one who was happy, as if that is the measure, and as if he wants especially a reputation for superior happiness. He recounts his deserts for such a reputation. He has enjoyed the fruits of what is thought to be noble at every age; his "power" (*dunamis*) has always increased; he undertook or desired nothing he did not obtain; he kept all he acquired. But what are these fruits of his deeds, and what did his success at acquiring and keeping power bring him? Or is his power itself, in the sense of his superiority over other men, itself the end? He continues: his friends have been made happy, his enemies enslaved, his fatherland from "living privately" became "foremost in honor in Asia." Does his happiness lie in using his vast powers for others? But the friends are ranked by their devotion to his own advancement. His chief friend, Chrysantas, won his ranking by being "even better for me than I am myself" (8.4.11). And the "fatherland" has been transformed from an independent "city" into dicey dependence within an empire that exists for Cyrus's "own special gain" (*pleonexia*, 8.5.24).

What Cyrus fundamentally sought was superiority over others, together with a reputation for being superior. And what is the advantage of that? The answer, I think, is not a reason but an extraordinarily forceful desire, an underlying force that stops further inquiry and remains unspoken by Cyrus. That is why I turn in the sequel to the early strivings and to the ferocity of the young Cyrus, at freedom in Medea. Still, two clarifying articulations occur later, apart from the final soliloquy. After two early victories Cyrus sends extra emissaries to the king of India. Xenophon explains: they "would say such things about him as he himself desired all human beings both to say and to hear about him" (3.2.31). Cyrus seeks honor, no doubt for his marvelous deeds of conquest and diplomacy, and from everyone: from "all human beings." Cyrus wants his superiority to be known to everyone and from everyone. Xenophon pronounces this wish. His Cyrus did not. He never says such a thing, neither to his own troops nor to the emissaries. At the time his duty was defensive, and he was subject to Cyaxares. But there may be a personal as well as a politic consideration. Might he, like Plato's Alcibiades, be unwilling to acknowledge even to himself his neediness, his dependence on the opinion of others? Later, as to his imperial quest, he gives a partial account to the Persian peers alone. They should obtain another army from home, "if at least the Persians desire that the rule of Asia, and its fruits, be theirs" (4.5.16). Cyrus is silent to his armies in general; if the Persians rule Asia they rule over allies as well as enemies. Besides, he has not obtained agreement for this offensive turn from his allies or even from his army in general. Actually, he is coy also to the peers and to the Persians at home. The rule will be decisively his own, not Persian, just as the worldwide honor he sought was for himself, not for the Persian republic or its army.

What accounts for this ambition? No doubt the descent from kings and even gods contributed, as did his Spartan-style military and republican disciplining. He, like Alcibiades, was free of the scars of necessity, even if he, unlike Alcibiades, was without the softnesses and self-indulgence of an upbringing in freedom and luxury. Still, Cyrus himself never relies on old titles in his decisive steps (cf. 2.2.19), although he uses his titles. (His imperial power established, he obtained Persian kingship by inheritance and

Medea by marriage.) This is not to deny that Cyrus's very quest is in a sense legitimate. He was defending his country, of which he was heir to the throne, and defending too its ally by royal marriage.[13] "The appearance of unjustly desiring what belongs to others is far from impeding us," as he put it at the start (1.5.13; cf. 6.1.26). This too might add to his confidence. Still, Cyrus from the start sought to render this army an instrument of imperial ambition. The reality of defensive war covered his actual enterprise. Cyrus was a legitimate ruler and defender of his country and its allies. But he did not understand himself that way.

What Cyrus does repeatedly acknowledge is the advantages for him of his Persian education. The public education and public living of the old republic, says Xenophon, had "whetted" Cyrus's soul for hunting and war; it was a moral education that "habituated" him to hardship for work in "common" (1.2.3–15). Cyrus himself praises in word and deed this training in justice, gratitude, obedience, austere self-control, and military virtue (7.5.74ff., 85–86; 8.6.10). He imports a version for his own imperial purposes, first for his new-model army and finally for the circle with whom he rules his new empire. But there was another part of Cyrus's Persian education that went beyond what was customary. He had to have benefited from the political rationality advanced by his father (1.6.2–46), although, admittedly, Cyrus himself never praises nor mentions this education in prudence. Nevertheless some parts of it are exhibited, whether in his father's lessons or in Cyrus's own discerning. Cyrus certainly shows himself a model of "being more prudent" about his friends' advantage "than they are themselves," which is central to those lessons, and a model too in contriving ingenious traps and disadvantages for his enemies (1.6.21–23, 35–41). But Cyrus uses his father's wary counsels to serve his own daring.

It is Cyrus's nature, not his descent, duty, or education, that accounts for his distinctive ambition. His father had much the same descent and education, but he shrank from imperial enterprise. Cyrus, however, was intimidating to his age-mates even as a youth and even in the midst of his republican education. When Xenophon says only that Cyrus then "seemed" superior in caring for the republic and in respecting elders and obeying the rulers

(1.5.1), we may take him at his reservation. The young Cyrus's subordination to equal ways and republican rulers was an appearance.

Xenophon provides a layered account of Cyrus's nature, to put it mildly. At the beginning we get a general description of body (or shape) and soul, the source being what is legendary ("in word and song") among the barbarians (1.2.2). Is this Xenophon's philosophic equivalent of a poetic legend, a version very different from both the bloodthirsty conqueror presented by Herodotus and the wrathful Achilles of the *Iliad?* Cyrus was "in form [*eidos*] most beautiful and in soul most benevolent, most eager to learn and most ambitious [*philotimatatos*]."[14] Ambition or love of honor dominates even in the legend. He "endured every labor and faced every risk," it continues, "for the sake of being praised." The legend is not of Cyrus as protector of the Persian republic, but as conqueror-founder of his own empire. Later Cyrus will call love of praise in his troops "the most warlike possession." It encourages taking on "every labor and every risk" (1.5.12). But what labors and risks are to be pursued? Why imperial war, especially?

It is the young Cyrus in Medea, freed from republican discipline and appearances, who displays the imperial future in domestic miniature and with it the underlying nature. One sees extraordinary charm, yes, but mixed with an unspoken love of mastery. The boy wins over Astyages, the master there, and this leads to an invitation to remain and the extrication of himself from both his mother ("at last," 1.4.1) and Persian equality. Now free to be on his own, the young Cyrus then wins over his agemates and extends his address to their fathers; he wins influence as a precocious broker of favor, interceding for both with Astyages. Then he wins over the master completely, by tending him and weeping over him when he is sick (1.4.2). The youth can then obtain what he most wants, a full-fledged hunt in the wild and a full-fledged part in a battle. We see the revolutionary in microcosm. The most striking scenes in Medea show Cyrus overturning the customs of both the royal hunt and royal warfare. He introduces equal competition in hunting, thus reducing in miniature the absoluteness of Medean monarchy (and anticipating his equal opportunity army). He overturns the forms of border warfare, instigating daring cleverness in tactics and daring ruthlessness in slaughter. At the end of this three-year visit the experienced old despot Astyages is speechless and astonished at the soul revealed, that is, at a Cyrus "mad with daring" (1.4.24). When such exploits reach the ears of his father Cambyses, the republican monarch immediately recalls Cyrus to the "customary" things in Persia. Cyrus cries at leaving Medea. A dozen years later, there is eagerness and no sadness when Cyrus departs Persia to return to Medea. Mastery suits his soul. A republic does not.

In this account of the boy becoming a young man we can see motives other than ambition, such as love of beauty and benevolence. But what dominates is an elemental passion for superiority, that is, for victory. While Cyrus was "pleased" with a beautiful robe, he was "exceedingly delighted" with learning to ride (1.3.3). The robe he gave away before he left. Horses, he solicited to take home. He would stay in Medea to learn horsemanship, he told his mother at age twelve or thirteen, thus to "be victorious for you over those who are good on foot" and to be an ally to his grandfather (1.3.15). Cyrus's challenge to superior riders can be understood in the context of this military ambition (1.4.4, 5). Probably his benevolence can also be so understood. While benevolence as well as ambition is mentioned as a motive for helping his fellows and their fathers, there follows a description of Cyrus nursing his grandfather: "He thus won Astyages over to the highest degree" (1.4.1, 2).

It is the hunting and fighting that clarify the underlying passion. Having quickly killed off all the wild animals in the king's park (1.4.5), Cyrus "passionately desired" a hunt in the wild. Warned against dangerous wild places and dangerous wild beasts, he forgets all caution at the sight of his prey, first risking life and limb in chasing a deer, and then, "like one possessed" (1.4.8), charging a boar that was charging him and spearing it dead. But this is not merely a passion to dominate. It is inseparable from a sense of the nobility of his prey: the deer leaping "toward heaven" as if with wings, the boar coming on at close quarters "just as they say courageous men do" (1.4.11). Cyrus wants a worthy, one could say, a wondrous, target. Compare the dark prince, who wanted to "hunt safely," with the game driven into cultivated and level grounds. There is no grandeur, no wonder, in the Assyrian's soul (1.4.16). We see one hunt planned by the dark prince. He would hunt alone, with the game ushered toward him.

Yet the grand desire has its own dark side. Are courageous men a still superior prey? Is conquering more desirable than hunting? The answer comes soon. In his very first battle Cyrus is carried away by "battle joy." Impatient to put on armor, entering the action at his own initiative, he cannot stand by while the Assyrians plunder "our" goods. He enters the fray and transforms it. Cyrus alone discerns a tactic to stop the plundering; he forces an attack. What stands out apart from the discernment is the furious delight in "striking down." Cyrus destroys the enemy even as they flee, and he leads his followers on an extended chase that strikes down all they reach and kills all that fall. Only his grandfather's command stops the blind slaughtering. One sees immense animal ferocity. Xenophon dwells on the lack of discernment: "Just as a well-bred but inexperienced dog rushes without forethought against a boar, so also rushed Cyrus, seeing only that he struck whomever he caught, with forethought for nothing else" (1.4.21, 23).

A final word-picture clarifies the mixture of wonder with passion for superiority. The battle over, Cyrus can only with difficulty be dragged away from gazing at the bodies of the slain. "Gazing" is a contemplating; the Greek, Wayne Ambler notes, might be rendered "gloating" (1.4.24, n. 46). This is contemplation in the style of the young Cyrus, a gloating over the fallen, who exhibit his full and even bloody mastery of men's souls. After the first hunt Cyrus had given Astyages the wild animals he killed. But he also left his bloody spears for the king to see (without himself calling attention to them). He wanted the master to acknowledge his warlike mastery—without having to reveal his need for such acknowledgment. The pleasures of the victor, the mature Cyrus will tell his troops, include those "to pursue, to strike, and to kill" (7.1.13). But the later speech is explicit in adding more rational pleasures, culminating in that of rule: "to have good things, to hear noble things, to be free, to rule." The young Cyrus exhibits the elementary passion and its cruelty

(1.2.2), prior to its more rational and political development and concealment.

All this helps explain, I think, the prominence of "power" in Cyrus's final soliloquy. While power is less an end than a means, it seems an end if one seeks above all superiority over others. The mature Cyrus conquered until he could reach no more men to conquer (8.6.21). His culminating counsel before his death is this: "And remember this last thing from me, that by benefiting your friends, you will be able to punish your enemies" (8.7.28). Enemies are more fundamental than friends if one desires above all to rise above others. This desire occasions Cyrus's "shame" at being ruled by inferior rulers and also his refusal to weigh the difficulties attending ruling in itself (1.6.8).

What then of a Cyrus as lover or cherisher of others, as opposed to conqueror or manager? This is a visible topic of the *Education*. While Cyrus (as a youth) cannot drag himself away from viewing corpses of vanquished soldiers, he refuses (when mature) even to view the most beautiful woman in Asia. Is this simply a sign of a man's self-command, a man who knows the overpowering and distracting effect of love? To avoid the distraction of beauty, Cyrus the general averts his eyes. So he tells Araspas, who proclaimed his freedom from the power of love (and was then overcome by Panthea's beauty) (5.1.8–17; 6.1.31–35). But such an explanation overstates Cyrus's warmth. Even as a youth he was cool as to love. Admittedly, there is talk of a boyfriend in Medea. But this fellow, Artabazus, seems a smitten admirer who looked on at a distance and who obtains nothing more than a couple of kisses, a laughing dismissal, and a false promise (1.4.27–28). From the start, it seems, Cyrus uses lovers for his own advancement. He uses yearning Artabazus for the whole imperial campaign, notably as a crucial emissary who induces the Medean cavalry to depart Cyaxares and join him (4.1.22–24). He strings him along until, the main campaign over, Cyrus kisses Chrysantas, the friend most devoted to Cyrus's rise (8.4.4–5, 10–11, 26–27). But this love too is not much of a love. Chrysantas's reward is not closeness to Cyrus but the satrapy of Lydia and Ionia (8.6.7), which are the westernmost provinces of the empire and far from the capital at Babylon. While Cyrus as king did spend the spring in Lydia, it was for the climate. There is no mention of any wish again to see Chrysantas (8.6.22).

We never hear of girlfriends. When we do hear of Cyrus's marriage, it is late, cool, and political. At one point Gobryas offers Cyrus his daughter, whom Xenophon calls "a marvel in beauty and stature" (5.2.7). Xenophon marvels at this beauty. Cyrus does not. He shows no erotic interest whatsoever in this maiden, or in any woman for that matter. Cyrus is not the loving type. During a bantering exchange Chrysantas calls him "a cold king" (8.4.22). Cyrus is seriously cold. He marries after his conquests are completed, and he marries Cyaxares' daughter as part of a trip to Persia and Medea to consolidate the old heart of his empire. This marriage is political consolidation. Is it love? Xenophon teases us. Some "talk" holds that this consort was beautiful, but "some writers" say that he married his mother's sister who, says Xenophon doubtfully but with emphasis, would "by all means have been an old woman." Given Cyrus's priorities, it doesn't much matter. "Having married, he immediately set out with her" for his capital (8.5.28), whereupon he turns to consolidate and expand the empire. Cyrus dies in Persia surrounded by his friends and the Persian magistrates (including his sons), with no wife present and no one named, except for his sons who are treated simply as heirs of empire. Cyrus dies profoundly alone except for his power.

What then of the "love of learning" for which Cyrus was also said to be legendary? The love is real, but the direction is given by ambition. As a boy he loved learning chiefly about horsemanship and hunting ("he loved the work"), and the conversations with his father had a political and especially a military cast (1.4.4–5; 1.6.2–8 and following). Admittedly, three of his closest youthful friends were the conspicuous lovers Araspas, Tigranes, and Hystaspas, and all three were also involved in some way with philosophy or wisdom. This shows something of Cyrus, who is described as a boy quick of mind, quick with words, eager to learn, and always asking the causes of things (1.4.3). He had been impressed as a youth with a certain wise man who was revered by Tigranes and who rather sounds like Socrates. Nor does he turn his back on such friends. These three are with him during the imperial quest. Still, their service is military, not conversational, and this reflects his characteristic demeanor. Cyrus had treated Tigranes coldly, for example, until he had extracted from Armenia the troops, the money, and the predominance he sought. It is true that Cyrus is shocked to hear that Tigranes' wise teacher has been executed by Tigranes' father. Yet it is also true that he urges "sympathy" for the father upon hearing of his "envy": the sophist had alienated the son's affections from the father. The passage reminds of a big cause why Athens killed Socrates. The Socratic-Armenian wise man had counseled only that Tigranes not be "harsh" to this father, who had acted out of ignorance of what was important for his son (3.1.38–40). Cyrus sympathizes more with the all-too-human passion of superiors for superiority over their own.

The only character in the *Education* who actually speaks of philosophy is Araspas. The occasion is not happy. Indeed, "philosophizing," and love too, seem to be culprits. Araspas had fallen in love with Panthea and eventually sought her by threats, despite his assurances that he was nobly impervious to the charms of beauty and love (5.1.9–18; 6.1.31–34). He attributes his fall to "philosophizing" with the "unjust sophist, love." There must be two souls, concludes Araspas, one good, and ordered to the rational Cyrus, and the other bad, and oriented to love (6.1.41, cf. 5.1.12). Cyrus ignores this opportunity to consider the soul in its complexity, turns to the business at hand, and treats Araspas's fall as an opportunity to use him as a spy. Cyrus had already expressed the apparently sensible view that human beings cannot resist beauty. But some decent or philosophic souls do resist or, like Tigranes and Xenophon himself, live well with love. It is true that Cyrus does favor a certain wisdom at the victory banquet. He is matchmaker in marrying the marvelous daughter of Gobryas to a friend, Hystaspas, who is an admirer of wise sayings (8.4.14–16, 25). Still, this Hystaspas most desires to be ranked first among Cyrus's friends. He is ambitious above all and completely dependent, although he is not as single-minded as Cyrus, or, for that matter, as Chrysantas. Nevertheless, Hystaspas does get the marvelous beauty and a future dose of Gobryas's sage sayings as well as the place Cyrus bestows on him. Cyrus himself gets neither the love nor the wisdom, such as it is.

In the *Education* Tigranes is the only political man of some independence who combines loving and wisdom. From him we learn something of the immense political restraint required. He shows a way less ambitious than Cyrus's, rational if not noble and perhaps wiser and more advantageous. While he joins Cyrus with the appearance of good will, he stays in the background. He seems determined to do what is necessary and no more. Other aides flatter Cyrus in their eagerness to keep the campaign going. Tigranes says only, "Never be surprised, Cyrus, if I am silent, for my soul has been made ready not to deliberate but to do whatever you order" (5.1.28). That is restraint. It shows in practice. After Tigranes brings his forces to join Cyrus's forces we hear very little of him. He neither seeks nor is given a leading assignment. He once warns Cyrus against danger. The circumstance had found him and his Armenians exposed to attack when generaled by Cyrus (3.2.8). He seems last among the generals in volunteering to build a siege weapon (6.1.21). At the victory feast Cyrus's inner circle vies for predominance and other benefits. Tigranes never speaks. Cyrus does bestow "feminine adornment" for Tigranes' wife because she "courageously campaigned" (8.4.24). Silence reigns as to Tigranes himself.

Unlike noble Abradatas, Tigranes never throws himself into the campaign. He had joined out of necessity; he had brought along the (new) wife whom he so much loves (3.1.36). The very rational Tigranes is a lover. But unlike Abradatas he seems not much a lover of the noble as such. We never hear that he shines in battle. While Tigranes defends shrewdly his father and the family dynasty and "would pay with his own soul" for his wife's freedom, these things are less for his honor than out of love and for his advantage, broadly construed. Compared to Abradatas, Tigranes' relation to his wife is more of love than of honor, and his action, more to his advantage than noble. While he is like Gobryas and Gadatas in political dependence on Cyrus, he manages to retain more independence for his *patria*. In general, Tigranes seems less dependent in his soul and policy because more independent in his thought. He obtains some success. That is, he emerged with his beloved and probably with his political inheritance, albeit within the constraints of Cyrus's empire. Cyrus permitted each of those "who willingly became his allies" to return, and as he consolidates the empire he does not appoint a satrap over Armenia. Tigranes' restraint in joining willingly reaps important fruit. Still, if a success, his is a limited success (as Cambyses' is a limited political success). Much later, in his dying distributions, Cyrus does include Armenia among his younger son's satrapies (8.7.11). If Tigranes had been alive he would not have been surprised.

Cyrus and the Ways to Happiness

What finally does Cyrus get? Cyrus would be happy, but he is most concerned to have the reputation of being happy. He seeks what is good, but especially the name or fame of having it. That priority proves to leave him content with a rather hollow happiness, as we can see by considering the paradoxes within Cyrus's last words and the appeal of other characters such as Croesus and Tigranes.

Cyrus's final soliloquy is a final set of orders, and first he orders the sons and friends gathered around "to say and do everything about me as about one who was happy" (8.7.6). It is all of a piece, with this concern for what people say, that no one is to view his dead (and powerless) body. No young Cyrus is to gloat over *his* fall (8.7.26; cf. 1.4.24). In addition, all who count in his kingdom, all the Persians and the allies (no less), are to be "summon[ed]" to his monument. All are to share in his pleasure that he can no longer be harmed and to do the things customary on behalf of a "happy man" (8.7.27). Is Cyrus happy? It must be some question even for Cyrus himself. Why else would he set forth reasons that "he thinks he knows" in the first part of his speech, which concludes, "How should I not justly obtain for all time the memory of being blessedly happy" (8.7.9)? At the end Cyrus too appeals for justice. Does he deserve the reputation he seeks, will he get it, and will it make him happy?

There is, first, a problem in getting the reputation. Cyrus

seeks a glory for all time, and the obvious difficulty is the problem of perpetuity. Why should new seekers of honor subordinate their name to that of an old seeker now powerless? Did the new king raise the monument as Cyrus ordered? Did he gather the great following to attest Cyrus's happiness? Xenophon does not say. What he does say does not bode well. The two sons "immediately" fell into dissension, cities and nations "immediately" revolted, and "everything" took a turn for the worse (8.8.2). Nor is the one other monument mentioned in the book, raised by Cyrus for Panthea and Abradatas, an encouraging precedent. It came to be called a monument for the eunuchs, that is, it was influenced by the palace guard of eunuchs that had come to power under Cyrus. New rulers, new names, new memories. Someone might object that the problem of perpetuity is solved through Cyrus's sons: "Now, if I die, I shall leave you alive" (8.7.8). The elder gets the kingship; the younger, certain satrapies. But Cyrus must suspect that the elder will "compete against my deeds" (8.7.12). In any event, Xenophon himself leaves his reader with a picture of a soft but savage post-Cyrus tyranny bent on exploiting a soft, resentful, and defenseless collection of subjects. Cyrus's order appears transitory, not perpetual. The whole seems ripe for an Alexander's picking. Xenophon notes too the surrounding monarchies, as if Cyrus's fame is not everywhere and for everyone, any more than forever (8.8.1; cf. 8.6.21). Any hope for honor from "all human beings" (3.2.31) is doomed to disappointment. Which is not to deny that Cyrus obtained a certain enduring glory. Many of Cyrus's establishments and customs remained in the Persia of Xenophon's time.[15] And Cyrus himself remained dimly legendary. But this is a dim and limited fame.

There is a bigger difficulty in the problem of happiness. Is it reasonable for an extraordinary man to find happiness in the opinion of ordinary men, precisely those incapable of judging the deeds of a superior man? Why should a superior so defer to his inferiors? It may be that love of honor from all men involves an attachment to all men, and hence benevolence or love of humanity.[16] But the effort to win all men also eviscerates friendship. Overcoming enemies is the primary thing, and helping friends, chiefly a means to extending one's empire. The deeper question, then, is whether the quest for popular reputation is wise, not whether reputation is widespread or can be perpetuated. Will Cyrus "justly obtain" fame for blessed happiness, as he wishes, or is he unjustly commanding untrue belief? Is it important to become legendary for happiness even when one is not truly happy?

Cyrus does justify his claim to happiness by his noble deeds, by the happiness he has brought his friends, and by the honor he has brought his fatherland. These claims ring hollow, even if sincerely made. To repeat, Cyrus ranks his friends by their service to his rising, benefits his friends to keep their loyalty, and sets his friends against one another to make them even more dependent upon him (8.2.26–28; 8.4.5, 10–11). Similarly, there is precious little evidence that he retained much affection or even gratitude for either his father or his fatherland. While he appreciated the good soldiers and rulers it produced, he treats it and these as his instruments. He undermines the republic that produced the peers, the extraordinary commoner Pheraulus, and the republican statesman-king Cambyses. He replaces it with an immense collection of toadying subjects and exploitative officials. Cyrus's chief happiness lies in his own increasing power ("always on the increase," 8.7.6) as well as his reputation. That is what his noble deeds, especially his imperial conquests, chiefly serve. The question remains: does his quest for power bring him happiness?

Cyrus is certainly aware of the trouble, pains, and dangers that beset such a quest. He urges his younger son to be content with three satrapies instead of the kingship. He can thus avoid the anxiety, war, and plots that interrupt "the leisure needed for taking delight" (8.7.12). It is an argument that had been addressed to Cyrus himself and at the critical point: just as he turned from defending Medea to annihilating the Assyrian host and seeking "the rule of Asia" (4.5.16). Cyaxares, the defensive battle won, had urged self-control upon him, especially in good fortune. We might then "grow old in happiness without risk" (4.1.15). Cyrus may parry various of Cyaxares' arguments, but he does not address this one. It is his second evasion of an argument about the limitations inherent in rule (his father's cautioning as to the inherent difficulties of ruling others being the first [1.5.7]). The second applies more obviously. Cyrus could well have been killed in the ensuing campaigns, notably when he fell with his stabbed horse in the second great battle (7.1.37–38).

Yet Cyaxares' moderation is no more compelling to Cyrus as a model of happiness than was his father's—and with reason. If the constraints of Persia repel him, he would be more repelled by Cyaxares' luxurious sluggishness, which must seem boring and contemptible to a serious man (1.6.8, 4.1.13, 4.5.51–52; cf. 1.3.10–11). Is not Cyrus correct in his disdain? After all, Cyaxares was a ruler who in any serious trouble proved inadequate, even in his own eyes. He wished "the dignity and honor" of a ruler, but he eased himself as much as possible from spending and fighting (5.5.34; 2.1.8–9, 2.4.11). Cyaxares lacked the ruler's art and temper. Wishing his officers to be loyal, he raged at them, threatened them, and earned a reputation for "savagery" (4.5.8–9, 12, 19). Wanting the Armenian to keep an alliance, he dithered and then would threaten his children (2.4.15). In general, Cyaxares wishes to be esteemed by the Medes as "better than they in everything" (5.5.34), but they disdain soft incompetence and laugh at his preoccupation with women (4.5.52). When Cyaxares realizes he has lost his power, he cries, says he appears "unworthy of rule," and compares himself to "a woman" (5.5.33). All this makes his criticism of Cyrus's attention to rule, however rational in itself, unconvincing. For what serious good comes of Cyaxares' restraint?

It is Croesus who affords a more appealing alternative and a more appealing illustration of the tension between enjoyment and the demands of ruling. He loves beautiful things, the arts, his wife and daughters, and his city and its families. No mere voluptuary, he is urbane in adversity. Nevertheless, Croesus too desired to be the "greatest" man in the world (7.2.23). After two defeats, and now at the mercy of Cyrus, Croesus believes he finally knows himself (7.2.25). But what he knows is that he is not fit to defeat Cyrus in being the greatest, not that being the greatest is not the thing to be. While he adopts the "most blessed" home life of "my good, refined, and delightful things" (7.2.27–28), this domesticity is forced upon him. For him too the alternative to a political life is the soft life of a woman, albeit his dear wife. If such a life relieves him of care and battles, as she had urged, it makes him in effect a prisoner. While Cyaxares becomes a puppet, Croesus has to become an exile from the family, home, and city he loves. The alternative to the political life, it seems, if not philosophy, is inevitably unmanly. If Cyaxares had been led astray by soft luxury, Croesus was betrayed by beautiful appearances. He was swayed by the flattery of kings, sought counsel from oracles (even while testing them), and examined too little the oracular pronouncements. While Croesus professes to "know myself" by comparison with Cyrus's superiority, he never speaks of Cyrus's superiority in soul, especially in intelligence and ambition.

Nevertheless, Croesus's soul is admirable in ways that Cyrus's is not. Croesus loves good and beautiful things, and he would defend what he holds dear. In his active way he is both more loving and more contemplative. There is something reminiscent of Socrates in Croesus, moved as he is by beauty, examining the gods and especially the Delphic oracle, desiring to "know myself." He seems a partial incarnation, in practical form, of the philosophic outlook. In this he is similar to the republican statesman Cambyses and the student prince Tigranes, both of whom speak in Socratic idiom and have a considerable life of friends, family, wisdom, and political loyalty. There are warm charms and attachments that the cold Cyrus lacks.

Of the three it is Tigranes who seems most to have an inner life of loving and of thinking. He had, after all, a Socrates-like teacher to cultivate his thinking, he travels outside the confines of his father's monarchy, he is not seduced by fripperies and appearances, and he, like Cambyses, reasons reasonably on the assumption that men generally pursue what they think to be their advantage. Tigranes and Cambyses are more aware than Croesus of the ways that necessity and nature limit the goodness of gods, family, and rulers. Unlike Croesus, Tigranes has managed to follow Cyrus voluntarily even if out of necessity. He sized up Cyrus well and did not give himself over to political rivalry. Unlike Croesus and unlike Cyrus also, Tigranes retained an independent life of love and thought as well as of ruling.

But does not Cyrus too appear aware that happiness requires more than a continual acquiring of power and reputation (7.5.45)? With Babylon conquered, "since labor-loving war has gone to rest," he speaks of his need for leisure: "If, however, to have great success entails the result that it is not possible to have leisure either for oneself or to enjoy oneself with friends, I bid farewell to this happiness" (7.5.42, 47). But the words are misleading, and intentionally so. This statement is a ploy to get his friends' consent for a royal palace and royal prerogatives. After the gambit succeeds Cyrus uses his time to consolidate his authority, that is, to achieve a victory over his enemies and indeed his followers. He surrounds himself with a corps of personal bodyguards (7.5.59–65), adds a personal military guard of ten thousand commoners fresh from habitual subjection in Persia (7.5.66–68), and makes the peers into servile dependents who obey on the double under threat of losing favor and property (7.5.70–86; 8.1.1–12, 8.3.19–23). Later he constructs his own governing apparatus after the model of a military hierarchy. This step again provides "leisure" (8.1.13–16). But again he uses the time to magnify his power and bamboozle his subjects. He introduces more new servility for the peers as well as a new and bewitching piety to help overawe subjects generally (8.1.13, 16–23, 40–42). This is his use of leisure.

We do see Cyrus banqueting and joshing with his closest friends (8.4.1–27). But how much enjoyment of friendship does this show? The gathering is a victory banquet and a breakup feast. As with all his hospitality, Cyrus uses this party to grade his subordinates and to get them to compete against one another and for his favor. While there is a certain banter and benevolence, there is chiefly a toadying rivalry together with fulsome obedience that extends to matchmaking. It is at this banquet of friends that his warmest friend calls Cyrus "a cold king" (8.4.22). When not hosting politic dinners Cyrus dines with Gadatas, in whose company he "took pleasure." This is the only such indication, Ambler notes, of Cyrus's pleasure in another human being (8.4.2). Gadatas is peculiarly loyal, selfless, and domestic—not exactly a barn burner of spirit and talk—and even he is Cyrus's companion merely at dinner. If Cyrus sought leisure, in short, it was leisure from small affairs so that he might give himself to "the most important affairs" (8.1.13).

As soon as Cyrus dominated the capital city, he set his forces in motion to consolidate his hold on his fatherland, Persia, and his uncle's Medea. As soon as he returned to Babylon, he first established his rule over the other parts of the empire and then set out with an immense army to conquer more and as far as possible. This was his use of leisure. Enjoying his friends and caring for his fatherland are little to Cyrus. Acquiring and keeping his power are almost everything.

Xenophon mentions two activities, apart from conquering, of the king Cyrus for himself. First, "he always spent his time in the warmth and coolness of spring," moving from palace to palace with the seasons. Second, he received from all over the empire what most would gratify him, and he then returned what was there lacking (8.6.22–23). The great Cyrus had disdained comfort, luxury, and trade. By toil and trouble he wins comfort, luxury, and trade. The mind seems so little occupied; the soul hardly attended to, except for the necessities of guarding and conquering and the virtuous habits bred in a Persia he has put on the road to destruction. No wonder Cyrus conquers without end. Activity is there as well as great renown. But it is an activity without a serious end, and it is renown in the opinion of those he disdains and enervates. Cyrus knew how to succeed, but he did not know what was best to succeed at. Here Tigranes, surely, and perhaps Croesus also were superior and happier. They were in their way gentleman-statesmen.

CHAPTER SIX

Obscuring the Truly Great: Washington and Modern Theories of Fame

T HE VERY NOTION OF gentleman-statesman is now of course much doubted, whatever Aristotle, in his far-off wisdom, might have said. This chapter and the final two address such doubts. In the final chapters I confront the sweeping modern skepticism as to both parts of the formula, both the allegedly superior character and the allegedly superior political wisdom. This chapter is less theoretical, deals with less radical theories, and is more biographical-historical. I mean to remind here that the gentleman-statesman is a familiar type still, although harder to see and appreciate in the shadows cast by our theories.

My example is the iconic American George Washington, still known and admired by many of his countrymen, if only through the historians. The modern interpretation I weigh is that of the American historian Douglass Adair. Adair was the author of a daringly wide-ranging essay, "Fame and the Founders," which argued that the greatest deeds of the seminal American founders were due to their love of fame. My plan is to confront Adair's general characterization with the greatest founder of them all, Washington, while relying on John Marshall's *Life of Washington*.[1] That old biography, which came out within a decade of Washington's death, better catches the statesman Washington's motives, I contend, than Adair's modern theory. Whatever the disadvantages of the *Life*, including a certain ponderousness, it has the advantage of an acute statesman-author who knew his subject at first hand. Marshall fought under Washington and was a political protégé, was of superior judgment and character, and himself knew high office as soldier, politician, and the "Great Chief Justice." He was himself a founder, at least the founder of his country's constitutional law.

What might seem merely particular differences, between two historians of different eras, can directly illuminate our big topic, the various theories of ambition. This is chiefly to the credit of Adair, a thinking man's historian, who sought to understand the founders' motives by recovering a great tradition of republican statesmanship. He too was engaged in an attempt at recovery, and he addressed in his own way the great political-philosophic alternatives, ancient and modern. Adair's is an architectonic inquiry into American developments often treated all too parochially. Nevertheless, his way is not quite my way. Adair looked to a republican tradition that incorporated almost seamlessly both modern and ancient theories of honorable ambition. His account has the big advantage of challenging directly the contrast I have developed, and it has another big advantage. His examples, unlike my Cyrus and Alcibiades, are not completely unfamiliar.

In what follows I first address Adair's theory of a seamless tradition, which, having been about at least since the philosopher Hegel, is certainly not his alone. Such an account, I argue, misses the decisive difference between the modern theory of enlightened leadership (Adair's chief source is the seventeenth-century Enlightenment philosopher Francis Bacon) and the ancient accounts (such as Cicero's *De Officiis*, which Marshall praises). My argument proceeds by setting these two authorities against one another. I take up in turn Bacon's rather Machiavellian discussion of leaders and their ambition, on the one hand, and Cicero's rather Aristotelian emphasis on virtue and republican duty, on the other. I then turn to measure Adair's account of the American founders against the founder Washington. I close with an extended discussion of Washington's motives and in particular of the way that he, according to some letters as well as Marshall's account, understood love of fame. Was Washington decisively moved by a love of fame, as Adair's account would make us think? Or was ambition subordinated, as Marshall insists, to duty, law, and the cause of free government? While Marshall acknowledged Washington's "ambition," he contended strenuously that the great man put duty and the "public advantage" before the "false glare" of fame (2:293).

I should make clear that Adair's thesis was a breath of fresh air when it appeared. He wrote during the 1970s, and there was a lot to recover from. Adair was particularly troubled by a previous generation of scholars who had largely obscured the founders' grandeur of spirit. He too is rebelling against modern theorists. Historians and social scientists like Charles Beard had explained the founders' deeds by their "interests," especially their economic interests as members of an upper class. Adair called attention to the "amazing self-consciousness about fame" of those old public men. He rightly called attention also, and here the argument got more complicated and theoretically interesting, to a certain republican tradition of fame. His basic reaction, then, was on behalf of political and political-intellectual motives in some complicated relation. In this he is surely correct. His special focus was on the great political-intellectual traditions that encouraged enlightened rationalism and popular self-government. Here, too, he is correct. The combination of ambition and the great cause of enlightened progress, political and scientific, surely moved the great founders. How can personal acquisitiveness account for the ambitious and semitheoretical free market republicanism of an Alexander Hamilton, who impoverished himself in office, or for the more democratic republicanism and humanitarian science that preoccupied Thomas Jefferson, who for those reasons and others could never quite keep his mind adequately on his own finances?

But is Adair right in his particular reaction? Can these things be explained by some version, however mediated, of the ambition for fame as such? I will contend that Adair is reductionist in his own way, that is, in tracing the founders' plans and accomplishments largely to a passion, albeit not one for gain. And this misreading is connected, I first argue, with a conflation of two republican traditions, only one of which does justice to the virtues of truly outstanding public men.

The thesis of one inclusive tradition is by no means simpleminded in Adair's hands. He certainly acknowledges differences between the ancient Cicero and Cato and the enlightened Jefferson and Benjamin Franklin. But the same fundamental political tradition, he maintains, turns both types to public-spirited works. Hamilton may have taken the great Caesar as a model to emulate;

Jefferson took the humane philosopher-scientists Bacon, John Locke, and Isaac Newton. But both participate in a "classical" and then "neoclassical" succession of politic views that turn ambition for fame into a reward for republican leadership. It is one great tradition that encompasses the framers, Tacitus's Roman history, and Plutarch's lives of the great Greeks and Romans. The thesis allows for a big change in the eighteenth century, for what one might call a scientific and humanitarian revolution. But this was a change in inclusiveness, according to Adair, not in tenor. Philosophers and scientists came to be included among those to be managed through ambition, and humane ends were developed for scientists and science. If Tacitus and Plutarch helped originate the old republicanism, it was especially Francis Bacon (1561–1626) who developed the new views as to useful science and the management of men. Nevertheless, what might seem Baconian innovation was not a break and not a new beginning. The new supplemented the old. The "antique" tradition explains a Hamilton, according to Adair, the Baconian variation, Jefferson's ambition to take as his purview the "advancement of humanity."

The Enlightened Seam

I contend, nevertheless, that Adair errs as to the essentially seamless character of the tradition of fame, chiefly because he errs as to the character of the enlightened innovations. Accordingly, he underestimates clashes and difficulties within the tradition and without—the French Revolution!—and even within the souls of modern republican statesmen. He underestimates in particular the superior virtue of Washington, and the pain and difficulties it caused him. Alternatively, Adair overstates somewhat the importance to the framers, and to admirable statesmen in general, of tradition and of theory.

I begin by considering Bacon's innovations as to honor and fame, which Adair holds paradigmatic for the modern development. Whether or not Francis Bacon is so seminal I need not argue, for at the very least the Baconian works on experimental science and worldly morals were representative and powerfully influential. (Jefferson put Bacon with Locke and Newton as one

of "the three greatest men who have ever lived.")[2] That Adair
perceived Bacon's importance, in the face of much mistaken
scholarship since the nineteenth century, is testimony to his seriousness and independence. That he appreciated the importance
of fame, of something like Nobel prizes, to Bacon's scientific enterprises, is at least as impressive. It is a great theme in Bacon's
vast corpus of writings, this mixing of fame seeking by leaders, in
physics and medicine as well as in statecraft, with security seeking
by peoples and indeed by humanity at large.[3] Nor can one doubt
that some such enlightened mix of private interest and public
good, whatever the origin, helps to explain the founding generation's self-consciousness about fame.

What I wish to prove is this: the mixture involves an innovation that was decisive, not merely secondary. Bacon's new understanding is not traditional, if only because it both incorporates a
critique of moral virtue and advances a new, amoral virtue of advancing oneself. It is then contrary to a Washington's uprightness. Bacon separates ambition for fame from that for honor and
true distinction, and he connects it instead to desire for preserving and empowering oneself. Desire for fame replaces love of
honor. The wish to be honorable as well as honored, to be worthy
of the honor, is dropped. Instead, the man of enlightened ambition is to seek a name that endures. It's a deal. He obtains a kind
of immortality by supplying his followers with enduring benefits,
private and public. Security is the end even for him, and a calculated fame is the way—not honor or glory as such and certainly
not honorable action or duty as such. In Bacon's marvelously circumlocutory prose: "Certainly *Vaine-Glory* helpeth to Perpetuate
a Man's Memory, and Vertue was never so beholding to Humane
Nature, as it receiveth his due at the Second Hand."[4]

Which is not to deny a concern for public-spiritedness, even
for republican service, in Bacon's argument. Adair's remarkable
insight is confirmed, to that extent. But Adair missed the new and
calculating spirit. One rises by serving, and clear-sighted rising
requires public servants whose clear-sightedness is not obscured
by considerations merely moral or honorable. Love of honor or
glory often bedazzles politic judgment. Calculated concern for
enduring power bedazzles it less. It certainly bedazzles less than

do moral scruples, Bacon seemed to think, including various and variously ill-founded ideas of justice, especially divine justice. Private interest, public gain, is the later formula, and Bacon's plan extends far beyond his seminal work, too little appreciated, in that quintessentially enlightened science, modern political economy. Enlightened self-interest well understood can also drive leaders to public duties. It drives them to breed powerful countries, if only because national power sustains their position and elevates their name. This new kind of knowing *politique* may smile at goodness, piety, nobility, and justice even as he adopts a suitable image. But although he disciplines all aims in accord with policy, his private aims require public policy, that is, national security and an efficacious government that satisfies its people.

The enlightened *politique* leads and founds republics. He favors large and expanding popular republics, not cities and certainly not gentlemanly cities. Popular nation-states are more stable with the people satisfied and can be better organized for war and industry with clergy and a landowning gentry class suppressed.[5] While few contemporary historians have gone so far as Adair in penetrating the untraditional thoughts beneath the veneer of traditional words, one must go farther to grasp the radically antimoral implications of Bacon's well-known "realism" and raison d'état: "We are much beholden to Machiavel and others that write what men do and not what they ought to do." Bacon was more open in his praise of Machiavelli than any other sixteenth- or seventeenth-century philosopher.[6] Adair gets much of this. He calls Bacon's *Essays* "a Renaissance equivalent of Dale Carnegie's success manual showing how to win powerful friends and influence the top people."

But these changes involve reinterpreting desire for honor into a passion for enduring superiority and adding the image making calculated to make oneself attractive and memorable. This is a decisive innovation. The new version is at once peculiarly selfish (an early individualism) and peculiarly dependent upon dominating the minds of others (an early modern politicization of life).[7] Bacon-style thinking thus involves two big theories, that of the autonomous (but dependent) individual and that of the domination of peoples by manufactured progress and tra-

dition (civilization or culture, as it came to be known).[8] The core
of the new outlook is an amoral ethic of getting ahead by parading one's usefulness, and it informs the scientist as well as the *politique* in his public relations.

I will say a word about Bacon's extension of this motive to science and his introduction of the special image of the humane
provider. Bacon is most famous for popularizing (some say re-
vamping) the experimental method. In his broader plans for the
role of science, the new experimental scientist is to be disciplined
by method to seek useful knowledge, the formulas which can be
paraded in their uses for health, wealth, and power. Scientists rise
by finding what Bacon calls the "laws of action": the formulas
that give us power over nature. In Bacon's utopia, set forth in his
sci-fi *New Atlantis*, the most prominent institution is an MIT-like
research institute, the purpose of which is experimental inquiry
that breeds power on the grandest scale. "The End of our Foundation," he writes, "is the knowledge of Causes, and secret motions of things, and the enlarging of the bounds of Human Empire, to the effecting of all things possible." But what keeps the
white coats in the lab is fundamentally the possibility of gain and
fame. While civil leaders rise by providing national security, freedom, and a rising standard of living, scientists rise by offering humane relief from the sufferings of mankind. They offer especially
technological affluence and scientific medical care. In the *New
Atlantis*'s vision of the new world, luxury, inventions, medicines,
and drugs abound, and the research establishment is the most
revered institution. Indeed, the chief scientist is the most revered
man, his prominence being paraded in a parade that reminds of a
procession of sacred priests and replaces the preeminence of
priests. The institute has its own hall of fame, which includes
both great inventions (such as "observations in astronomy") and
the statues of "all principal inventors." Indeed, "upon every invention of value, we erect a statue to the inventor, and give him a
liberal and honorable reward."[9] Bacon's more worldly and efficacious theory of ambition is part of a comprehensive plan for
progress.

Who can doubt that this project and even this psychology had
a big influence over more than a few statesmen of the founding

period? Franklin is the exemplar, I suppose, even more than Jefferson. Franklin was a projector in Bacon's fashion, himself a member of the Royal Society more or less modeled on Baconian plans for experimental science and scientific institutes. The Franklinian projects extended to an American version, the American Philosophical Society. It was to aim for "useful knowledge," that is, to "increase the power of man over matter, and multiply the conveniences or pleasures of life."[10] Still, the relevant point here is that Franklin followed too the moral and political side. His writings develop the arts of the self-made man and the civil science of mutual negotiation and useful society. His most important work, the wonderful *Autobiography*, is all about an easygoing and democratic version of advancing oneself and of the work ethic, two of the many innovations in Bacon's *Essays*. Franklin treats his own turn to scientific research under the heading, "the Rise and Progress of my Scientific Reputation."[11]

Nevertheless, this enlightened account of fame seeking does not actually characterize accurately the framers' own motives, at least in the most distinguished cases. Whatever the influence of this Enlightenment philosophizing on a Franklin, even then regarded by many contemporaries as a slippery fellow, it did not shape a Washington, at least as Marshall understood his motives. How could it? Wouldn't a glory-seeker on many occasions get less fame from founding a republic than from lording it over a people as one alone?

There is evidence, unfortunately, on the side of the lords and emperors. The most famous man of Marshall's time was the emperor Napoleon, who destroyed many republics, beginning with his own. The very famous Julius Caesar is famous above all for erecting an imperial rule over Rome and its empire. "Master of the world," Cicero calls him in *De Officiis*, who rose by destroying the republic. Machiavelli, an authority on this subject of rising to glory, gave advice to princes as well as republics. If he tells princes to maintain their fame by founding republics, he also shows them how to destroy republics in order to found their own state. Adair did not weigh adequately the depth of Bacon's Machiavellianism. Bacon took as a model Julius's successor Caesar Augustus, who

fed on the republic's collapse, and on Julius's beginnings, to pre-
side as emperor over the world.[12]

Now Adair himself had illuminating doubts as to his own thesis. His rejoinder relied on the introduction of a new form of
goodness, "humanity."

Adair worried about the danger from an "ethically neutral"
passion for fame. He says flatly what neither Machiavelli nor
Bacon, who aimed for an effective truth, could say flatly: one
should avoid the "bitch-goddess, success." The framers, he maintains, avoided her. For they and their tradition deferred to the
"wise and the good," those who kept the distinction between
"virtue and vice."[13] This is an insistence in the spirit of Marshall's
Life. But it seems an admission at odds with Adair's chief contention—that the greatest framers were moved by the passion for
fame. Was it a devotion to justice and honorable conduct that finally shaped Washington's public actions, as Marshall maintains?
Or was it ambition for fame, as Adair maintains and Marshall
sharply denies? This is not a quibble, for Adair's article at times
denies to the framers what he seems here to require. Although he
upholds here the standard of virtue, elsewhere he disparages as
"elitist" and "ethically reactionary" the love of honor: the disposition that causes a man of honor to shrink from what is base or
wrong.[14]

To these criticisms Adair has a pregnant reply: the framers es-
poused a new kind of goodness. They and their tradition inno-
vated as to goodness itself, for theirs was a "horizontal" understanding of good that encompassed humanity at large. This new
view is more "inclusive" than devotion to honor or other aristocratic standards. It makes the leader's desire for widespread ap-
plause newly appropriate. There is deep truth in Adair's observation as to the invention of "humanity" as replacement for the old
virtue.[15] But a new difficulty appears, one that will occupy us until this book's end. What is the quality of an idealism that abstracts from the distinction between virtue and vice?

Suppose Adair means by humane and inclusive ends the relief
of the sufferings of humanity, say, or the rights of man. Even at
this horizontal level, what is it besides the passion for fame that

keeps a man humane and devoted to human rights? Marshall speaks of justice, devotion to equal rights, and patriotism. These are limitations, within the soul, of the desire for fame. Adair does not. Also, there is a price to be paid for going the horizontal route in morals. Would Adair not have to give up the traditional understanding of virtue and vice that he wishes to retain? Machiavelli had given it up, substituting the mixture of force and fraud he called *virtù*. Bacon gave it up, mixing ambition and acquisitiveness with foresighted industry in his self-made man. But Adair would not give it up, and the biographer of Washington, Marshall, certainly did not.

Indeed, Marshall's letters show him anxious about a decline in character among the new republic's political class and about a new primacy of success and of political righteousness. Is there something nefarious "lurking beneath our institutions"? "To what," he asked a correspondent, "are we to impute the disregard of those maxims which time has rendered venerable, which early impressions had surrounded with a sort of religious reverence, & whose utility has the sanction of true experience & consent of the ages? . . . Does the execrable doctrine that the end will justify the means derive its prevalence from temporary causes or from such as are permanent & deeply rooted in our system and habits? Does the no less execrable doctrine that merit as a partisan will excuse the want of every virtue & of every moral quality belong to man in all situations or does it derive peculiar strength from particular causes in operation among ourselves?"[16]

Such anxieties help account for Marshall's intense efforts during his last thirty years to immortalize Washington as a model for his countrymen. Even when over seventy-five years of age he was still painstakingly revising the *Life*, first reducing five bulky volumes to two and then condensing again for a one-volume school edition (which was reprinted twenty times).[17] He addressed especially the ambitious. The actions and character of Washington supply lessons for those "who are candidates for fame" (5:380). The concluding summary of the hero's character develops the theme: "If Washington possessed ambition, that passion was, in his bosom, so regulated by principles, or controlled by circumstances, that it was neither vicious, nor turbulent." Washington was finally governed not by "personal aggrandizement," or "an avidity of power," but by duty, country, and honor. In accepting his great offices he yielded chiefly to a general conviction that his country would be benefited. Washington in office was then above both pretension to honors and the arts of popularity. He mixed an "innate and unassuming modesty" with a "high and correct sense of personal dignity" and a "just consciousness of the respect due to station" (5:379–80).

A Tradition to Fit a Washington

What Marshall looked to as explaining Washington was not a seamless tradition but an old-fashioned and indeed Roman seriousness about virtue. None of Marshall's surviving papers or works praise much any of the modern philosophers except Edmund Burke, who was, after all, a critic especially of the Enlightenment's calculating philosophy. But Marshall twice commends Cicero's *De Officiis* to his grandsons; it is "among the most valuable treatises I have seen in the Latin language."[18] There is in fact an uncanny resemblance between the duty-oriented spirit of Marshall's *Life of Washington* and the rather austere and even Stoic *De Officiis* ("On Duties" or "On Offices"). One must first acknowledge, of course, that Marshall was also gravely devoted to individual rights, representative government, and other parts of the modern constitutionalism of Locke, Montesquieu, and William Blackstone. There was more than one outlook, if not a seamless outlook, within his capacious soul. Still, as to ethics he praises especially Cicero's austere version of the classical moral tradition. This has political significance. The *Life* eulogizes the republican gentleman-statesman, which is what the *De Officiis* itself encourages.

Cicero's *De Officiis* is a book on duty that dwells on the honorable duties involved in free public life. It does have a Stoic tone. Duty and justice are the themes, not pleasure, happiness, honor, or glory. Still, we are given a popular or at least political version of Stoicism. The particular theme of the *De Officiis* is the priority of one's office to the seeking of one's own advantage (*utile*), whether that advantage be money, pleasure, or fame. Admittedly, one can find quiet qualifications if one looks. Cicero eventually acknowledges the attractions of fame, especially to the high-spirited. He shows himself advancing his own just reputation (2.84, 87, 88; 1.2−4).[19] He instructs repeatedly in the just ways a young man can win fame and glory (2.42−43, 85; 3.45−46). But the work's obvious advice, given first and foremost throughout, is to "discharge the duties prescribed by justice" (2.43). The work magnifies not greatness but "true and wise greatness," of the sort "that regards the *honestum* [honesty, integrity] to which nature disposes as consisting in deeds, not in fame" (1.65). The big warning is that glory seeking leads away from the public good. A general declined a necessary withdrawal because it would be "dishonorable" to himself (1.84). (Marshall's *Life* mirrors the example [2:121].) Cicero warns especially against great glory seekers, those who promote wars "out of hunger for glory" (1.74). He warns above all against Caesarism, the immense glory seeking that is satisfied only in being "master of the world" (3.83). The desire for fame can be bad for your republic. In the extreme case, which was Rome's case, it destroys the republic. The general lesson is this: citizens of a republic must do their duty whether the consequences be glory or dishonor, victory or death, pleasure or pain. Self-government requires this, and dignity, noble self-respect, requires it as well. Cicero's spirit is moral as well as political.

What distinguishes the *De Officiis* from the paradigmatic work on moral virtue, Aristotle's *Nicomachean Ethics*, is the twin focus on Stoic dutifulness and free politics. Cicero acknowledges a model in a book on duties by the Stoic Panaetius, and his initial discussion of philosophic schools advances "stoicism" as the most "probable." This is notable. Elsewhere, as in *De Natura Deorum*, Cicero criticizes the school he here praises. Is Stoicism preferable here because it suits his prescription of duties? *De Officiis* appears in the form of a hortatory letter to Cicero's son, while works such as *De Republica* and *De Natura Deorum* appear in the more philosophic form of dialogues. However that may be, *De Officiis* advances *honestum* as either the only good or the most important good. The book sharply deprecates pleasure, especially *voluptas*, and it sharply attacks the Epicureans for upholding pleasure as the good. In the Epicurean teaching "justice totters or rather, I should say, lies already prostrate; so also with all those virtues which are discernible in community and general human society" (3.118). Cicero goes so far with Stoicism in the *De Officiis* as to declare pain not really evil. It is true that qualifications emerge on this topic, also. He allows for a more subtle understanding of Epicurus on pleasure and eventually acknowledges that bodily pleasures at least give "spice" to life. He also advances now and again the claims of greatness of soul (praising the Aristotelians), of philosophic inquiry (repeatedly deferring to Socrates), and of a life retired from politics. It is also true that in book 3 Cicero does what, according to him, his Stoic predecessor did not do. He at least considers the apparent conflicts between *honestum* and *utile*, between what is our duty and what is to our advantage, between duty and pain or death. But from the start of *De Officiis* Cicero disavows philosophic inquiry as to the *summum bonum*. Most of the qualifications mentioned, along with many others, appear quietly, whether between the lines or in the course of other arguments. The distinctive task of *De Officiis* is to set forth the common duties of life, and to the end it tends to give these priority.

It is hard to say how much the priority of moral duty in *De Officiis* depends on the priority given to free politics. A republican spirit certainly suffuses the work, despite the fact that the republic Cicero loved and defended was already doomed. Caesar committed "murder of his patria" (3.83), and, despite the murder of its murderer, Cicero thought the republic dead. Still, he does not turn his readers away from worldly troubles. He does the opposite. References to our obligations to God or the gods are conspicuous by their absence, even if not altogether absent. Nor does Cicero say much about duties to kin and friends, although his gloominess about politics leads him a little in that direction. He dwells chiefly on duties to fellow citizens. "No social relation is more close than that which links to our country" (1.57). It is true that he attends also to what is owed humanity at large, relying on a natural law, or at least a law of peoples, that reminds of Stoic universalism. But he uses this universal doctrine chiefly to criticize Rome's unjust domination of its neighbors, even under the republic, and to criticize especially the new military captains who would dominate even fellow citizens. The most important duties are of the citizen, and especially of the gentleman-citizen who governs by consent and by sharing. It may be that it is Cicero's republicanism that finally distinguishes the *De Officiis* from the more moral and philosophic teachings of Aristotle and of the usual Stoics.

The reasoning behind the preference for republican freedom is worth noting, if only because Marshall's Washington also held "the most precious rights" to be those of popular self-government. Self-government as Cicero understands it is connected with the primacy of reason. For it is intelligence and reasoning that lead human beings to stand up for what they think true. Intelligence and reasoning lead to independence and to "greatness of soul" (1.13). But they lead also to special respect for those able to judge independently and reasonably. Cicero's republicanism moves toward both republican self-government and government by those judicious and wise. It leads also toward respect for the most knowing, whether or not they are involved in governing. While insisting on the primacy of active statesmanship, *De Officiis* takes many opportunities to bring out the uses of philosophy and philosophers, especially Socratic philosophy and Socrates: "As Socrates used to express it so admirably," for example, "the nearest way to glory—a short cut, as it were—is to strive to be what you wish to be thought to be" (2.43; cf. 2.67–69). *De Officiis*, like the *Education of Cyrus*, the two *Alcibiades*, and the *Politics*, educates free citizens to look up to philosophers and not disdain them or kill them. But its principal task is to foster the justice and noble spirit needed for free politics, which requires simplification and moralization of instruction as well as a salutary philosophy. An unequivocal Stoic defense of duty helps put the almost natural ambition for fame into its political place.

Honor, Duty, Country: American Particulars

While Marshall's *Life of Washington* itself occasionally points to some peaks of conduct above what his free country permits, it never eulogizes some philosophic Socrates, and it concentrates on the moral qualities that distinguish the republican statesman. Washington exemplified the real distinction, which forever ex-

ists, "between wisdom and cunning." Washington's were immense powers of judgment, but they were themselves subject to
"ends" that were "always upright" and "means" that were "always
pure" (5:378–79).

Here is a key example, which I have used before. A correspondent had urged Washington to offer himself for the presidency in
1789, while acknowledging that the general's "just fame" would
be stained should the new system falter (4:250). Washington was
terse in reply. He was by no means so "solicitous for reputation" as
to "seek or retain popularity at the expense of one social duty, or
moral virtue." On the contrary, if the "good of my country" requires "my reputation" to be put at risk, so be it (4:250). He might
decline to run, yes, but on one ground alone—if some other person, with "less pretence and less inclination to be excused," could
fulfill the duties as well as he could. It is hard to believe, Marshall
remarks, that "ambition" did not tempt such a commander to become the supreme magistrate. But one cannot reduce an extraordinary human being to "the motives" that "usually guide the
human mind." Washington, profoundly disinclined to return to
public office, yielded "to a sense of duty, and deep conviction of
his obligations to his country" (5:245–46).

The point of all this is not that love of fame or notice is per se
bad, or that a man should not struggle to obtain the name and
honors he deserves. The point is that Marshall restricts his praise
to those who sought nobly a just fame, especially those who in
their actions benefited their country. The *Life* offers a variety of
such tributes. They go not least to honorable warriors. Marshall
praises at length the famous generals the Marquis de Montcalm
and James Wolfe, who both fell before the walls of Quebec
(1789), in the climactic struggle in North America between France
and Britain. Enemies they were, but alike "fearless of death" and
passionate for "victory and fame" (1:352). And he can praise a
dashing American lieutenant who died while pursuing "military
fame" with "the ardour of a young soldier." Contrast this with his
treatment of Napoleon, the most famous man of his time.
Napoleon was a strategic "genius," something Marshall never
says of Washington. But Napoleon was a "tyrant." With all his
fame and genius, Napoleon was justly opposed. He was "the ter-

ror, and justly the terror, of the world."[20] Washington, admittedly, was "more solid than brilliant" (5:374). Yet in his loftiness and dignity he disdained glorious victories and public acclaim, too, when contrary to justice and his public duties. Though far from being "regardless of popular favor," he "would never stoop to retain it by deserving to lose it" (5:377).

It must be said that Washington, great as he was, was probably not Marshall's exemplar of the great statesman. If one judges by the *Life*, that honor seems reserved for William Pitt the elder, later Lord Chatham, under whom Britain warred so successfully against France in Quebec and elsewhere. In the whole *Life* Marshall gives very high praise to only two political leaders besides Washington. John Smith, captain at the early colony of Jamestown, truly had "the character of a commander." He made the new colony prosper every time he controlled it. He and his projects, however, were repeatedly undermined by envious rivals (1:26–38). Pitt, on the other hand, was a great man who found a worthy platform. He succeeded in infusing energy and daring that made a great empire victorious over an ancient rival. An "inglorious scene," of a sluggish and defeated Britain, was succeeded by a period of "unrivalled brilliancy." Victory followed victory. Marshall dwells as much on loftiness in the man as on energy in the country. Pitt had an "exalted" opinion of his countrymen; his plans were "grand"; the secret was his "talents" and an "independent grandeur of character"; his was a "proud elevation" of soul; Pitt was "great in his spirit" and "lofty in his views" (1:320–22). All this goes beyond anything in *De Officiis*. Even more than the *Life*'s concluding eulogy of Washington, Marshall's quick portrait of Pitt reminds of Winston Churchill and of the first and classic picture of the great-souled man in the *Nicomachean Ethics*.

The *Life* also supplies, by contrast, a little portrait of "false pride." The traitor Benedict Arnold (3:253, cf. 252–58) is the illuminating counterexample to Pitt and Washington. Arnold was not without grandeur. He had been a hero on a quite grand scale, and he tried to turn traitor on a quite grand scale, or at least a large scale, partly from greed and perhaps largely from inability to tolerate even deserved dishonor. At the start of the war he had been a leader in the ingenious capture of crucial forts at Ticonderoga and Crown Point. Later he commanded the bold American expedition against Quebec, which nearly succeeded despite being a desperate venture, and he manufactured impressively a fleet on Ontario. As military governor amidst the elegance of Philadelphia, however, vanity and dishonesty brought him down. Arnold lorded it in luxury without the fortune to support the show. He lacked, Marshall wrote, the principle and correctness needed for peaceful life. Arnold's was a false pride. He was drawn to extortion from private parties, then to theft from the public funds; the eventual result was court-martial and reprimand. This humiliation his proud temper could not abide. Arnold turned to recover his position by grand revenge. He would inflict a "mortal wound," "the ruin of the American cause" (3:254, 252). He would turn over West Point, the fortress that barred British armies from dividing the colonies by coming up or down the Hudson. After the project failed by a hair, Washington considered Arnold's state of mind and concluded he would be feeling no remorse. Judging from his treason, his stooping, and his peculations, Arnold, "hardened in crime," is "lost to all sense of honour and shame" (5:264).

Such discussions are unusual in the *Life*. The vices on which Marshall concentrates are less grand defects and more failures in the common duties, the duties that are needed in the generals and officials of a free country. The relevant point is this: hunger for fame and reputation often leads astray. It leads generals especially away from what judgment and the public good would dictate. This general stayed too long besieging Quebec and lost an army; he was reluctant to "encounter the obloquy" of giving up a post even when it could no longer be defended (2:121; cf. 5:345, 349–50). That general delayed detaching troops to another general, despite orders; he cherished a favorite enterprise that would bring "splendor" to his reputation. Generals such as the Marquis de Lafayette and Washington showed the correct way. At Yorktown Lafayette waited for the arrival of Washington and the main army, rejecting exhortations to an early attack by the French admiral on the spot, his countryman. While a victory through his own forces would have given "unrivalled brilliancy," the cost would have been much blood. Lafayette did not "for his personal glory" sacrifice the soldiers confided to him. Similarly, Washington in Philadelphia never hesitated to detach a major contingent of troops to another general, thus, for example, to block John Burgoyne's march down the Hudson from the north. Here it is that Marshall concludes that "the fame of being himself the leader of the victorious army, did not, with false glare," dazzle Washington's "estimate of the public advantage" (2:293). Other generals were dazzled.

THE PATRIOT CHIEF

The "most marked" quality of Washington was his patriotism, and Marshall's discussion helps to clarify, I think, the distinctive role of patriotic and liberal principle in regulating American ambition at its peak. Whatever Washington's aspirations for himself, he served first the "glorious cause": "the rights of mankind and the welfare of the common country" (2:54; cf. 4:147, 153). One cannot understand true ambition and true pride, it seems, without understanding true justice and finally true republicanism. For Washington, and for Marshall too, the "choicest rights of humanity" are those of republican self-government, that is, of men "legislating for themselves." American aspirants for fame can be proud of themselves only if they serve the thing truly glorious: the "preservation of the exalted rights and liberty of human nature" (1:187; 4:135).

Marshall calls Washington a "patriot chief." He is particularly impressed that as the revolutionary war ended Washington managed to keep his army from overthrowing the republic and making their captain the dictator (4:68ff., 73ff.). It was a near thing. The army had become the infant republic's greatest force, and it was about to be unhappily disbanded without assurances of pay, including substantial back pay. Officers and men alike had suffered much, and they had endured much from weak and suspicious democratic governments. They had plenty of grievances, grievances that could be exploited by a popular and victorious general bent on dictatorial glory. As Marshall tells the tale, only Washington's acquiescence was required for a march on the capital. But Washington did not acquiesce. He suppressed. He suppressed a rebellion that perhaps he alone could have suppressed. It was only the last of a series: a series of convulsive army mutinies in face of the state governments' failures adequately to recruit, pay, feed, and clothe—above all, to pay (3:220–21, 336; 4:65).

Such failures suggest a more disturbing reason why in such a country justice and patriotism should take priority over love of fame. Public life may not allow much fame. It should not depend on a commodity in short supply from a fickle audience. Washington as commander in chief had some grand plans. Almost all fizzled because the government or governments did not supply the means. The general wanted to attack (2:30, 32); he wanted to prove himself worthy of command by a striking action (2:74, cf. 80; 2:161, 234, 266, 280); he saw "a glorious occasion" for striking a blow or the "prospect of a glorious offensive campaign" (3:423 n. v). All these occasions and many others came and went, and the cause, according to the *Life*, was want of a timely and adequate supply of arms, provisions, and troops. Great actions and great honor foundered on a lack of political energy (3:206) and on a populace generally unwilling to sacrifice. The army and its general's ambitions were often sacrificed instead.

Actually, the problem was worse, if Marshall is right. Political leaders would often demand glorious actions and daring projects even while "the army was reduced to the last extreme for want of food" (5:220–21). Overconfident after the occasional victory, various members of the continental congress called for a march on the British in heavily defended Philadelphia, or they demanded an attack on distant Canada. Thus: the "false brilliant" of public opinion. This false fame, too, Washington resisted. He did instead the one thing necessary for his country. He saved his ragged army and kept it in the field until an ally arrived, and this despite forces inferior for most of the war. An extreme example of the austere devotion needed was that of General Nathanael Greene, in North Carolina. Greene "never obtained a decisive victory, and yet obtained, to a considerable extent, even when defeated, the object for which he fought" (4:43).

Humiliations continued into peacetime. After the war the state governments evaded payment of the debts by which their independence had been financed. Their conduct was "disgraceful": "blots" upon the national honor, anathema to a Washington (4:192). A more serious problem was popular suspicion and envy of the ambitious and honorable, not least of the officer class that had suffered most and sacrificed most during the fighting. Marshall recounts at surprising length the sharp controversy over plans for an association of the officers, a Society of Cincinnati. His sympathies are obvious. The society issued from "the finest feelings of the human heart" among companions in "virtuous suffering, danger, and in glory" (4:134ff.) But there arose a vociferous suspicion of "a race of nobles"(4:137). Washington confronted artfully both the officers and the people. Wishing to avoid a division between them, he tried to remove from the society's constitution the most undemocratic features, including the hereditary principle and a power of adopting honorary members. Here, according to recent accounts, he failed.[21] But suppose Washington had not been a patriot chief, a chief superior to, but subordinated within, a republic of equal rights?

As to this very delicate problem, the problem of an honorable patriot's devotion to a not very honorable country, Marshall is circumspect. This is, after all, a public man who near the end of his life took care to burn all of his correspondence that he could reach. He was particularly discreet in later life, being chief justice, and having lost an earlier hope that an essentially sound democratic majority need only be trimmed of its excesses by the federal constitution.[22] But flashes of light show in letters that survive. In 1813, when Marshall had been chief for a decade, he says he is "mortified" at his country's servility before Napoleon.[23] Napoleon did not think enough of the Americans even to pretend to do what they, in justifying an accommodation, had said he had done. Marshall burns at the "tame unmurmuring acquiescence" of the Madison administration, and he burns at the general "infatuation" of his "countrymen." But he wrests some control: "This is a subject on which I do not trust myself." Beneath the black robes, the black letter reasoning, and the historian burned fires of spirited honor and justice. For a country's sake, for liberty's sake, patriotism and duty are needed in the ardent and honorable, especially when loyalty cannot be accompanied by pride.

Despite all the simplicity and charms that Albert Beveridge recounts in his delightful old biography, it is also true that there burned in Marshall's heart something of the austere dignity and fierce sense of honor of an old Roman republican. If I read right, the one popular militia strongly praised in the *Life of Washington* is that in which the people were "genuinely attached to the revolution"—and attached also to a "high spirited and intelligent gentry" (3:184). Some such American mixture of popular patriotism and honorable character, together with capacious judgment, was what the author found in Washington.

CHAPTER SEVEN

Honorable Greatness Denied (1):
The Egalitarian Web

THESE LAST CHAPTERS turn to address the skeptics, especially the intellectual critics. There are many. While admiration for a Nelson Mandela, a Franklin D. Roosevelt, and a George Washington may arise almost naturally in decent citizens and appreciative historians, many present-day intellectuals and academics would challenge such estimates in principle. This chapter and the next examine the principle, or, rather, several of the critical principles and their complicated origins. The egalitarianism and relativism of the present may seem compelling on their face, but they are also contradictory on their face. How defend equality as a principle when all principles are merely subjective values or historically relative? Besides, these present-day beliefs are not necessary truths, self-evident as they may now seem, but derivative effects. They arose out of questionable contentions at various stages in the development and fraying of modern political philosophies. My effort in these concluding discussions is not chiefly rebuttal—an adequate argument would call for much more—but reminder, a reminder of how we got to the questionable outlooks that now seem so obvious.

Perhaps the most thoughtful of contemporary critiques are the relevant contentions of John Rawls (1921–2002) and Hannah Arendt (1906–75), two thinkers who much influenced post–World War II academicians in the United States and Europe. Their teachings were complex, sometimes changing over the years, and the sketches that follow may well be flawed in some details, despite my intention. I ask the reader to remember my broad purpose, which is to call to fresh awareness the big premises.

As a preliminary, however, I again address some everyday objections to a revived appreciation of great statesmen. For these are often not only common but also reasonable.

To begin with, my concern in this book is not with ordinary political disputes, as to whether Harry Truman deserved the presidency, for example, or should be ranked among the great presidents (as I happen to think). Such differences among partisans and historians are the stuff of political life, and the stuff too of the political judgment and intelligent political history that can weigh sensibly the controversies. These rankings and weighings, however, presuppose what our behavioral and egalitarian theories deny, that some political figures are superior in judgment and character. Everyday political enemies can acknowledge that. The British monarch George III eventually called his tormentor Washington "the most distinguished of any man living," "the greatest character of the age."[1]

Neither do I deny or minimize the dangers to free politics that grand ambition often poses. The danger can be genuine. But serious statesmen themselves often address this threat, and it is certainly provided against by a Plato or Aristotle. Washington was famously self-conscious as to his role as exemplar in popular self-government. He was appalled at the idea of restoring some kingship, and this foreshadowed his resignation as chief of a victorious army adoring of him and resentful of its incompetent political masters. Charles de Gaulle, the twentieth-century rejuvenator of France, devoted himself similarly to the republic; he disdained similarly a dictatorship. Kemal Atatürk, often overlooked as the extraordinary founder of modern Turkey, himself sought to stir up democratic parties, even a democratic opposition. As for the classical philosophers, my earlier chapters tell the tale. Aristotle, whose account of magnanimity illuminates a Washington or Churchill two millennia later, is also the Aristotle who would cabin the passion for superiority. His *Ethics* and *Politics*, I argued, work to sober grand claims to honor and rule. They remind of the priority of true worth and of justice, of the case for free and nonimperial politics, and of the superiority in most circumstances of a rather democratic republic, a middle class, and middle-class virtue.

Actually, the classical reflections on greatness are a sobering antidote to certain unbounded modern theories of leadership still in the intellectual air, despite the discrediting of the Nietzschean *führer*. I have in mind romantic celebrations of Napoleonic genius, longings for some leader to provide for humanity's basic needs, and paeans to a dictatorial transformer of civilization, whether Robespierre, Lenin, Hitler, or Che. Yes, everyday extremes of class strife and tyranny are always with us. But the distinctively modern extremes, of half-theoretical tyranny and total war, were much influenced by theorists. It was Nietzsche, Marx, and Lenin who led their followers toward resolute doubt as to any scruples that did not serve the revolution. The only morality, it was said, is the revolutionary, republican, or humanitarian morality. This terrible error the ancient thinkers did not make.

Sometimes it is said that our experience of modern tyrannies should make us skeptical of political greatness. That reaction is a big mistake. The same experience points in the opposite direction. What of FDR, Churchill, Truman, and Reagan, of Ernest Bevin and George C. Marshall? These were great public men who led the allied democracies to confront and then defeat the tyrannical dictators and their empires. Such experience teaches the evil not of greatness but of evil greatness. It teaches too the indispensability of first-rate statesmen of free government, of men good as well as great (as old Aristotle might have put it).

Still, such suggestions may seem elitist, in contravening the equal dignity of every person, and absolutist, in not respecting the subjectivity and uniqueness of personal values. I turn to such theories. To avoid straw men, I address the versions set forth by Rawls, who revived liberal political theory with his *A Theory of Justice* (1971), and Arendt, well known for *The Human Condition* (1958) and other attempts to sustain freedom by correcting liberalism. Rawls shows how the equal dignity of persons requires rejecting the claims of allegedly superior persons. Arendt, reacting to bourgeois "mediocrity," does recur to "human greatness." She seeks, however, a solution compatible with both equality, greatness for "everybody," and individuality, greatness as "unique personal identities."

Greatness as Injustice:
John Rawls and Equal Respect

Just now it is an "egalitarian form of liberalism"—the self-description is Rawls's—that most fuels the intellectuals' animus against claims of moral superiority.[2] This is not the plain man's inclination to plain-Jane equality, if only because the new idealism originates with academic professors such as Rawls and Richard Rorty. Nor is the new creed simply antiaristocratic, any more than simply democratic. It developed out of the complicated tradition of progressive liberalism, socialism, and other projects for humane and worldwide progress. From such a viewpoint, aristocracy appears as but passé oppressors, a class whose alleged virtue is as obsolete as feudalism and the Dark Ages. The contemporary proponents of equality are worried about the powerful "elites" who rise through modern mobile society. No doubt this is reasonable in plenty of cases. But the animus against elites, both modern and traditional, tends toward the sourly indiscriminate. It rarely differentiates clearly between good people and bad, between the civil servants, entrepreneurs, and statesmen who are estimable or outstanding and those who are indolent or exploitative.

The new egalitarians suspect superiority in power as "domination," and they suspect especially the few of wealth and corporate power. While taking as given the establishment of modern democratic systems and approving at least tacitly their intellectuals, representatives, and unelected judiciary, they nevertheless seem often skeptical of all establishments. They are doubtful not least of the original constitutional establishment of limited government, a free enterprise economy, and rights to life, liberty, and acquiring property. Rawls denies any "so-called private sphere," praises the objections raised by "Hegel, Marxist, and socialist writers," denies any right to own "the means of production," and sets out the alternative of social ownership.[3] While this reformed liberalism aims for social justice, equal dignity, and equal citizenship, it is marked more by its animus: a radical suspicion of classifications that imply any moral or social superiority. One sees an underlying and laudable intent to sustain liberalism amidst the contemporary philosophic turmoil. Yet the most visible effect is exhortations to indignant and liberating reform rather than exhortations to law-abidingness and patriotism.

The most influential version is Rawls's own *A Theory of Justice* (1971), together with the three editions of his *Political Liberalism* (1993; paperback, 1996; posthumous expanded edition, 2005).

Rawls kept tinkering and restating until his death, but the original equalizing impulse remained central. He would raise the equal rights of the old liberalism to "a higher level of abstraction," a level of abstraction that cannot abide inequalities hitherto tolerated. *Theory* had pressed toward a universal political-social equality. Inequality is permitted, but only as "functional" to an "egalitarian" end, "the greatest benefit of the least advantaged members of society." The later Rawls became a bit more circumspect. He dwells on political equality, allows for equal opportunity to obtain admittedly unequal political powers, and in general confines the scope of liberal principles to constitutional and political essentials.

Still, the effect of the focus on equality remains pervasive. Equal respect, provision to all of the means to equal respect— those are the watchwords. Justice involves the "basic structure of society," including equalizing definitions of family and of the relations between man and woman. Indeed, it involves all the important economic and social prerequisites for equality among citizens. The gist is twofold. First, citizens must regard each other as equally reasonable as to constitutional and political essentials. Second, all must be assured of the "primary goods," that is, the "all-purpose means" such as wealth and education that are the "social bases of self-respect." Rawls continued to maintain that the "greatest benefit" from any "social and economic" inequalities must go to the least advantaged. Within its scope this egalitarian justice is to take "complete priority," with no exceptions, over every contrary or contradictory value, moral scruple, or commandment: secular or religious, narrowly political or thoughtfully comprehensive.

At the root of all this "equal division" is what Rawls came to call a universal "criterion of reciprocity." The liberal citizen, and especially his officials, judges, and candidates, is to treat all other citizens as if equally entitled to be regarded as reasonable. More precisely, he and they are to act according to reasons that "we might reasonably expect" all adults, "as free and equal citizens, might reasonably also accept." Beneath all this complexly abstract wording is a simple iron requirement: the true liberal must treat others as if "everyone's being fully reasonable."[4]

Is this requirement reasonable? or is it irrational? If all citizens are to be judged equally reasonable for the important purposes of justice, then judging citizens as unequal in merit or worth is unjust. Whatever differences of ability and character there may be, they don't deserve differential rewards. Rawls accepts this implication. He insists on it, and he defends it with a deterministic psychology or sociology. Differences of merit or character there may be, but they are not relevant to justice. They must be attributed to nature or society, not to the individual. The point extends to ordinary virtue, such as the work ethic. Ordinary Americans tend to think that the person who rises by his own hard work to sobriety, distinction, or wealth deserves (much of) the fruits of his labor. Rawls denies it. The attack on unequal desert repudiates rewards for hard work (Locke's liberalism) and moral effort (Kant's). For Rawls, it has been said, "there is no such thing as an earned lunch."[5]

Instead, there is a sweeping political attack upon all such moral and political-economic distinctions. *Theory* put it most unqualifiedly: justice is politically and morally prior to "the good" and hence to the distinction between good and bad human beings: "What they are entitled to is not proportional to nor dependent upon their intrinsic worth" and "None of the precepts of justice aims at rewarding virtue." Later reformulations do not differ much: "Distribution in accordance with moral desert, where this means the moral worth of character," cannot be "a political value" for liberalism. To legislate according to unequal deserts violates the equality that all citizens, regarded as equally reasonable, might be reasonably expected to accept.[6]

That is doubtful. For in fact this doctrine differs much from the ordinary American citizen's respect for his fellows. Let us grant that decent citizens indeed suppose that even a vicious criminal should be fairly judged, not punished like a dog. He is a human being with reason, not a dog being, and, however vicious, he ought to be reasonably judged and have a chance to speak up for himself. It follows, however, that the decent person respects less those with less of the distinctively human qualities and more those with more. He respects less the inconsiderate, lazy, brutal, and dishonest, such as that criminal, and more those with a bigger share of considerateness, industriousness, fairness, and honesty, such as an FDR or a Washington. Ordinary decency leads to moral indignation toward nastier types and admiration and deference for the higher.

But "the ideal of the person" leads Rawls toward denying this differential respect, and this is not changed by his later ideal of equally reasonable citizens. "Democracy aims for full equality for all its citizens," and this means that, for political purposes, at least, "all are (more or less) above reproach." If all citizens must be regarded as above reproach with respect to basic justice, it would follow that all citizens must be regarded as basically just. One must treat others as if there were no basically unjust citizens. Rawls moves toward this irrational conclusion. Everyone's "sense of justice" is to be thought "equally sufficient" in relation to what is expected of him or her. The "criterion of reciprocity" demands that liberal citizens be regarded as (almost) equally just and (almost) equally entitled to respect as capable of judging reasonably.[7]

If all liberal citizens are to be thus respected, we owe little special respect to our governors, even to superior statesmen. What is most needed is egalitarian pressure on any government. Hence, the priority of suspicion and reform. It is not merely that Rawls objects to "our present constitution" and "society's basic structure." (He mentions unfair distribution of wealth and the absence of public funds for health care and political campaigns.) The point is a more generalized attitude. All institutional acts and laws "should always be regarded by citizens as open to question."[8]

A late little monograph, *The Law of Peoples*, exhibits vividly this mix of suspicion of elites with faith in peoples. Unjust war, writes Rawls, is always to be blamed on the leaders, "never" on the "people." For democracy leads to harmony among democracies, we are assured, and if true democracy comes to be worldwide, we can expect the "realistic utopia" of "democratic peace." Rawls draws the happy consequences. There will be "no need for armed forces" since peoples don't attack themselves and no war since peoples have "no cause" to go to war. Only "Monarchs" and

"Royal Houses" would war for such things as territory, "true religion," "power and glory," or "a place in the sun."[9]

One might think this vision of democratic reasonableness contradicted by everyday experience of mobs and the street, and certainly by the ancient Athenian democracy, whose imperial energy so impressed the historians Herodotus and Thucydides. Whatever Rawls thinks of mobs and fanatics, he certainly rejects the Athenian precedent. Those "democracies" of slavery and male dominance were not democratic. They were actually autocracies of few over many.[10] But the reply does not meet the objection. For the more widespread the citizenship, according to the ancient historians, the more widespread had become the ambition and desire for gain. Democratization explained the increasing energy for acquisitions. "As soon as they got their freedom," Herodotus observed, "each man was eager to do the best he could for himself."[11] Might more democracy mean what it meant among those ancients, more imperialism?

What underlies Rawls's idealistic and anti-imperial optimism about all humans is a psychological supposition: malleability. Supposing that human nature is "permissive," he denies any naturally overweening desire for gain and superiority. True, Rawls quietly allows "unspecified" limits on malleability. The lack of specificity, he nevertheless seemed to think, allowed him to assume that the "average citizen" is capable of "equal respect" for others. This seems a misstep. The limit, if unknown, might forbid just such an assumption. Be that as it may, Rawls thought it possible to assume that all will abide by reason in the sense of "fair terms of cooperation." And if it is possible so to assume, Rawls asserts, we must so assume. The "ideal" of equal respect requires us to "assume" the capacity for equal respect. This is a more audacious move. "Moral psychology" is to be deduced not from "human nature" but from "a scheme . . . for expressing a certain political conception of the person and an ideal of citizenship." The wish is father to the thought. If I am correct, it is this mix of assumptions, ideals, hopes, and inferences that enables Rawls to assert that "all citizens' sense of justice is equally sufficient relative to what is expected of them."[12]

Presuming the self-government of citizens, and the dangers of leaders over them, Rawls is characteristically doubtful about the role of statesmen, especially outstanding statesmen. There may be the occasional mention of "qualifications" for "public office" or other "positions," especially for judges, but the emphasis goes the other way. We need not rely much on "scarce motives and abilities." If Rawls allows rewards for unequal contributions, his reluctance is visible, and he abstains from recommending the particular reward, unequal honor, wanted by those politically ambitious. The indices of his major books contain no references to ambition, honor, or greatness, or to leadership, founders, or framers. The texts themselves attend little to those who led in shaping, preserving, reforming, and defending his own liberal democracy. In a late writing he denies explicitly that the American founders were of special distinction. Those allegedly distinguished founders are not to be regarded as superior to citizens today who, living under a constitution, can in their own time "fully reflect on it" and so "freely execute it." Washington, father of his country to most Americans, is to Rawls another equal citizen full of big thoughts. It is as if a democracy arises by a voluntary general agreement or contract (with principles defined by some liberal tradition), and then the people generally preserve themselves. Rawls actually says this fatuous thing: "Liberal peoples are both reasonable and rational," just like "citizens in domestic society." Liberals are to "assume" that if "we" grow up under "reasonable" institutions, "we shall affirm those institutions when we in our turn come of age, and they will endure over time." We are to assume, that is, that democracies don't fail, or if they fail, as did Weimar Germany, it is because "traditional elites" somehow failed to accept the creed of democratic justice.[13]

The elites are always at fault. This faith in equal statesmanship (if I may use the term), like the moral-psychological assumptions, seems hopeful. Consider FDR's manipulations to bring his people to war against fascist imperialism abroad, or Abraham Lincoln's struggles to keep the Northern democracy devoted to the liberal cause and to make the Union war against the slave power. But Rawls supposes that a historically developing consensus can move us beyond such necessities and such superior governors. The few desultory mentions of Lincoln in *Political Liberalism*—there are none in *A Theory of Justice*, and none of FDR in either—are mostly concerned with extending Lincolnian principles farther, to women's rights, for example.

Nor does Rawls afford much respect to everyday and lesser leaders, whether political, economic, or popular. *Political Liberalism*, I believe, mentions unequal rewards only for judges—they who understand "more deeply" the principles of justice—and even in that case Rawls immediately reminds us that differential ability implies no differences in worth or justice. One looks in vain for discussions of the decent and competent civil servant, businessman, editor, and union leader—of the political and semi-political executives, leaders, and writers who can help guide sensibly a modern democracy's public and private sectors. And what of West Pointers, distinguished by honorable patriotism, and in general of the men and women who serve in the most honorable and most dangerous services? It is true that *The Law of Peoples* touches on the patriotism of soldiers. But this is chiefly to deplore exploitation of patriotism for dubious wars and purposes and to voice suspicions of superior officers.[14]

Still, it is to Rawls's credit that the *Law of Peoples* gives some space to "statesmanship," affords praise for Lincoln and for George Washington too, and even prescribes some toleration of "decent hierarchical" and "benevolent absolutist" societies not themselves liberal. One welcomes many of these concessions to practicality. But one should not overstate their extent. They seem to be merely provisional, that is, for the "non-ideal" world of the present. And they may not go very far. It is in the nonideal world in which we live now, for example, that unjust wars are always to be attributed to leaders and *never* to the (irreproachable by his definition) peoples.[15]

More generally, this hesitant advance toward good sense has a precarious place in a teaching fundamentally skeptical of common opinion. The seminal *Theory of Justice* had been emphatic. Acknowledging a certain moral common sense, it demanded that liberals find their orientation elsewhere. "Ordinary meanings" of "justice" and law indeed exist, but these are not to be taken as the liberal meanings. The crucial case I have touched: the supposition that good people are more deserving than the mediocre or bad. "Common sense" often supposes that "the good things" in life "should be distributed according to moral desert." But, to repeat, "what [people] are entitled to is not proportional to nor dependent upon their intrinsic worth." This, in the face of Rawls's acknowledgments, first, that ordinary moral meanings have "deep intuitive appeal" and, second, that his new meanings of "justice" are by no means "self-evident." Despite the intrinsic appeal of ordinary morals and the unobvious appeal of his fundamentals, Rawls's liberals must suppress intuitive morals in favor of that "Archimedean point" which is the "ideal of the person." Rawls's late recurrence to ordinary prudence, as in praise (however faint) for democratic statesmen, is at odds with a very principled and egalitarian departure.[16]

The point holds despite Rawls's famous change of basis: the turn to "freestanding" liberal principles that originate in the "public culture" of existing democracies. By this, perhaps, he might have recurred to a liberal version of ordinary good sense. But he remained tied to principles that violate liberal common sense. Not many sensible citizens or statesmen in America, and no liberal philosopher of the status of Locke, Kant, or Mill, had supposed that without law and punishment "all citizens' sense of justice" can be "equally sufficient relative to what is expected of them."[17]

While Rawls was determined to foster "consensus," his arguments, I fear, have actually fostered something very different. They have encouraged a certain divisiveness and zeal in both his opponents and his followers. His egalitarian version of the liberal creed cannot but offend the successful, the wealthy, and the ambitious. But it grates too upon the aspiring middle class, the moral, the patriotic, and the religious. Besides, it breeds dogmatism. Its beginning insists on an egalitarian "criterion" as a fact, when it is not a fact, and as a universal requirement, when few liberal democrats hold it or could possibly hold it. The later Rawls tries to be more tolerant. But while he allows for "a family" of political conceptions of justice, the "limiting feature" of this family is Rawls's fundamental dogma, the "criterion of reciprocity." Rawls could have surveyed the true family of liberal ideas—the

Democrats' and the Republicans', Lincoln's version and FDR's, Locke's version and Kant's, and so forth—thus to criticize some public doctrines and put weight behind those more idealistic, sensible, and politic. He could have reasoned politically or dialectically. He does not. While he calls his a "political" understanding of liberalism, the indexes to his major books have no entry for political parties. This is a politics of doctrinal correctness rather than of sensible self-government: "The conception of political justice can no more be voted on than the axioms, principles, and rules of inference of mathematics or logic." Judges declare and administrators minister, while legislators and other officials are especially engaged to "follow" and "explain" the "public reason."[18]

These are invitations to doctrinaire partisanship, and they are exacerbated by Rawls's attempt to divide off his liberalism from its comprehensively philosophic progenitors. At first his project was set within the liberal philosophic tradition. *Theory of Justice* had relied on a diluted version of the old social contract theory, thus to derive "uncontested principles" from some "original position" of free and equal individuals. But *Political Liberalism*, acknowledging a "serious internal problem," gave up the attempt. Perhaps Rawls recognized that "uncontested" was a bit hasty, in light of Rousseau, Marx, and Nietzsche. What is certain is that he lost faith that liberal philosophy could win the philosophic contest. His problem was not with the liberal ideal but with philosophy: he doubted that any philosophy could establish itself as true. The problem seems to be relativism, the skepticism as to rational knowledge of right and wrong that besets modern philosophy and science.

Now impressed with the "pluralism" of "comprehensive" alternatives, now doubting the possibility of a philosophic resolution, still wishing to defend liberal idealism and constitutionalism, Rawls's response was politic evasion. His way out, his foundationless island amidst the relativistic flux, is a liberalism "political," not "metaphysical." He would draw his principles from the "culture of civil society," "not from philosophy" or the "concept of truth." But this postmodern gambit has the difficulty mentioned. Subjective choice cannot be evaded, whether in selecting from the various democratic ideas or in turning to democratic or civic culture rather than republican or high culture. Relativism reappears, although disguised beneath an alleged "fact," as if Rawls's were the obvious and necessary doctrine.[19]

Nevertheless, Rawls seemed certain to the end that his replacement of "Enlightenment Liberalism" with political liberalism would at least yield big rhetorical dividends. He could thus finesse not only the abyss confronting philosophy, but also the special religious objections to enlightened philosophy. Without the baggage of those enlightened doctrines of nature and reason, political liberals will be more persuasive to the pious as well as less doubting of themselves. But will they? How can liberals be more persuasive if the reasoning for their position is removed? Can liberals appeal more to alien parties, peoples, philosophies, and religions if they proclaim no ability whatsoever to "engage" them in argument?[20] Most unlikely. And then there is the effect on liberals: liberal irrationalism. Giving up on reasonable persuasion, disdaining appeals to the most thoughtful of their own tradition and of other traditions, this postmodern species of intellectual becomes doctrinaire purveyor of a political religion. The new liberals must insist upon their criterion of equal reasonableness, however contrary to experience. They hunker down within the familiar confines of a fundamental text while dismissing as alien, or even "mad," the most thoughtful politicians and thinkers of other traditions or even of their own. One may safely conclude thus: the new liberalism's antipathy to superior statesmen and to human excellence is peculiarly zealous, parochial, and antiphilosophic. But one may conclude as well that it is also, in its own worried eyes, baseless.

Political Greatness as Domination:
Hannah Arendt and Liberated Liberalism

Hannah Arendt confronted the difficulty that Rawls's tent of liberal custom had been designed to put out of mind. Of a generation prior to Rawls, Arendt too was concerned to defend the humane and "egalitarian" modern regimes, of which the American seemed the best. But how could that be done in light of the crisis of "modernity" as such? Her writings, unlike Rawls's, range widely over the modern political world and are deeply informed by the internal development of modern philosophy. Deep apprehension runs through them. A "growing meaninglessness," a "general relativism," is the "hallmark of the modern age." This, according to *The Human Condition*, Arendt's most comprehensive book. No modern country can avoid the crisis, certainly not the quintessentially modern United States.[21]

Behind modernity is a historical process away from the old "absolutes." It is a movement away even from everyday labor for daily necessities, although toward private-oriented lives obsessed with work and with conquering nature. But for what, all this industry and mastery? The modern way, having departed from religion, tradition, and authority, proves to lead to a void. Arendt gives reasons. There is a process of "alienation" from the earth and even from the "world," a process that shows itself most precisely in our vaunted science and philosophy. Mathematical and experimental physics looks for the processes that give us power. This is as if we "dispose of [the world] from the outside." It is as if there is some "Archimedean" starting point beyond man's senses and beyond his prescientific awareness generally. The result is a "specifically modern nihilism" as to the meaning of our mastery and of the everyday world that surrounds us. To fill the void, modern philosophy from the start had combined its fundamental doubt as to common sense with the vast project of progressive civilization. It planned the economy of unlimited growth and free enterprise, technological easing of life, and a ministering nation-state. But these too endanger life, Arendt thought, at least an active life. The mix of Cartesian skepticism with Hobbist state building results in "mass society" and smothering institutions. Modern "society" requires tent vision or tunnel vision, limited by a man-made horizon of subjective aimlessness, distracting entertainment, timid careerism, and an "attitude of consumption." All this led Arendt to severe judgments. Progress is a "superstition." The danger of the Modern Age is the "deadliest, most sterile passivity history has ever known."

The roots of the crisis, nevertheless, are deeper and older than the great modern revolutions, including the revolutions in science and philosophy. They are as old as Greek science and philosophy, according to Arendt, who in this follows Martin Heidegger. Whatever the historical events and processes underlying these changes, the identifiable culprit is our "apolitical" inheritance from Plato and Aristotle. These celebrated ancients should not be celebrated, according to Arendt, if only because they took Socrates' equivocal devotion to philosophizing and turned it unequivocally to the devaluation of action. It is true that Arendt, unlike Rawls, would retain the old Socratic equivocation and thus, for a few, the philosophic life. But as to politics, at least, the whole Western tradition is now "a field of ruins," and the rot begins with "Greek thought" and its abstraction from political life. To correct the problem, the seamless tradition of Western thought (the so-called Great Tradition) has to be confronted and overturned.

For Arendt, as for John Rawls, there is a political way out from the toils of modern political thought. Her way is a life of "action," free from governance by philosophic abstraction. This differs from Rawls's way, of action governed by liberal abstractions. In her turn to political action, Arendt, unlike Rawls, departs not only from philosophy but also from modern "government." She departs from the fixed public institutions defined more or less according to the prescriptions of liberal constitutionalists such as Locke, Montesquieu, and the rest. In this respect she turns away from the liberal politics Rawls would protect and toward "original," prephilosophic politics, even the citizen "participators" of the Greek city. In the face of philosophic crisis as well as "mass culture" and "mass society" she would return to the action exemplified in the *polis*'s "agonal" contests for distinction. She speaks of the "glory of great deeds." The "shining brightness" of Greek civic life seems a model of "human greatness." Arendt could appear midwife of a radical recurrence to citizen politics, classical republicanism, and high ambition.[22] Yet her citizen politics ends up strangely near the politics of constitutionalism and liberal individualism. Her way, like Rawls's way, proves peculiarly skeptical of political excellence and peculiarly devoted to equality. Why?

A funny thing happened on the way to the forum. Arendt's recurrence to the ancient *polis*'s greatness is decisively constrained by two famous modern doctrines, individuality and the equality of all persons. To begin with, her "action" involves essentially the "uniqueness" of the actor, not the qualities or character. What is important is the "who," in "contradistinction to 'what' somebody is," that is, in contradistinction to someone's "qualities, gifts, talents, and shortcomings." Unique personal identities are the point, for they start something new. The important thing is a new "story" that changes the world by inserting "a miracle" into its otherwise automatic processes. Accordingly, equality enters, and on an egalitarian scale. For by action "everybody" may distinguish himself as new in breaking with the everyday. Admiration, and miracles too, are for everybody, since they need only "self-disclosure" rather than some character, quality, or divinity. Indeed, the root of the new is mere birth. Action is rooted in "natality," that is, in the birth-origin of everybody.

While Arendt talks of greatness, this greatness is only freedom, and freedom is not some rational or political capacity but merely the "sheer capacity of beginning something anew." It is not the quality of the something and certainly not any superior quality. Arendt expressly decries any "delusion of extraordinary strength."[23] But is greatness still greatness if without superior accomplishment, strength, or qualities?

The question arises conspicuously with respect to the more obviously political side of Arendt's project. Confronting the "crumbling edifice of religion, authority, and tradition," she would reestablish "authority" for "republican" politics by celebrating the act of founding. She celebrates political beginning as such. This does not mean, however, praise for the acts of singular founders or of superior founders. Founding is an act of citizens in common. Acting as "participators in government" (Jefferson's phrase), it is their "mutual promises" that begin an order. Precisely by their creative act they constitute an authority capable of replacing the now-absent "absolute," whether divine or traditional. Arendt replaces popular "consent" to a constitution with citizen creation of an authoritative horizon, demotes an enlightened constitution as the object of consent, and demotes any supposition of specially enlightened and virtuous planners. "The act

itself" is the important thing, not a government or the wisdom of
the governmental plan. What is to be preserved is not a fixed constitution, the fruit of modern revolution, but the "spirit of foundation" and "the revolutionary spirit."

What then of Washington, Hamilton, and Madison? Arendt,
like Rawls, is dismissive. Those "founding fathers" are to be seen
as but symbols of popular engagement, thus to encourage reverence not for themselves but for the popular spirit. She finds it
"unpleasant" to think, with Martin Diamond, that the founders
might have thought themselves Solons, of "more virtue and wisdom" than the run of citizens likely to follow. Nor does she, more
than Rawls, allow any such unpleasant truths to disturb her principles. What counted in the framing "was neither wisdom nor
virtue, but solely the act itself," which is an "egalitarian" act.

Arendt's is to be an egalitarian republic, and her turn to classical republicanism is but a feint compared to her devotion to the
modern "revolutionary tenet": "Every member of the modern
egalitarian society is to become a 'participator' in public affairs."
Her direction, then, is basically to a democratized and liberated
liberal democracy. Arendt may attack liberalism's identification
of "freedom with security," but she certainly holds that "the *raison
d'être* of politics" is a "freedom" that goes hand in hand with universal interdependence and citizen equality. She, like Rawls, recurs at decisive points to the impartial generality of Kant. She
too, in effect, advocates equal respect for persons irrespective of
qualities.[24] But to understand fully the egalitarian bent—the denial of goodness as well as greatness—one must grasp the radical
dismissal, going beyond Kantian reformulations, of ordinary
morals.

How can Arendt so simply ignore such old absolutes as prudence, wisdom, and decent character? Simply put, her thinking
incorporates modern moral relativism; it does not overcome
moral relativism. She is explicit. Whatever her celebration of action for freedom and equality, she also insists that neither greatness nor action be measured by moral standards. Usually she puts
quotation marks around "moral." "Moral systems . . . can hardly
be taken for granted" and, indeed, "higher aims," as in traditional

morals, are "unknowable." Accordingly, the action she commends is not to be done out of "goodness," nor is it for "the common good." "Fear," "distrust," and "hatred" are "principles" of action, as much as glory, love of excellence, and love of equality.[25] In all this Arendt separates herself from Kant's moral liberalism, as had Rawls. She goes farther than Rawls.

For her, ordinary morals are not only baseless but also bad for you. Great and radiant deeds require liberation from the "normal," from the everyday processes, whereas morality as she interprets it is but the norm and hence but everyday and utilitarian. This is antibourgeois and antidemocratic relativism with a strange amoral moral edge—with a Heideggerian (and Nietzschean) flavor. It is more like antimoral liberation than relativism. The result is a big negative for politics: political "achievement," action for the common good, is bad. A focus on achievement is common, all too common.

This critique of citizen public-spiritedness has a governmental complement: ruling is bad. Contrary to what seems obvious to most citizens, (good) ruling is not the preeminent locus of (true) greatness. There should be no "rule" by persons, according to Arendt, any more than by external morals, for rule by persons, as by morality, is "domination." Arendt's politics, not unlike Rawls's, tends toward a "togetherness" without government. Rule leads to repression or at least "limitation" and thus to mediocrity within oneself and to domination by others without. Ambition to rule, however good the purpose, is evil.

In her more theoretical flights Arendt even denies that "rule over others" is political. Yes, she acknowledges, there is a common misunderstanding on this point. But that she blames on the philosophic tradition, especially on Aristotle. In elevating philosophy Aristotle had snuck in the distinction between artful rulers and subordinate ruled, thus putting on stilts the hierarchical order he had absorbed from the old-fashioned family. Arendt corrects the repressive tradition, especially that sneaky Aristotle. She equates rule and its coercion with violence, and her politics are of persuasion or debate alone. (Like Rawls, she seems often to presuppose that the unruled are not unruly.) The question of legitimate or rightful authority is politically irrelevant, she says, and whatever the actions of some founding legislator, a Washington or a Solon, they are prepolitical.[26]

Nevertheless, this strange politics without superiors leads to a peculiarly strange dependence of citizen upon "society." The performer needs an audience. While public life is diversity— "everybody" seeing and hearing "from a different position"— only "publicity" assures the performer's immortality and even his "reality"! "The political art *par excellence*" is more like the theater, then, than the arts of ruling and being ruled. Politics is "a kind of theater where freedom could appear."

Here, at least in one discussion, Arendt seems to permit some room for the "strong." She alludes to "artists," in conjunction with "culture." This has political consequences. She alludes to a political "elite" with "taste," and with specifically "political qualities," an elite chosen within this realm of freedom, or even self-chosen. In another context, that of the American founding, she can even praise power in the people only when "authority resides in the senate," that is, in some such elite. The provision of this "public space," this "realm of freedom," is the "end" of a republic. How this is compatible with the priority of uniqueness as such, or with her thematic denials of the importance of the politically wise and virtuous, I do not venture to say. But it is certainly true that at times she ends up restoring a place for liberal government. Despite her attacks on ruling, and on "limiting and protecting" peoples by boundaries, Arendt recommends a people "constitutionally ruled." Indeed, she (like Rawls) favors the judiciary, academy, and press, that is, the "public institutions" least subject to popular action and most fit to impose liberal principles.[27] The critic of liberalism is as to politics its stepchild. John Rawls, by comparison, is more forthright and politically sober.

While Arendt's political thinking has its difficulties and paradoxes, one must remember that she thought she had a higher calling. She sought to restore "wonder," "higher and more meaningful activities," to a world reduced to doubting subjectivity and to historical and economic processes. Arendt tried to apply to practical life, it seems, Martin Heidegger's evocation of our mysterious awareness of the world. But in moving from Heidegger's mysterious Being to the "emerging, shining quality" of action, her thinking aggravates the practical problem of relativism.[28] In her case, as in Rawls's, there are difficulties in a search for practical meaning that ignores common meanings. If all stories are "radiant" and "great," that includes stories boring, debased, or tricked out (my car, my drool, Vegas!). Does not her solution aggravate the mediocrity of mass society she diagnoses? If "togetherness" as an audience actually fixes our very "reality," as she at times asserts, and the tastes of liberated individualists are to rule, then Arendt's reality will be a vanity fair shaped by consumerism, celebrities, self-promoters, sensationalism, and manipulators.

The graver implications arise when Arendt denies moral qualities while retaining moral words. She praises as "hero" anyone who performs—a unique "who"—and expressly denies any need for "heroic qualities." She defines courage simply as the "willingness to act and speak at all," as "disclosing and exposing one self," while saying also that courage "may even be greater" if the "hero" happens to be a "coward." This is denial of virtue, albeit by paradox and confusion. Amidst such lessons there is the occasional more sensible remark. Urging forgiveness of all choices, itself a rather perverse view, she suddenly backs off: we should not forgive "crime and willed evil" or "radical evil." But this turn to moral distinctions contradicts the usual insistence that "greatness" not be measured by "moral standards." The problem is shown in her reply to Gershom Scholem, who had criticized the coldness toward Jews of her book on Israel's trial of Adolf Eichmann, chief of the Gestapo's Jewish section and murderer of untold numbers. She has changed her mind: she declines any longer "to speak of radical evil." Even in *The Human Condition* she had said that radical evil is beyond punishment as well as forgiveness. The doer should do away with himself. Airy and unpolitical advice, cold as to justice and policy both. *The Human Condition* contains another example of such moral obtuseness. Expanding on her turn to greatness (in an antimoral sense), Arendt repeatedly quotes Pericles' funeral address: seeking glory may be by "evil" as well as "good" deeds. Pericles had been eulogizing bloody victories in foreign lands that memorialized Athens's imperial sway.[29] His defense of imperial "tyranny" does not go easily with Arendt's attacks on imperialism and on domination generally. Her liberated skepticism seems to undermine not only our discrimination as to leaders good as well as great, but also her own egalitarianism.

Arendt once noted impressively the "loss of common sense" amidst the "introspection" and the disappearance of a "common world" fostered by modern philosophy. Aristotelian wonder, she said, has been replaced with Cartesian doubt. Her own attempt to recover life's "splendor," however, remains beset with such doubts. Finding the philosophic tradition since Plato discredited by modern rationalism, she, like Heidegger, would deconstruct the tradition.[30] Yet she retains a ruthless denial of traditional morals, an insistence on the equality of individuals irrespective of their qualities, and a denial of the political superiority of such as Churchill and Washington. All or some of these views violate common sense, none are shared by Plato or Aristotle, and in these problems, as in others, Arendt is enmeshed in the modern difficulties that she would overcome.

CHAPTER EIGHT

Honorable Greatness Denied (2): The Premises

I compared the moral writings of the ancient pagans to very proud and magnificent palaces built only on sand and mud. They extol the virtues, and make them appear more estimable than anything else in the world, but they do not adequately explain how to recognize a virtue, and often what they call by this fine name is nothing but a case of callousness, or vanity, or desperation, or parricide.

— DESCARTES, *Discourse on Method*, Part I

Mankind has never been in this position before. Without having improved appreciably in virtue or enjoying wiser guidance, it has got into its own hands the tools by which it can unfailingly accomplish its own extermination. . . . It is therefore above all things important that the moral philosophy and spiritual conceptions of men and nations should hold their own amid these formidable scientific evolutions.

— WINSTON CHURCHILL, *Thoughts and Adventures* (1932)

How we got to the complicated doubts and paradoxical denials of a Rawls and an Arendt is itself a complicated as well as a disputed story. There is, nevertheless, an underlying dynamic of modern political theories at work. So I mean to outline with key examples. I sketch in turn a representative early modern critique of virtue and especially superior virtue (Hobbes's), the leading attempt, in reaction, to recover morality by a teaching of equal dignity (Kant's), and finally the explosive Nietzschean reaction against both Hobbesian bourgeois security and Kantian idealistic equality. It is this final reaction that has led to both relativism and the postmodern efflorescence of antirational liberation, will, and self-expression. I acknowledge easily that such a genealogy, especially without the proper qualifications, is no adequate weighing of such serious thinkers. Still, to repeat, it can make us aware of some doubtful premises in the family tree.

Greatness as Vainglory and Aggression

The pursuit of peace requires that men be regarded as equal. And therefore the eighth precept of the natural law is: everyone should be considered equal to everyone. Contrary to this law is pride.

— Hobbes, *On the Citizen*, 2:9

Whatever the complicated origins of modern skepticism about human excellence, there is one clear voice at the start: the attack by the great Thomas Hobbes on ancient and biblical virtue and not least on the ancients' praise of magnanimity. What old Aristotle called magnanimity is but foolish and dangerous "vanity," according to Hobbes. It is only "vain-glory," natural self-love magnified by self-estimation.[1] To add to such ordinary pride a supposition of superior worth, what Aristotle encouraged, only multiplies the exaggeration and the danger. Self-glorification blinds to one's real dependence on others, and it fosters both outrageous claims for oneself and indignant reactions from others.

It follows that the ancient teachings of gentlemanly and republican spiritedness, so much praised in the Renaissance, are in truth daggers in the heart of civil society and peace, everywhere. Hobbesian enlightenment expressly departs from moral opinion and the ancient philosophers, especially as to political life and claims of superior desert. His laws of reason prescribe giving up one's claims to rule over oneself or others; Hobbes constantly attacks the "vain esteem of ourselves" as deserving to rule. Both the claims and the pride undermine obedience to the one sovereign who protects society and ensures security. Accordingly, Hobbes denies the pretensions of "gentry" generally, not merely of feudal aristocracy, and he denies any distributive justice that would award honors and offices to the worthy.[2] Aristotle's *Nicomachean Ethics* and Cicero's *De Officiis* had eulogized, to an extent, noble pride. Hobbes's *Leviathan* is "King of the Proud." Arendt could find here the home of the enemy.

Admittedly, Hobbes's exuberantly cynical acid is a variation on earlier attacks by Machiavelli, Bacon, Montaigne, and others. Machiavelli in particular had taken the antimoral step of questioning "high" ambition and any aspiration to something noble and good. His counsel in *Prince* ch. 15, which has been touched before, is of effectual opportunism. To preserve one's state and get on in the world, take one's bearings from the necessary passions, what men generally "do," and not from what they think right, what they "ought to do." Perhaps it was he who inaugurated the modern philosophic animus against "gentlemen" generally; he was especially against the chivalry empowered by faith, territory, and castles.[3] Accordingly, to Machiavelli, and to such quasi-followers as Francis Bacon, honor is only a glorification of the self, not a tribute to inherent virtue, and superiority is chiefly relative to others, without any ranking in accord with superior worth of soul. Vainglory, as Hobbes would later put it, is an "internal triumph of the mind," an "imagination of our own power over the power of him that contendeth."[4]

Machiavelli and Bacon had nevertheless thought that ambition so reduced was useful. It could be serviceable to oneself and politic in managing others. Glory brings immortality, albeit a man-made immortality, which faith, as they seemed to suppose, would not. "*Vaine-Glory* helpeth to Perpetuate a Man's Memory," Bacon wrote. And it can be politic: "by Glory one Courage sharpeneth another," since "all Bravery stands upon Comparisons." All the Machiavellians were great projectors of enterprises, and in any "great Enterprise, a Composition of *Glorious* Natures, doth put Life into Business."[5] They would mix princes with peoples, the enterprising with the security loving. They retained something of the old and obvious political mix of the ambitious with the ordinary.

This political mixing Hobbes rejects, the Machiavellian version as well as the Aristotelian. His innovation is an unwavering attack upon all glory seeking, and he does this, remarkably enough, despite admitting a powerful natural root. Hobbes grants that in the race of life the only goal is "being foremost," that "all the heart's joy and pleasure lies in being able to compare oneself favorably with others and form a high opinion of one-self."[6] In face of the force and pleasure, nevertheless, he denies the utility, personal as well as political. Vainglory, precisely by its pleasure, blinds to reason. It blinds, that is, to long-term calcula-tion, which is Hobbes's version of reason (calculation, but no in-tellect). Vainglory fosters "the irrational desire to reject future goods for the sake of present goods," and thus it endangers the crucially necessary thing, peace and order.[7] Here is a form of pe-culiarly modern "rationalism," a farsighted but self-denying cal-culating, which is in fact oriented not to the kinds of things we discern (Hobbes denies that discerning) but to a passion: fear. The state of nature, in Hobbes's famous diagnosis, is a state of war. Our natural condition is fundamentally painful, not pleasur-able, a source of apprehension, not of potential happiness. Over-coming that fearful state requires conquest of the honor-seeking side of our human nature. Conquest of nature begins with heart and thought, especially with the ambition to be and to be thought superior.

Here is an early stirring of the doctrine of human malleability, the doctrine that modern egalitarians adopt. Hobbes did not share all the hopes that resulted from Rousseau's expansion of the doctrine, for he thought that fear dominated or should dominate mankind. Nevertheless, a certain utopianism shows in his own politics. There is a void as to generalship and leadership. With Machiavellian *ambizione* excluded as well as Aristotelian magna-nimity, who will be the great soldier, general, and founder? Hobbes's political science says much of legal sovereignty and doctrinal supremacy, but it says little about who will dare to step into the military and political breach. Hobbes is the theorist of war and society who says, "When armies fight, there is on one side, or both, a running away" and who allows to any man the right to resist likely death—even if required justly and by his own government.[8]

To grasp the case for these doctrines is to see several of the de-cisive premises that moved or repulsed later modern thinkers. I attend first to Hobbes's humanitarianism and then to his critique of morality, his general epistemological critique of common opinion, his turn from ordinary and diverse opinions to introspection and a "physical" psychology, and finally his resolve to find a certain foundation, surer than ethics, for a useful political science.

Hobbes's cynicism as to traditional morals is matched by a solicitude, often unappreciated, for basic human needs. His is a seminal humanitarianism. Hobbes the authoritarian planner of the administrative state is also Hobbes the humane, and the link between the two is obvious and should be pondered. His attack on political and moral greatness is partly a humane reaction to Machiavelli's brutal models. Not for Hobbes the glory-seeking Roman republic that was Machiavelli's model. Rome "plundered nearly all the world,"[9] and "no large or lasting societies can be built on the desire for glory." "You," says Hobbes, as if exhorting humanity at large, should "measure justice by the laws of a commonwealth and not allow ambitious men to get power over yourselves by shedding your blood."[10]

Hobbes's humanity, however, goes much beyond the topical or the anti-Machiavellian. It goes beyond, too, the antibiblical turn that suffuses his thought and that of other Enlightenment thinkers. Hobbes's critique of greatness extends to a resurrection of justice, contrary to the Machiavellians, and to a transformation of justice, contrary to the ancients as well as the Bible. He is a "natural rights" theorist in the precise sense. He replaces traditional natural law and the traditional priority of duty by an individual freedom to provide for one's own necessities.

If vanity blinds, it is moral righteousness that makes vanity zealous and doubly dangerous. Hobbes has in mind the religious wars, as does Rawls in our time. Unlike Rawls, he has finally in mind dangers from human pride and self-righteousness generally. His fundamental solution is not toleration (that by itself might bring anarchy), but antimoral reform as well as an antimoral supreme sovereign. This explains the priority of deconstructing any conviction of superior worth, justice, and righteousness. Hobbes is the political thinker who praises the social life of the bee, which organizes by instinct, over that of man, precisely because the bee lacks private judgment and the wish to be thought superior.[11] It is spirited claimants to virtue and righteousness, not Machiavellian princes, who are especially in Hobbes's sights.

The result is his devising of laws of reason that are essentially laws of peace and inoffensiveness. His fifth law, in its final formulation, is "COMPLAISANCE, that is to say, *that every man strive to accommodate himself to the rest.*" This is a prescription to be nice, whatever the quality of those about one. It is, then, a proscription of the magnanimous man's moral disdain. Every man is to "*acknowledge other* [sic] *as his equals.* And the breach of this law, is that I call PRIDE." A humane code of equal respect replaces the old opinions, which held that "a private man" might determine whether a public command "be just or unjust," and which caused all those deaths through civil and religious war.[12]

In developing the equal natural rights others later expanded and elevated, Hobbes focused on basic needs for survival and peace, not on equal dignity as such, and certainly not on Kant's moral dignity. The Hobbist arguments for equality are famously undignified. Men are equal in being equally able to kill one another, or, at least, they must be esteemed equal in order to be induced, self-lovers that they are, to agree to the government that prevents them from killing one another.[13] If Hobbes thus restores a concern for justice that the Machiavellians had left out, or at least left obscure, his is a new justice focused on the poor fearful individual's concern for his elemental needs. The point is not duties to others. It is certainly not pride in one's superior deserts. The root is in fear of death. For whatever the diversity of desires, death endangers them all, at least all worldly desires. (Fear of violent death, in particular, illuminates our exposed condition—and that we can do something about.)[14]

At its start, then, Hobbes's critique of noble pride turns on an unmoral psychology, an "individualism" moved above all by flight from our natural human condition. We are not to live up to the demands of some higher rational or spiritual part of the soul, but we at least can be enlightened to flee obvious dangers, to respect others in their needs, and to acquiesce in an artful shelter. Still, for his new and amoral foundation Hobbes has to infer a right from the passion of fear—an "ought" from an "is." This questionable inference the ancient political philosophers did not have to take, since they began with our opinions of good and bad, prudent and foolish. It is one faulty step toward our relativism of "values."

Hobbes has a deeper critique of traditional morals than mere insistence upon basic necessities. He had to, since honest dealing may be a duty even if inconvenient, dangerous, or rather often unperformed. To show that one has no moral obligations in the ordinary sense, Hobbes denied any intuitions at all of what is noble, fair, or shameful. There is only a diversity of passions and tastes: "Men are different and so some things are not good to them all." We are only dealing with different "names,"[15] not with a hierarchy of goods, pleasures, and souls. Accordingly, and contrary to the "ancient writers," an "oligarchy" of the rich is "not distinct from aristocracy."

Ultimately, at the peak above intuitions and opinions to which Plato thought dialectic led, there is, for Hobbes, no peak. There is no best life by which to judge the others: "For there is not such a Finis ultimis, (utmost Aim), nor Summum Bonum (Greatest Good), as is spoken of in the Books of the old Morall Philosophers."[16] Goodness is not what is best by nature, since Hobbes's science rules that out: "The question of who is the better man has no place in the state of mere nature." Philosophy is not what is best, since reason is invented markers and intellect does not exist. Hence, because there is no activity satisfying in itself, "life is a race."[17] While Hobbes is not a relativist, his sweeping critique relativizes traditional morals. What he substitutes, his new and enlightened "laws of nature," are but rationally invented prescriptions for peace—deductions from the natural right to life. (Unless, Hobbes says, I suppose God to enforce them as laws.) Having done all this, Hobbes can proceed in his doctrinal fashion to reassign names, even the name "magnanimity." Life may be a race, but "to break through with ease" in the race "is magnanimity."[18] Hobbesian magnanimity is "a feeling" of power enough "to obtain one's ends in an open manner," that is, without "little helps" and "hindrances" such as "cruelty."[19]

By what warrant does Hobbes simply deny as imaginary the claims of ordinary duty and turn for his orientation to the powerful passion of fear? A conspicuous argument is from introspection. Hobbist introspection is familiar enough still from various later psychologies: he would look beneath our opinions to the necessary motions, the "real" forces, beneath. As necessary and alone real, they are in everyone. "When I shall have set down my own reading" of a human being, he says, anyone else can observe whether he "also find not the same in himself." Indeed, each can find within what moves all: "He that is to govern a whole nation must read in himself, not this or that particular man, but mankind."[20] Still, this move by itself is not only tendentious but also insufficient: the moral or religious man who looks within is likely to find the duties prescribed by his morals or his religion. Besides, this introspection is less a fresh reading than a reading under tutelage, as one can tell from the start of Hobbes's famous *Leviathan*. Hobbes's introspection is through the lens of his epistemology.

The first chapters of the *Leviathan* are not about morals, the heart, or politics; they are "Of Sense," "Of Imagination," and of speech, reason, and science. A preliminary account of knowing is the vestibule to Hobbes's thought, as it is for many early modern thinkers, probably beginning with Bacon. Before trying to understand anything else we must understand that thoughts are but impressions of bodies on our bodily senses and imaginings. Such a critical screen, Hobbes seemed to think, could rule out supposed moral intuitions and supposed divinations of "spirits," "grace," and "visions." This is epistemology with critical intent. "Good" and "evil" can then be disdained as but aspects of appetites and aversions, as can "*pulchrum*," "*turpe*," and all equivalents, such as "fair," "noble," "beautiful," "gallant," and "honorable," or "foul," "deformed," and "base." *Honestum, consensus gentium*, common decency, and the like—all are but "stupidity of the vulgar."

So much, then, for any supposed decent intuitions of the honest man. With such a screen and such a psychology, Hobbes proceeds to his famous reductions. "Admiration" is but "joy from apprehension of novelty" (shades of Arendt), "nobility" is merely "power" (shades of Nietzsche), and so forth.[21] Still, this epistemology has its own difficulties, now well known. The screen, for example, depends on general notions and suppositions that are certainly prior to it, such as "man," "body," and "nature," and perhaps excluded by it. The screen depends on knowledge it excludes. This cannot be an adequate account of our knowing, es-

pecially of the prescreened knowing against which we measure
the adequacy of the screen.

What seems finally to determine Hobbes's critical thinking as
well as his politics is a political-theoretical bent: a determination
to find a reliable political science. His first major political work
announces the principle at its start: it would "put such precepts
down for a foundation, as passion not distrusting, may not seek to
displace."[22] Hobbes wishes a solid foundation, one that accords
with the most common forces within, and this especially accounts
for his settling on the semirational passion of fear. This also accounts, at least to some extent, for his turn from moral opinion.
As to good and bad, men always dispute, and for this the "[an-
cient] philosophers had no remedy." Hobbes has the remedy. It is
a political science that leaves "no place for contrary disputes" because it begins with "definitions," not opinions, and because the
key definition of right incorporates concern for the fear that most
moves men.[23] The old philosophers "had not observed that the
goodness of actions lies in its tendency to peace." The secret of
political agreement is a common denominator, and this common
denominator. In the language of *Prince* ch. 15, once again: take
one's bearings not from the truth but from the truth that can
work, the *verità effetuale*. Moved by a new hope for certain reform,
and on the rock of critical thinking and fear duly enlightened,
Hobbes constructed his realizable ethics: "those qualities of mankind, that concern their living together in peace and unity." The
"books of the old moral philosophers" are to be replaced by his
new and enlightened "*summa* of Moral philosophy."[24]

IMMORAL PRIDE, MORAL EQUALITY

Every human being has a legitimate claim to respect from fellow
human beings.
    Rightful honor consists in asserting one's worth as a human being
in relation to others. . . . This duty . . . is an obligation that follows
from the *right* of humanity in our own person.

— KANT, *Metaphysics of Morals*[25]

For Immanuel Kant the dismissal of serious morality by Hobbes
and others of the seminal Enlightenment was a scandal and scan-

dalously indefensible. Kant famously recurs to what might seem a premodern orientation by moral and rational duty. Yet his was less a return than a further innovation, a recasting of duty that incorporated his predecessors' critique of classical and Christian morals and their dedication to individual freedom and security. He accepted these two fundamentals, despite his revulsion at the foundation in self-interest. Kant thus informed the philosophy of equal rights with a new idea of righteousness, and it is this idealism of equal dignity that underlies the recent morally edged attacks on moral and political greatness.

Decent intellectuals had been rightly horrified at twentieth-century tyrants influenced by nineteenth-century theories, and they had to be troubled at heart by a present-day relativism that could not defend decent and free politics. Chastened by fascist and communist tyrannies, they looked past the toxic mists surrounding Nietzsche and Marx to Kant's clear insistence on moral respect for the individual. It is true that some, such as Friedrich Hayek and Milton Friedman, returned to the philosophies of Locke and subsequent political economists, but most postwar thinkers thought pre-Kantian liberalism insufficiently "idealistic" (as Rawls put it). If the proposition that all men are created equal was to be a pearl beyond price and worthy of the full measure of devotion, Kant had supplied the most appealing moral and philosophic defense.

Kant's defense of the equal dignity of persons is simple to affirm but famously complicated on the inside. On the one hand, he followed Rousseau's rebellion from the early moderns' reliance on self-interest. He, like Rousseau, asserted the priority of morality—"virtue, the sublime science of simple souls," Rousseau had said—and the priority, too, of a freedom from another's "necessitating will" rather than of simple preservation.[26] On the other hand, Kant, like Hobbes and Locke, attacked morality as commonly known, albeit for a very different reason.

While the "hotchpotch" of ordinary morals is insufficiently definitive, as the earlier liberals had argued, for Kant it is also and above all insufficiently pure. Ordinary honesty and decency mix a natural appetite for happiness with mere and uncertain opinions as to duties. The mixing as well as the uncertainty is the problem.[27] Supposing with Hobbes that natural appetites are but "physical" and lack any component of intellectual intuition or higher inclination, Kant turns for a standard to pure reason, understood as universal law prescribed to nature: "Act according to a maxim capable of being universalized." This constitutes Kant's new moral law, a formal rational ideal that is separable from appetite and sensibility as well as from mere opinion. Whatever the formality and purity, the direction is clear: Kant is "establishing the rights of man."[28] He transforms the old and primary liberal teaching, of natural rights to life, freedom, and property, into a rational moral law that commands equal respect for all rational persons.

Nevertheless, Kant, like Hobbes, still supposed he had to confront the old morals and its champions, and one finds a refreshing liveliness in his weighing of Aristotle's ethics in particular. He, unlike Hobbes, retains more than a grudging respect for Aristotelian "perfectionism." Badly flawed as it was, Kant judged it next best to his own idealism. For Aristotle's moral teaching is genuine, not merely instrumental, and is on a human scale, not measuring man by models far above, especially models that foster "lust for glory and domination, and are bound up with frightful ideas of power and vengefulness." Without being merely calculating or chiefly otherworldly, the Aristotelian account of moral virtue preserves the claims of scruple and the authority of reason from the feelings below. Unlike enlightened orientations by happiness, self-interest, and a moral sense, it preserves the dignity of "a will good in itself," and it brings the moral question before the only authoritative court, "the court of pure reason."[29]

Nevertheless, the old "virtue ethics" is hardly more than a semblance of rational morals, at least in Aristotle's version. (Kant has his own doctrine of virtue, a virtue circumscribed by the law of equal respect.) The problem is the reliance on ordinary moral opinions. Beginning with popular scruples, Aristotelian ethics is not very rational and only mixedly moral. It is "empty," "indefinite," and "circular," and it provides "no decisions" as to moral matters.[30] It is empty as to the perfection of nature, according to Kant, since it lacks an absolute standard outside of nature. It cannot define what all should do, moreover, because it limits itself to what a person of character and judgment would do in particular circumstances. In these respects it lacks what Kant provides, a universal maxim of reason that provides for all and for all circumstances. Aristotle's ethics seems empty of clear principle, indefinite amidst the variety of precepts, and circular in resting on the moral intuitions that decent people chance to have.

Still, the crucial point is that virtue ethics shares the disabling defect of "popular" ethics, "heteronomy." It mixes the opinions we hold with the desires we experience.[31] Aristotle had himself divided magnanimity into a general inclination to what is worthy and just and particular inclinations that manifest more directly the passion for superiority. In general, he fell into what Kant thinks the "misbegotten mongrel" of empirical ethics, "patched up from some mixture of limbs" in "a dream of sweet illusions."[32] The decisive sign is that Aristotle's is an ethics of happiness as well as of moral virtue. For happiness is of our whole nature and thus, as Kant would say, of our merely natural appetites as well as of reason's dictates of duty. Aristotle "failed" like all previous moralists because he, like they, lacked what Kant found: "the autonomy of the will." Acting according to rational law frees man from merely natural cause and effect, and if it subjects him to law, it is to a law of reason imposed by himself. By moral freedom he is free, rational, and autonomous.[33]

Just this Kantian universalizing of moral freedom undermines the superior man's claims to preeminence and superiority, perhaps as much as did the rough Hobbesian critique of morals. Kant's moral freedom permits no claim to superiority to others or over others, in the fashion of the Aristotelian great-souled man. This is despite a Kantian restoration of pride, moral worth, and honor. A man may take rightful pride in beating down his various natural appetites, according to Kant. Kant encourages a moral pride, if not exactly a noble pride. Pride in one's self-restraint, done out of respect for the moral self-determination that is highest in oneself and others, is not mere vainglory, contra Hobbes. Such restraint is true worth and deserving of honor. Nevertheless, the worthy victories are only within, not in prominence relative to others. This is a redefinition of pride, worth, and honor with a view to equal dignity and republicanism, and it rules out fundamental inequality, whether moral or political. For authority is rightful only by consent and as manifestation of universal law, wars violate the rights of others, and worth is moral worth, which is respecting oneself and others according to the universal law. Love of honor thus pales into "equal respect." And why not, since everyone, no matter how moral, has within himself a perpetual struggle between what is right by reason and what he wants by nature? Who can throw the first stone? Be that as it may, all are bound by the law of equal respect for all.

Kant distinguishes accordingly and sharply between ambition and rightful love of honor, as Susan Shell has shown.[34] The distinction may fly in the face of the Greek word for ambition, *philotimia*, which means love of honor, fame, or reputation. For Kant, however, ambition for distinction in this sense is merely comparative. He seems to follow Hobbes's reduction of ambition for honor to desire for power relative to others. Ambition (*Ehrbegierde*) is the arrogance (*Hochmuth*) of those who want others to feel inferior. True love of honor, then, is fundamentally respect for one's own independence. It involves standing up to insults (you peasant!) and to attempts at subjection in general. Honor and pride, it seems, are basically means of defense. (Hobbes *redux*.) They are means especially to defend one's freedom. (Locke *redux*.) Love of honor is the external face of proper pride, which is "to yield nothing of one's dignity in comparison with others."[35]

From Kant's point of view, then, ambition is a vice, and Aristotelian magnanimity verges on the worst vice. It seeks a superiority that directly violates the fundamental law of equal respect. Magnanimity is the external face of improper pride, which demands that others concern themselves with one's own self-importance. No one (however meager of outlook) is obliged to "revere" a human being (however grand of outlook), for the only proper "reverence" is for "oneself," or rather "for the law" within oneself prescribing equality. Revering that law is "a universal and unconditional duty."[36]

Kant thus infuses with righteousness the Hobbesian suspicion of inequality of soul, and in effect he extends its reach. Since every individual is of a "worth that has no price,"[37] any individual anywhere deserves respect irrespective of his status or even his qualities. The magnanimous man's contempt for the mean and nasty is worse than misplaced; it is a terrible vice. While one perhaps cannot help "inwardly *looking down*" on some rather than others, any "outward manifestation" of this is an offense. One owes basic and primary respect to any man, Kant says, "even though by his deeds he makes himself unworthy of it." That is, even if depravity should make men not equal in dignity, one has the duty to treat them as being equal.[38]

This doctrine of moral equality thus prepares the sweeping and universal equality and freedom, the "autonomy," that Kant encourages as a moral cause. Humanity must be understood as making up a "kingdom of ends,"[39] a world community of all rational beings. Accordingly, the doctrinaire philosopher Kant drew the moral-political corollaries now well known: the duties to make a world of self-determining democratic republics, of united nations, and of cosmopolitan and humanitarian morals. These moral and political lessons are to be spread by any "teacher of the people," such as the philosopher Kant himself, and by "free professors of law" who are "natural announcers and interpreters."[40] Rawls and his fellows in many countries are Kant's progeny, spreading in their own ways the idealistic version of enlightened plans and hopes.

To support these vast idealistic hopes, however, Kant took a harsh realistic step rarely accepted by today's neo-Kantians. He outlined a doctrine of historical progress through *realpolitik*. This momentous invention, of a historical process, was in part theoretically compelled. Kant had adopted the modern (Baconian and Hobbesian) doctrine of natural cause, a motion necessarily producing effects. His proposal for a "universal history" begins with the supposition that "human actions" must be "determined by natural laws, as is every other natural event."[41] Nevertheless, this theory of causation accounts for only part of the doctrine of history. For Kant's "Idea for a Universal History" is "with a Cosmopolitan Purpose." The historical process, this History with a big H, can be finally understood only by reference to the supreme law of human intelligibility, which is not natural necessity and not human power but the decisive law for moral beings, the human moral law. The strange result is a hypothetical History of progress that relies on man's interests and vices to lead him toward freedom, peace, and humane morals.

This is the optimism about systems in history that has so influenced "progressive" liberalism. A "nation of devils" might become a rational republic if only their interests are calculated and managed intelligently.[42] Nations generally might become more peaceable precisely as their increasing power throws them nearer ever more terrible wars. And peoples might move toward cooperative mores with the spread of avarice and the pressures of globalized commerce.

Admittedly, this grim invisible hand does not determine the future, as it did for some of Kant's successors. His theory may prefigure the full-fledged Hegelian and Marxist philosophies of history, but it is not the same. For any necessary determination would remove the priority of individual moral choice, of the moral law, which remains crucial for Kant (but not for Hegel and Marx). Nevertheless, Kant's protophilosophy of history encouraged his progressive followers in the impolitic supposition that their ideals are realizable because history is on their side. It encourages them to slight the obstacles to a universal liberal democratic politics, for example, and to slight the necessity of good government and good governors for any decent politics.

I close by pointing to certain problems that bring out two Kantian premises: the priority of formality in the theory of moral freedom, and a quasi-Hobbist sensualist epistemology that denies an intellectual intuition of the fair or fitting.

There are well-known questions about Kantian autonomy as a moral principle: is it moral? and is it too principled? A choice may be free but bad, one might think, and a maxim might be rational for some in some circumstances, but not for all in all. Kant, however, insists that autonomy is rational and that reason in its fundamental form must be supposed universal law. He seems to have drawn these suppositions from what he thought was required for any knowing according to the "model" science of Newtonian physics.[43] Whatever the problems posed by that derivation and by difficulties as to the Newtonian interpretation of nature, there remains the big question: whether by formal universality a practical proposition is a moral prescription. Mere universalization might universalize evil, such as theft or cannibalism, unless qualified by some substantive understanding of what is good. A Kantian might reply that this objection makes impossible human society or denies the supposition that all men are ends in themselves with equal rights. But the reply introduces substantive suppositions foreign to formal universality as such. The difficulty reappears in the principle of equal respect: should I fundamentally respect the bad person as a potentially rational person equally with the good? Kant himself had difficulty with this morality. "One cannot help [disdaining the vicious] inwardly," he wrote in a late work, and yet one is obliged to acknowledge "the dignity of humanity," at least externally. According to Pierre Hassner, Kant's major works display a visible and systematic wavering between the universal principle of human dignity and an inconsistent esteem for the good man in particular.[44] The universal imperative takes the name "moral," in short, but whether it encompasses morals is a question.

Kant's theorizing, like Hobbes's, depended upon an epistemology that sharply distinguishes the merely empirical from the purely rational.[45] The crucial *Groundwork of the Metaphysics of Morals* begins, like the *Leviathan*, with epistemological critique, and Kantian moral treatises generally are pervaded by a distinction of sense impression, without intelligibility or form, from "pure reason," which prescribes universal laws. Experience may teach us of the mechanical motions of bodies in nature, Kant allows; "With regard to moral laws, on the other hand, experience is, alas! but the source of illusion, and it is altogether reprehensible to derive or limit the laws of what I ought to do by our experience of what has been done."[46] Whatever the other difficulties in such a separation of our "oughts" from experience, it also abstracts from an obvious moral competence. Decent people have an eye in particular circumstances for the fitting or correct thing to do. For Aristotle, that discernment, admittedly shaped by correct dispositions, is near the core of moral judgment. For Kant, epistemology rules that discernment out. It is true that Kant, unlike Hobbes, allows for certain inklings of the "noble" and "sublime." But it is also true that he aesthetizes and sensualizes such impressions. An alleged awareness of grandeur or height of soul, for example, is interpreted as but "sublime" feeling, and it is then reinterpreted with a view to universal law. It is "a feeling for the beauty and dignity of human nature as such," and "the more universal the principle," the more "sublime and noble the virtue."[47] Nobility is not only diluted but also universalized, and this involves again the moral dubiousness of universality: if everyone participates in the sublime and noble, the morally ugly and ignoble participate too.[48]

Whatever the inner problems, Kant's teaching has led to particular difficulties for the appreciation of a Churchill or a Washington. The protophilosophy of history and the scheme of general laws abstract from the superior respect due statesmen who are great as well as good and good as well as formative. Extraordinary men can seem no longer important, for the progressive can expect an inevitable growth of peace, democratic republics, and a world community. He need not even care much who rules, so long as peoples and governments are idealistic and have the right constitution. Still, the big blinder is the amoral morality and its psychological presuppositions. For these obscure the actual wishes of men such as Churchill and Washington, whose claims to rule and honor involve a wish to be genuinely outstanding, in truth. For Kant, however, honor is but "a delusion" that hides one's desire to dominate. The claim to great honor is, what Bacon's enlightened cynicism had earlier maintained, but a "solicitation of followers."[49]

Greatness Unbridled — and With a Vengeance

One will never understand the contemporary suspicion of "elites" without coming to grips with the influence of Friedrich Nietzsche's rebellion against liberal and democratic equality. Nietzsche did not deny greatness—on the contrary—but he made it so repulsive that decent people, and anyone devoted to a free country, harbor understandable suspicions. Like Hobbes and Kant, Nietzsche promoted a future-oriented project. But he was revolted by the security-oriented society and equality-oriented idealism they had promoted. His project was to engender philosophers of the future who would reestablish the rule of noble and grand human beings. To do this in the face of "modern ideas" (44), he would break the bonds of Kantian-style equal dignity as well as all equalizing moralities and semimoralities.[50]

Nietzsche's rhetoric flays; his new rulers are ruthless. The superman of great "will to power" is also a "man of prey" (197). If this suprahuman being of the future is of delicacy, elevation, and thoughtfulness beyond vulgar glory seeking, he is probably also inseparable from the Nietzschean counsels of cruelty, domination, and a master race. The free peoples of Europe and America were not aware during World War I that "it was from Nietzsche," as Charles de Gaulle observed, that the audacious German generals, "like all thinking Germany, had drawn their philosophy." But they were certainly awakened by the more thoroughly fascist dictators of World War II, especially the dictator who prided himself on a triumph of the will.[51] Besides, neither Nietzsche nor his followers hid their ferociously antidemocratic critique, which extended beyond modern society and "the democratic movement" (242) to ordinary people, their "slave morality," and their "slavish" biblical religions (195, 199). If this is what the culmination of philosophic culture promotes, why not resist such a poisoned chalice and, if need be, philosophy altogether? A strategy for evading deep thinking is what postmodernists, especially liberal postmodernists, attempt.

One can't get rid of moral and political relativism, however, by averting one's eyes. The deeper reason for contemporary evasions is the conviction that liberal thinking cannot be rationally defended, and here Nietzsche the philosopher is invaluable in clarifying our doubts and their peculiar grounds and limits. Modern epistemology and science lead to relativism, as Arendt maintained, and these are inextricable from the foundations of modern philosophy, including liberal philosophy. Nietzsche confronts this. He considered himself a physician of a sick culture. He thinks through not only the skepticism, but also the will to subject the world to our command, doctrines that pervade the works of Kant as well as of Bacon, Hobbes, and Locke.

To the critical thinking of his modern predecessors Nietzsche adds a disquieting historicism and a pervasive extension. His is a "natural history" or "genealogy" of morals. This is a variation on the submoral historical determinism that had developed, from Rousseauian and Kantian roots, into the full-blown Hegelian and Marxist philosophies of history. But Nietzsche saw that epistemological-historical critique could not be limited to moral intuitions, religious visions, and antique physics. Modern historicism undermines the constructive side of modern thought itself, including its doctrines of nature, science, humanitarianism, rights, equality, and progressive history. It undermines any rational defense of "values," a word Nietzsche makes prominent. But "values" determine how we see the world. "Interpretation," "perspective," is all (34). There are "no moral phenomena, only a moral interpretation of phenomena" (108). With Nietzsche, historicism becomes decisively critical and can no longer sustain the Kantian and Hegelian hopes. One could go beyond Nietzsche, perhaps, and say that the initial modern turn, to "what men do" from "what men ought to do," had come home to roost.

Nietzsche took no joy in the newly bleak human landscape since he thought the relativism of values a "deadly truth." It is a "nihilism" that looks up to nothing and thus saps man's will and aspirations. Relativism thus encourages what is already upon us: a dark and nauseous age of mere safety and consumption. In the face of a dire situation, in which for the first time nothing is given to guide and inspire, Nietzsche looks for a philosopher-creator who can give man a goal, that is, who can create transforming values. Like Hobbes, Nietzsche turns to real passion, not mere opinion. Like Hobbes's, his is a philosophy of power. But unlike Hobbes, his priority or very foundation is "will to power," especially the passion of the strong for domination. To an extent this reminds of Machiavelli's original prince. Nietzsche also takes Cesare Borgia as a model for his "man of prey" (197), and he praises Machiavelli's "long, difficult, hard, dangerous thoughts" (28). But Nietzsche would restore the spiritual and philosophic heights Machiavelli had disdained as politically ineffectual, unsafe, and perhaps imaginary. If Nietzsche too relies on strength of passion or will, it is a high, almost idealistic passion for a spiritualized discharge of force (13). A great man has to be "the actor of his own ideal" (97), and, indeed, such a man's strength is less in dominating others than in overcoming the corroding force of nihilism within. Nietzsche's is a peculiarly fragile and insistent redirection to the noble and high. Creating light and height amidst the darkness, but in full knowledge of man's utterly exposed situation, the new thinker-creator teaches the future of man as his will.

The nerve of Nietzsche's diagnosis contrasts "truth" with "life." Truth is that provided by modern sciences such as physics or philology. It is merely "objective" and at most knowledge of "the mechanics" of "nature." Life is different, since it depends upon aspirations for the noble and great, upon, that is, a horizon of values. Nietzsche certainly respects modern "probity." The scientist's painstaking honesty is perhaps the best of modern virtues (206, 207, 227). But it is not enough. Probity is merely the necessary condition for the philosopher-creator who can overcome this "mechanical doltishness" as to human things. The modern sciences catch only something of man and nature, while aggravating the intellectual and moral crisis.

Nor can one "go back" to some premodern science or philosophy. Here Nietzsche accepts the epistemological-scientific critique of dialectical philosophy and of the Bible's revelations. But he also radicalizes, in the way that is followed by Heidegger and Arendt. The old teachings are not only baseless, but also responsible for the mass democracy that degrades modern man. Hobbes and Kant had attacked the ancient philosophers' defense of pride and inequality. Nietzsche attacks Plato and Aristotle for undermining pride and inequality. His genealogy of morals treats Christianity as "Platonism for the people" and "Socratism" as the first cause (190, 191). From Socrates came cobwebby and tricky dialectics, "the allegedly rational morality" that has undermined the confidence of master classes down through the ages. For Nietzsche, Alcibiades is an exemplar (200); he, at least, resisted Socrates' inveiglings. Nietzsche thus radicalizes the Enlightenment's moral critique by attacking all rational restraints, enlightened as well as traditional, and by blaming the whole philosophic tradition, especially the Socratics, for the defects of all morals, enlightened as well as traditional.

Nietzsche does season his indignation with appreciation. Greatness as he understands it requires a deepening and development of soul, and for that the ancients' moral discipline, so different from modern freedom and equality, was indispensable. Nietzsche's may be a "profound" psychology—he would descend to the "depths"—but it is a historical-moral depth psychology. Nietzsche is the complicated sort of atheist who praises Blaise Pascal and the "grand style" of the Old Testament (45, 46, 52, 229, 250–51). A long development under biblical law and ancient morals has made the soul broader, more ingenious, and more intellectual. The history of morals has "spiritualized" the soul.

Nevertheless, the time for "gratitude" is past. Indignation is duty now, for morality, piety, truth, and objectivity exacerbate the mass society of repulsive mediocrity. If one accepts Nietzsche's genealogy of morals, as Arendt did (more or less), there is no place to turn for rational enlightenment as to morals and politics. This exacerbated relativism is the gravest difficulty Nietzsche poses for any effort at recovery.

The result of this unsparing diagnosis is a political-moral critique and construction matched in extremity only by that other historical-practical philosophy, Marx's. Humanity faces an apocalyptic "abyss," which can be overcome only by the transforming domination of "supermen."

"God is dead," in Nietzsche's famous maxim, by which he meant that belief in God is dying and with it support for all goals. We confront a world increasingly without "meaning," that is, without any natural or supernatural standard by which to live. The "abyss" is this nihilism or relativism (289). But "man is a rope across an abyss," in the famous words of *Thus Spake Zarathustra*. If he does not go forward, he goes back to animality, or he falls. Nietzsche shows the dark possibilities of the doctrine of human malleability. Indeed, the situation is very dark, for the very possibility of man as noble, philosophic, and strong is now at stake, and perhaps for the last time. Hence Nietzsche's apocalyptic-historical tone. Given the advance of democracy and the fragility of higher types, the future of mankind lies in the balance. The philosopher-creator must take responsibility for the future of man.

"Caesar with the soul of Christ," a "Caesarean trainer and mover of culture" (207) are but two Nietzschean formulations of the "philosophers of the future." Would one smile at the extremity? Recall then the plans of Hobbes, Locke, and Kant to enlighten their countries and every country, or Bacon's launch of "a total reconstruction of sciences, arts, and all human knowledge," including knowledge of "logic, ethics, and politics."[52] Machiavelli compared himself to Columbus, who discovered a new world; Bacon's model was Augustus Caesar, ruler of the world. We are living within the remains of such projects. Nietzsche's is another version of the modern philosopher-founder who understands the world chiefly to change it.

Nevertheless, Nietzsche's version is antirational and more extreme, and more extreme because antirational. His model is less a legislator of enlightened doctrines than a prophet-figure: a legislator for humankind, indeed, but one more religious than political and philosophic. *Thus Spake Zarathustra* is the title Nietzsche gave to the work he most admired. This remaking of the transforming side of modern political philosophy is of course connected with his rejection of reason as guide. Locke and his brothers in enlightenment had held up reason as "our only star and compass." Nietzsche finds only dusk there and no guidance. A Zarathustra leads while knowing of the abyss, even if, out of delicacy and to lessen his pain, he wears a mask of lightness (40). Still, whatever the differences from his enlightened predecessors, Nietzsche too orchestrates a flight from a state of nature to a willfully man-made world. But his construction has the burden of the subjectivity, the relativism, of a world merely willed. Neither nature, nor reason, nor history can guide us. Nietzsche even acknowledges his own teaching to be perhaps merely his own, the result of a deep but still subjective spiritual *fatum* (231). Can it then be a philosophy for the future? or for a class by nature strong, spiritual, and noble? While at times Nietzsche speaks of returning "man to nature," he also says that nature is "indifferent" as to human values (9).[53]

Whatever these difficulties in the new creator, the superman is Caesar as well as Christ, "commander-legislator" as well as philosopher-prophet. Indeed, Nietzsche radicalizes the ruling side as well as the transforming-philosophic. While this new Caesar has elements of nobility, generosity, and philosophic

heights, elevations that Machiavelli's all-business prince was to
put aside, he is also more "terrible" (a word Nietzsche often uses
as praise). Machiavelli's enlightened executive might be ruth-
lessly ambitious and had to lay his foundations in terror, but he
was also to think incessantly about satisfying his followers, not
least "the people." Machiavellian ruthlessness was limited by
Machiavellian "humanity." But Nietzsche, in restoring prominence to the great, foments a bitter contempt precisely for the
virtue of humanity. Indeed, he advances cruelty and criminality
as marks of elevation and resolution (109, 110, 229) and holds
before himself a mission of ennobling by vast transformations of
all men and their world. Accordingly, he, unlike Machiavelli,
Hobbes, Locke, and Kant, trumpets an animus against ordinary
people. He dismisses not only moral scruples but also the limited
goals his enlightened predecessors had substituted: popular comfort and security, popular empire, and popular rights and self-
government. It is fair to acknowledge that Nietzsche conceals
somewhat the harshest teachings and counsels a certain tolerant
humaneness from the heights. But these do not gainsay the emphasis on resoluteness in the cruelty and the "experiments"
needed for the transformations he plans.

Charles de Gaulle, inquiring as to Germany's peculiar willfulness
and unexpected collapse in World War I, had blamed certain
traits of its chief generals. These "eminent" Germans, he wrote,
exhibited in common "the characteristic taste for immoderate
undertakings; the passion to expand their personal power at any
cost; the contempt for limits marked out by human experience,
common sense, and the law." Precisely as Germany inaugurated
the world crisis, her key leaders were rash, selfishly ambitious,
and disdainful of reasonable limits. But far from combating or
concealing such inclinations as "defects," de Gaulle observed
wonderingly, these men considered them "forces" to be system-
atized. This error crushed Wilhelmian Germany at the decisive
moment: "One may perhaps find in their conduct the imprint of
Nietzsche's theories of the elite and the Overman . . . who with
his exceptional character, his will to power, his taste for risk, his
contempt for others who want to see him as Zarathustra—ap-

peared to these impassioned men of ambition as the ideal that they should attain."⁵⁴

In Nietzsche's thinking, noble greatness of soul, evicted from politics by earlier modern thinkers, comes storming back. One is reminded of other theories of restoration. Rousseau, Kant and the Scottish "moral sense" school all tried in one way or another to bring back moral intuition and duty. Hobbes and Locke in their own ways had restored a concern for justice. But all of these enlightened thinkers would define the good and right effectually, in terms of necessary feelings or laws. So Nietzsche. If Hobbes built justice on revulsion from death, and Kant built morality on a universal law, Nietzsche himself would restore high and spiritual conduct on the basis of will to power. This paradoxical master moralist eulogized both Shakespeare and "the blond beast."

Nietzsche's proposals and diagnoses alike invite us to look to more moderate accounts, whether in examples such as a Washington or in the historians and philosophers who took seriously what is good and true as well as what is strong and great.

To encourage such looking is what this book is about.

Notes

Chapter 1. Introduction: Honorable Statesmen and Obscuring Theories

1. Bowman, *Honor: A History* (New York: Encounter Books, 2006); quotations are to 38, 39, 40, 46, 47, 61.

2. Sharon R. Krause, *Liberalism and Honor* (Cambridge: Harvard University Press, 2002); quotations are from 7, 8, 23, 24, 51, 53, 144.

3. Alexis de Tocqueville, *Democracy in America*, trans. Harvey C. Mansfield and Delba Winthrop (Chicago: University of Chicago Press, 2002); quotations here and following are from 589, 604.

4. Leo Braudy, *The Frenzy of Renown: Fame and Its History* (1986; repr. New York: Vintage Books, 1997), 6, 9–10, 588.

5. Braudy, *Frenzy of Renown*, 13. Other quotations in this and the following paragraphs are drawn from 7, 8, 13, 16, 48, 585–97.

Chapter 2. The Gentleman-Statesman: Aristotle's (Complicated) Great-Souled Man

1. Quoted by Richard Brookhiser, *Founding Father: Rediscovering George Washington* (New York: Free Press, 1996), 103. The epigraph is from John Marshall, *The Life of George Washington*, 2d ed. (Philadelphia: James Crispy and Thomas Cowperthwaite, 1850), 2:446–47.

2. "I set out in this campaign, with the intention of conducting it strictly as a gentleman, in substance at least, if not in the outside polish. The latter I shall never be, but that which constitutes the inside of a gentleman I hope I understand, and am not less inclined to practice than others." Speech at Springfield, Illinois, July 17, 1858, in *The Collected Works of Abraham Lincoln*, ed. Roy P. Basler (New Brunswick: Rutgers University Press, 1953), 2:513. Thanks to Steven Kautz and Thomas Schneider for the source.

3. The derivation is express in *Magna Moralia* (1207b 21–25), which is sometimes attributed (although not by ancient commentators) to a pupil of Aristotle's. See the introduction by St. George Stock in volume 9 of *The Works of Aristotle*, ed. W. D. Ross (Oxford: Oxford University Press, 1915), xix–xxiii.

4. "Aristotle is the founder of political science because he is the discoverer of moral virtue." Leo Strauss, *The City and Man* (Chicago: Rand McNally, 1964), 27.

5. Brief accounts: Peter Simpson, "Contemporary Virtue Ethics and Aristotle," *Review of Metaphysics* 45:3 (1992): 503–24; Richard Ruderman, "Aristotle and the Recovery of Political Judgment," *American Political Science Review* 91:2 (1997): 409–20; Susan D. Collins, *Aristotle and the Rediscovery of Citizenship* (Cambridge: Cambridge University Press, 2006). Collins chronicles the slighting of magnanimity in particular: chap. 2, esp. 61–66. The recurrence to "virtue ethics" is often traced to G. E. M. Anscombe's trenchant critique of British moral philosophy: utilitarianism and semi-Kantianism leave out morals; see "Modern Moral Philosophy," *Philosophy* 33:124 (1958): 1–18. This attribution cannot be precisely true, even for the English-speaking world, since Anscombe leaves conspicuously undecided the question whether to recur to biblical law or Aristotelian ethics. Also, Harry Jaffa's *Thomism and Aristotelianism* had already tried to decide that question in favor of Aristotle's ethics, including the Aristotelian accounts of magnanimity and of the place of the divine in morals (Chicago: University of Chicago Press, 1952), 116–66.

6. Amélie Oksenberg Rorty, *Essays on Aristotle's Ethics* (Berkeley: University of California Press, 1980), 33. In the 357 pages of text in Richard Kraut's *Aristotle on the Human Good* (Princeton: Princeton University Press, 1989), there are, if I count right, eleven sentences devoted to magnanimity and ambition both, 337–38, 308n35. Eight of them deal with supposed connections of these virtues to practical and theoretical reason, that is, to book 6, in which Aristotle discusses neither these virtues nor the supposed connections. Kraut's book has three sentences on magnanimity and ambition as such. If its index is correct, Kraut's later study, *Aristotle*, has four one-sentence mentions of magnanimity, and none of ambition (Oxford: Oxford University Press, 2002).

7. Such references are to the *Nicomachean Ethics* and to the standard divisions from Bekker's nineteenth-century edition. I have used the Greek text in the Loeb Classical Library (*Nicomachean Ethics*, trans. H. Rackham [Cambridge: Harvard University Press, 1975]), occasionally corrected in light of John Burnet's edition (London: Methuen, 1900, reprinted by Arno Press [New York, 1973]). I have relied chiefly on the translations by Joe Sachs (Newburyport: Focus Publishing, 2002) and Terence Irwin (2d ed., Indianapolis: Hackett, 1999), while also consulting those of Martin Ostwald (New York: Macmillan, 1962) and W. D. Ross (*Works of Aristotle*, vol. 9 [Oxford: Oxford University Press, 1954]). I'm grateful to Irene Flowers Eide for correcting my references and my Greek.

8. *Life of George Washington*, 2:445–48.

9. *Douglass's Monthly* (October 1861), quoted in Philip S. Foner, ed., *The Life and Writings of Frederick Douglass* (New York: International Publishers, 1952), 3:37.

10. Quoted by W. F. R. Hardie, *Aristotle's Ethical Theory* (Oxford: Clarendon Press, 1968), 119. Hardie had second thoughts about slighting greatness of soul: *Phronesis* 23 (1979): 65.

11. As to the needs of liberal democracies, consider Churchill's "Can Modern Communities Do Without Great Men?" Exploring this theme in the pivotal

time of the early 1930s, Churchill worried especially about the vast new war powers supplied by science and collective social organization, the unstable new economies, and a peculiarly modern spiritual hunger. In retrospect, he foreshadows his own superior deeds in World War II. *Thoughts and Adventures* (London: Thornton Butterworth, 1932), 264, 229–80.

12. *An Abstract of a Book lately Published; Entitled, A Treatise of Human Nature, &c.*, in *An Inquiry Concerning Human Understanding*, ed. Eric Steinberg (Indianapolis: Hackett, 1977), 126. Quoted by Nasser Behnegar, *Tough Liberals: John Locke, David Hume and the Epistemological Foundation of Freedom* (forthcoming).

13. See the descriptions collected by Brookhiser, *Founding Father*, 116–19.

14. GW to Henry Lee, Jr., *The Papers of George Washington*, Confederation Series, Dorothy Twohig, ed. (Charlottesville: University Press of Virginia, 1992), 6:530–31.

15. Jefferson to Madison, June 9, 1793, *The Papers of James Madison*, Congressional Series, William T. Hutchinson et al., eds., 17 vols. (Chicago: University of Chicago Press, 1962–91), 15:38, 27.

16. Letter to Karl Löwith, August 20, 1946, translated in *Independent Journal of Philosophy* 4 (1983).

17. Which, among other things, leads Jacob Howland to contend that the *Ethics'* discussion indicates that true greatness of soul is "Socratic self-knowledge." "Aristotle's Great-Souled Man," *Review of Politics* 64 (Winter 2002), 27–56.

18. R. A. Gauthier notes that Philopon, Eustrates, and other ancient commentators understood Aristotle's position to be that magnanimity is finally an equivocal term (*Magnanimité: L'idéal de la grandeur dans la philosophie païenne et dans la théologie chrétienne* [Paris: Librairie Philosophique J. Vrin, 1951], 57n2). Gauthier himself supposes a development in Aristotle's thinking that ends equivocation: the truly magnanimous man is finally Socrates. According to him, the *Eudemian Ethics* sets forth magnanimity as a separate virtue concerned with "greatness" and thus synthesizes the two inconsistent definitions of the *Posterior Analytics*. Then the *Nicomachean Ethics*, elaborating the virtue, so brings out the magnanimous man's indifference to fortune that only the magnanimity of Socrates remains. Honor seeking is then by the ambitious man alone, not by the magnanimous man, 55–117. I am grateful to Crystal Cordell for her researches on these matters. Howland, I think, refutes this thesis: "Aristotle's Great-Souled Man," 44–48.

19. James Thomas Flexner, *George Washington*, 4 vols. (Boston: Little Brown, 1965–72), 2:469.

20. Cf. Howland, "Aristotle's Great-Souled Man," 31–32, 41–43: the great-souled man (like the philosopher) is said to be a lover of the noble and also an instrument of the city and thus of its conventions. I believe he is both of these, but not chiefly or merely either.

21. *Seven Pillars of Wisdom, a Triumph* (Garden City: Doubleday, Moran, 1926 [private], 1935 [general]), 563.

22. Carnes Lord, *Education and Culture in the Political Thought of Aristotle* (Ithaca: Cornell University Press, 1982), 35.

Chapter 3. Imperial Ambition in Free Politics: The Problem of Thucydides' Alcibiades

1. I'm grateful to Judge John C. Wheatley for improvements of this chapter's prose, to Benjamin Lorch and Nicholas Starr for help with the translations, and to Henrik Syse and Gregory Reichberg, of the International Peace Research Institute, Oslo, for soliciting the first version for their Thucydides Workshop (February, 2005).

2. Plutarch, "Alcibiades," in *Lives*, vol. 4, trans. Bernadotte Perrin (Cambridge: Harvard University Press, 1986), xxii.5.

3. Thomas Hobbes, *The English Works*, 11 vols., ed. Sir William Molesworth (London: John Bohn, 1843), 8:viii.

4. Jacqueline De Romilly, *Thucydides and Athenian Imperialism*, trans. Philip Thody (New York: Barnes and Noble, 1963), 3. De Romilly shows the inherent difficulties confronting historical accounts that do not attend to Thucydides' "carefully finished result" and especially to his own "intellectual attitude," not least his "political judgment" (5–10; 153–54). Which is not to say that the text supports her conclusions that Thucydides "despises Alcibiades' policy of alliance with Argos" (227; cf. 196–97), that he thinks "force" to determine "all human relationships" (294), or that book 8 "minimizes" Alcibiades' influence (227). For a model of serious reading and more faithful interpretation, see Christopher Bruell, "Thucydides' View of Athenian Imperialism," in *American Political Science Review* 68 (1964). For an argument for such a reading, see Leo Strauss, *The City and Man* (Chicago: Rand McNally, 1964), chap. 3.

5. I use, with occasional corrections, the translation by Charles Forster Smith in Thucydides, *History of the Peloponnesian War*, 4 vols. (London: William Heinemann, 1920). There are useful aids in *The Landmark Thucydides*, ed. Robert B. Strassler (New York: Free Press, 1996).

6. Xenophon, *Hellenica*, trans. Carleton L. Brownson (London: William Heinemann, 1918), II.1.25–26; Plutarch, "Alcibiades," xxvii–xxxviii.

7. Steven Forde, *The Ambition to Rule: Alcibiades and the Politics of Imperialism in Thucydides* (Ithaca: Cornell University Press, 1989), 55–56; Clifford Orwin, *The Humanity of Thucydides* (Princeton: Princeton University Press, 1994), 111, 128n20.

8. See W. Robert Connor, *Thucydides* (Princeton: Princeton University Press, 1984), 165–66.

9. Forde, *Ambition to Rule*, 12–67.

10. Ibid.

11. *Posterior Analytics*, 97b15–26.

12. Jonathan Price, *Thucydides and Internal War* (Cambridge: Cambridge University Press, 2001), 11–21. Price devotes a book to Thucydidean "internal war," a book that discusses helpfully the scholarly treatment of *stasis* (civil strife). But does the *History's* civil strife essentially involve contested language rather than political partisans, and internal war among the Hellenes rather than among classes within the cities (11–59)? Orwin offers a measured critique in *Humanity of Thucydides*, 177n10.

13. Orwin, *Humanity of Thucydides*, 175–82.

14. Peter Pouncey, *The Necessities of War: A Study of Thucydides' Pessimism* (New York: Columbia University Press, 1980), 109.

15. Plutarch, "Alcibiades," xvi.5.

16. De Romilly, *Thucydides and Athenian Imperialism*, 227.

17. Forde, *Ambition to Rule*, 104, 122–23f.

18. Ibid., 187, 183–97.

19. I largely follow Forster Smith's translation and with him reject some translators' reliance on ms. B to say that this is Alcibiades' "first" service to the city. How could that be, in light of the Argive alliance and Alcibiades' imaginative generalship, however brief, in Sicily?

20. Plutarch, "Alcibiades," xxxiii.2.

Chapter 4. The Soul of Grand Ambition: Alcibiades Cross-Examined by Socrates

1. I have relied on the Loeb editions of the Greek: *Plato* (vol. 8), ed. and trans. W. R. M. Lamb (Cambridge: Harvard University Press, 1955). Nicholas Denyer's edition of the first *Alcibiades*, with commentary, has been a boon: Plato, *Alcibiades* (Cambridge: Cambridge University Press, 2001). For translations of the first *Alcibiades* I've used chiefly Carnes Lord's version, in *The Roots of Political Philosophy*, ed. Thomas L. Pangle (Ithaca: Cornell University Press, 1987), 175–221. As to the little-known second *Alcibiades*, I've mostly turned to Amy Bonnette Nendza's unpublished translation, for which I am very grateful. But I've looked also at David M. Johnson's useful edition and translation of both dialogues: *Socrates and Alcibiades, Four Texts* (Newburyport, Mass.: Focus Publishing, 2003). I thank Irene Flowers Eide for cheerful and expeditious help with the references and with the Greek.

2. Denyer, *Alcibiades*, 14–26; Pangle, *The Roots of Political Philosophy*, 1–20; Johnson, *Plato and Alcibiades*, xiv, xviii. For an early and outspoken expression of the critical stance as to the two *Alcibiades*, see Friedrich Ernst Daniel Schleiermacher, *Schleiermacher's Introductions to the Dialogues of Plato*, trans. William Dobson (Cambridge: J. and J. J. Deighton, 1836), 165–68, 328–36. The major recent criticisms of the historical critics are these. Their assertion that early custodians of manuscripts were sloppy seems to be a mere speculation. It is a speculation that neglects the greater familiarity of the ancient librarians and philosophers with the texts, their history, and their arguments. Moreover, the old librarians and philosophers had more reason than modern historical scholars to be concerned for the genuine article; they thought that Plato's texts might contain the truth. Nor were the old scholars uncritical. They too excluded certain texts as not Plato's. But a long succession of such authorities, including very great students of Plato, accepted the two *Alcibiades* as part of the traditional canon of thirty-five dialogues. Also, the stylistic differences sometimes alleged are decisively inconclusive, since similar differences exist among and within dialogues that modern scholars acknowledge to be Plato's. The substantive differences alleged are at least as inconclusive, both for a similar reason and because it is hard to know Plato's true teaching. It is famously hard to know which arguments, or which difficulties in argument, are to be attributed to Plato and which to the foibles of a character he is examining.

3. This was the old judgment of Diogenes Laertius (*Lives of the Eminent Philosophers*, III 59, 62). See *The Philosophy of Plato*, in *Alfarabi's Philosophy of Plato and Aristotle*, trans. Muhsin Mahdi (NY: Free Press, 1962), 53–54; *Proclus: Alcibiades*, trans. William O'Neill (The Hague: Martinus Nijhoff, 1965).

4. Mark J. Lutz, *Socrates' Education to Virtue* (Albany: State University of New York Press, 1998), 111. Cf. *Symposium* 213c6–d6.

5. Alcibiades, born in 451 BC, is said to be not quite twenty in the first *Alcibiades* (123d7). Denyer estimates its dramatic date to be 433 BC (Denyer, *Alcibiades*, 189). Lamb supposes the dramatic date of the *Protagoras* to be 432 BC (W. R. M. Lamb, "Introduction to the Protagoras," in *Plato, Laches, Protagoras, Meno, Euthydemus* [London: William Heinemann, 1952], 87n1).

6. Compare to this emphasis on greatness Mark Blitz's suggestion that Alcibiades seeks, with some qualifications, to "stand alone"; the first *Alcibiades* is an experiment with a soul that "recognizes nothing outside itself." See his "Plato's Alcibiades I," *Interpretation* 22, no. 3 (Spring 1995): 339–58, esp. 343–44, 349, 356–58.

7. Compare the suggestion of Christopher Bruell that the Alcibiades of the second dialogue worries about his injustice, an anxiety aroused by the first dialogue. See Bruell's indispensable *On the Socratic Education: An Introduction to the Shorter Platonic Dialogues* (Lanham, Md.: Rowman and Littlefield, 1999), 10–48. I am much indebted to these explorations.

8. For Socrates' effort to produce other guardians, from the sophists and orators themselves, see Devin Stauffer, *The Unity of Plato's Gorgias: Rhetoric, Justice and the Philosophic Life* (Cambridge: Cambridge University Press, 2006).

9. The Alcibiades of the first dialogue only tacitly accepts "tyranny" as descriptive of his aspirations. See Charles Rubin, "Ambition Ancient and Modern," in Leslie G. Rubin, ed., *Educating the Ambitious*, Politikos (1993), 2:51.

10. *Lives* xxvii.1, xxxii.1–3, trans. Bernadotte Perrin (Cambridge: Harvard University Press, 1986).

11. See the discussion of Diotima's speech in Steven Forde, "Political Ambition in Thucydides and Plato: The Case of Alcibiades," in Rubin, ed., *Educating the Ambitious*, 23-25.

12. Paul Friedländer, *Plato*, trans. Hans Meyerhoff (New York: Bollingen, 1964), 2:232.

13. *On the Socratic Education*, 28.

14. Cf. Denyer: Socrates' "philosophical wisdom, such as it was, consisted in an appreciation of his own ignorance." *Alcibiades*, 3, and the commentary on 117b12 and 113b1.

15. See the conflicting opinions of Denyer (*Alcibiades*, 236–37), Lord (in Pangle, *Roots of Political Philosophy*, 317n37), and Johnson (*Socrates and Alcibiades*, 53n74).

16. Irene Flowers Eide and Jeffrey Pearlin pointed this out to me.

17. *On the Socratic Education*, 45–46.

18. I follow the editors who attribute to Socrates the question about nobility. See David Johnson's note to 109c5, in *Socrates and Alcibiades*.

19. In actuality, Alcibiades did not avenge himself when returned to Athens and in power, according to Plutarch; even when driven out a second time he tried

to aid Athens in its danger. This distinguished him from, say, the untutored (and radically vengeful) Coriolanus. *Lives,* "Alcibiades," xxiii.2, "Alcibiades and Coriolanus," ii.3–5.

20. So some argue. But if this is a decisive revision of judgment as to the youth's promise, why does Socrates subsequently treat Alcibiades as a comrade in inquiry, even after the silly celebrity-worship of Spartan and Persian royalty (*I* 124b–d)?

21. Blitz, "Plato's *Alcibiades I,*" 353.

22. Even in professing his concluding allegiance to Socrates, according to Denyer, Alcibiades resorts to the prose of sophistic oratory. *Alcibiades,* 246 (commentary on *I* 235d 8–9).

23. Euripides, *Phoenician Women,* 858–59. Johnson interprets the quotation to suggest that Socrates refuses to sacrifice Alcibiades to the city (*Socrates and Alcibiades,* xx). But is it Alcibiades, or more promising students, who will be the true sons of the philosopher Socrates? Still, Socrates may engender enlightened guardians as well as truer sons, and these, too, an Alcibiades as well as a Plato, are in danger from the creeds of Teiresias.

24. *Phoenician Women,* 15–20, 865–94.

25. S.v. Sir William Smith, *A Classical Dictionary of Greek and Roman Mythology,* rev. G. E. Marindin (London: John Murray, 1919).

26. This remarkable observation was made by Bruell, in *On the Socratic Education,* 45–46.

27. See *Leo Strauss on Plato's Symposium,* ed. Seth Benardete (Chicago: University of Chicago Press, 2001), 209–12.

28. In real life Alcibiades is said to have so managed Ammon as to produce a prophecy to persuade to the Sicilian expedition. Plutarch, "Nicias," in *Lives* (New York: Modern Library, 1932), 637; Denyer, *Alcibiades,* 107.

Chapter 5. Imperial Grandeur and Imperial Hollowness: Xenophon's Cyrus the Great

1. Xenophon, *The Education of Cyrus* , trans. Wayne Ambler (Ithaca: Cornell University Press, 2001). I have benefited much from Ambler's excellent translation and notes, and I owe particular thanks for the opportunity to examine the work before publication.

2. I am grateful to Thomas Schneider for many corrections, and to Christopher Nadon for allowing me to see, prior to publication, his excellent *Xenophon's Prince: Republic and Empire in the Cyropaedia* (Berkeley: University of California Press, 2001).

3. See, for example, Geoffrey Ellis, *The Napoleonic Empire* (New York: Palgrave Macmillan, 2003), 109; Desmond Seward, *Napoleon and Hitler* (New York: Viking, 1989), 302; David Gates, *The Napoleonic Wars, 1803–1815* (London: Arnold, 1997), 272; Allen Schom, *Napoleon Bonaparte* (New York: HarperCollins, 1997).

4. *Napoleon* (French and European Publications, 1993).

5. "Napoleon, asked once what was his program, had replied: 'I just go ahead and my progress is the result of my movements.'" Kemal Atatürk quoted

this and commented: "Those who 'just go ahead' finally knock their heads against the rock of St. Helena." Atatürk liked to compare Napoleon's advance on Moscow with the Ottoman advance to Vienna—"at the expense of the country's internal welfare." Quoted in Patrick Kinross's extraordinary *Atatürk, The Rebirth of a Nation* (London: Phoenix Paperback, 1964), 477–78.

6. *History,* trans. George Rawlinson (London and New York: J. M. Dent and E. P. Dutton, 1927).

7. *Memorabilia,* trans. Amy L. Bonnette (Ithaca: Cornell University Press, 1994), I.3.8–13.

8. *Anabasis,* III.1.4–7.

9. *Memorabilia,* IV.8.11.

10. I am grateful to Crystal Cordell for pointing out this and other relevant details.

11. See the discriminating discussion and references in Nadon's *Xenophon's Prince,* 30–42.

12. Pheraulus labors to hide this with specious arguments, that hand-to-hand fighting with shield and sword, for example, is "by nature" (2.3.9–14). He is probably a "plant." Pheraulus had been known to Cyrus, is of a superior nature, is the only commoner to rise to the inner circle, and is preternaturally devoted to Cyrus (2.3.7, 8.3.2, 5, 6, 28).

13. Leo Strauss, "Restatement on Xenophon's *Hiero,*" in *On Tyranny,* ed. Victor Gourevitch and Michael Roth (New York: The Free Press, 1991), 182.

14. Or most loving honor, 1.2.1; cf. Ambler's n. 10.

15. Ambler counted over twenty such indications (vin7).

16. According to Leo Strauss's account of the Xenophontic view, the political man is moved by love of honor and thus attaches "absolute importance" to human things. He wants to be "loved by all human beings regardless of their quality." The philosopher, who loves the truth, is attached to "a particular type of human being, namely to actual or potential philosophers or to his friends." Strauss, "Restatement on Xenophon's *Hiero,*" 198, 200.

Chapter 6. Obscuring the Truly Great: Washington and Modern Theories of Fame

1. The texts used are Adair's title essay in *Fame and the Founding Fathers,* ed. Trevor Colbourn (New York: W. W. Norton, 1974), 3–26, and John Marshall, *The Life of George Washington* (Fredericksburg, Va.: Citizens' Guild of Washington's Boyhood Home, 1926). References in the text are to this edition, which reprints the revised text printed in two volumes in 1832 but adds the introductory history of the country and the five-volume format, both from the first edition (1804–07). On the writing and publication, see "Editorial Note" in *The Papers of John Marshall,* ed. Charles F. Hobson (Chapel Hill: University of North Carolina Press, 1990), 6:219–30. One could probably make my same argument by relying on what is now usually judged the best biography, James Thomas Flexner's *Washington, The Indispensable Man* (Boston: Little Brown, 1974), or on other astute recent works such as Joseph J. Ellis's *His Excellency, George Washing-*

ton (New York: Knopf, 2004), and Marc Landy and Sidney M. Milkis's *Presidential Greatness* (Lawrence: University Press of Kansas, 2000), 12–39. Still, Marshall's thematic attention to character helps.

2. To John Trumbull, February 15, 1788, in *The Papers of Thomas Jefferson*, ed. Julian Boyd, 25 vols. to date (Princeton: Princeton University Press, 1950–), 14:561.

3. The *Essayes or Counsels, Civill and Morall*, ed. Michael Kiernan (Cambridge: Harvard University Press, 1985), #55; *New Organon*, #129; cf. Bacon, *Advancement of Learning*, aII, iv, 4.

4. *Essayes*, "Of Vaine-Glory," #54.

5. Compare Bacon's *Essays*, #29, with Machiavelli, *Discourses*, 1:4–6, 10. For arguments supporting this sketch of Bacon's views, see Robert K. Faulkner, *Francis Bacon and the Project of Progress* (Lanham, Md.: Rowman and Littlefield, 1994), 183–200.

6. *Advancement of Learning*, II, xxi, 9; for further argument see *Bacon and Progress*, 59–83.

7. These theses are argued in *Bacon and Progress*, 51–56, 127–40.

8. Hence the importance of history and the management of *traditio* ("wisdom of transmission") in Bacon's *Advancement*. See *Bacon and Progress*, 30–41, esp. 30–31, 33–34; 161–81.

9. Jerry Weinberger, ed., *New Atlantis and the Great Instauration* (Wheeling, Ill: Harlan Davidson, 1989), 71, 82.

10. See especially "A Proposal for Promoting Useful Knowledge among the British Plantations of America" (1743), in *Franklin's Writings*, ed. Jared Sparks (Boston: Hilliard, Gray, 1836–1840), 6:16.

11. *Benjamin Franklin's Autobiography*, ed. J. A. Leo Lemay and P. M. Zall (New York, London: W. W. Norton, 1930), 130.

12. *Bacon and Progress*, 128–33.

13. Adair, *Fame and the Founding Fathers*, 11.

14. Ibid., 10.

15. For a (circumlocutory) example: Bacon, *Essays*, #13, "Of Goodness and Goodness of Nature." For an interpretation: *Bacon and Progress*, 62–65.

16. Letter to John Randolph, June 26 (no year) (ALS, Virginia Historical Society), quoted in Robert K. Faulkner, *The Jurisprudence of John Marshall* (Princeton: Princeton University Press, 1968), 136.

17. James A. Servies, *A Bibliography of John Marshall* (Washington: U.S. Commission on the Bicentennial, 1956), 60.

18. To John Marshall, Jr., November (December?) 7, 1834. Reprinted in *The Nation*, 72, no. 1858 (February 7, 1901): 111–12. Cf. *Jurisprudence of Marshall*, 144n36. One must note that much of Marshall's correspondence was destroyed.

19. I use the Loeb Classics edition, trans. Walter Miller (Cambridge: Harvard University Press, 1956), while very occasionally changing the translation.

20. *Papers of Marshall*, 7:415.

21. I follow Ellis's summary of the matter in *His Excellency*, 158–60.

22. See *Jurisprudence of Marshall*, 147–65, esp. 149, 159ff.

23. To Timothy Pickering, December 11, 1813, *Papers of Marshall* 7:416–17.

Chapter 7. Honorable Greatness Denied (1):
The Egalitarian Web

1. Quoted in Richard Brookhiser's *Founding Father* (New York: Free Press, 1996), 103.

2. John Rawls, *Political Liberalism, Expanded Edition* (hereafter *PL* 2005) (New York: Columbia University Press: 2005), 6, 82. Thanks to Christopher Kelly and Lucas Swaine for important aid with the intricacies of Rawls's doctrines. The conclusions are mine alone.

3. *PL* 2005, lvin34, 410n50, 471; *A Theory of Justice* (hereafter *TJ*) (Cambridge: Harvard University Press, 1971), 274, 324–31, 262–65.

4. *TJ*, 11; *PL* 2005, 11, 16, 17, 35, 46, 58, 201f., 301, 447, 456; *Political Liberalism* (hereafter *PL*) (New York: Columbia University Press, 1993), 6–7, 46, 82; *The Law of Peoples* (hereafter *LP*) (Cambridge: Harvard University Press, 1999), 13–14, 41. See generally the discussions indexed under "difference principle" in these works.

5. Clifford Orwin, "Welfare and the New Dignity," *Public Interest* 71 (Spring 1983): 91. See references in the previous footnote.

6. *TJ*, 12, 310, 311; *PL* 2005, 456.

7. The remarks quoted in this discussion are from *PL*, 80–81; *PL* 2005, 472.

8. *PL* 2005, 407, 431.

9. *LP*, 8, 26, 47, 95.

10. *LP*, 29n27.

11. Herodotus, *Histories* V 66, 78; cf. Thucydides, *The Peloponnesian War* 2.41.4, 61.4, 63.2; 4.61.5; 6.33.5, 64.1; 6.24–6.32, and Machiavelli, *Discourses on Livy*, I.5.3; I.6.3, 4.

12. *PL*, 81–88, xvi–xvii, 187–88; *LP*, 7. The supposition of malleability seems ubiquitous among today's leading proponents of equality. "Human nature in general" does not exist, according to Arendt (*Human Condition*, 193); there is "nothing to people except what has been socialized into them," according to Richard Rorty (*Contingency, Irony, Solidarity* [Cambridge: Cambridge University Press, 1991], 177, cf. 187–88).

13. *PL* 2005, lix, 403, 456; *PL*, 87, 79; *LP*, 7, 25.

14. *LP*, 95n9.

15. *LP*, 4–5, 95, 97–98; *PL* 87.

16. *TJ*, 24, 310, 311, 578, 581, 584; *PL*, 86, 87, 189.

17. *PL*, 80–81, xvi–xvii, 10, 12, 13.

18. *PL* 2005, 386, 388n22, 395, 442–45, 450, 486.

19. *PL* 2005, 382, cf. 406; *PL*, 29–35; see too the introduction (xii–xxx) and all of Lecture I, "Fundamental Ideas," 3–46.

20. *PL* 2005, xx, xxxvii, 441, 442, 406, 486; *TJ*, 118–92, 585.

21. *The Human Condition* (Chicago: University of Chicago Press, 1958, paper ed. 1989) (hereafter *HC*), *Between Past and Future* (New York: Penguin Books, 1993) (hereafter *PF*), a republication of the Viking Compass edition (New York, 1968), itself an expanded version of the 1951 original (Viking Press and Faber

and Faber, London). References in this paragraph are to *HC*, 12–29, 257–65, 280–325; *PF,* 17, 28, 72, 78–79, 91–141 esp. 114 ff., 211; *The Origins of Totalitarianism* (San Diego: Harcourt Brace/Jovanovich Publishers, 1973), vii. Thanks to Lucas Swaine and Jakub Franek for very helpful criticisms of an earlier version of this essay on Arendt's egalitarianism.

22. *HC*, 35, 41, 46, *PF,* 8, 25, 145, 147, cf. 152ff., 173, 179–99, 263–64.

23. *HC*, 9, 57, 176–79, 184–92, 194, 236, 247; *PF,* 152, 153, 169, 174–79, 202, 213, 223, 261–62.

24. *HC*, 41, 176, 234; *PF,* 33, 44, 134, 146, 151, 148–49, 155–56, 195, 220–21, 242, 246–47; *On Revolution* (hereafter *OR*) (New York: Viking Press, 1963), 202, 204, 223, 247, 255, 268 (cf. 275), 279–85.

25. *PF,* 78–79, 152, 224; *HC*, 205, 229; other references in the paragraph: *HC*, 74–77, 223–30, 194–96, but cf. 30–33, *PF* 14, 115–16, 162, 164–66, 215–16, 222, 242; *OR*, 152.

26. *PF,* 92–119, esp. 116–17; *OR*, 170–74; *HC* 13–20, 26–32, 188–90, 194–98, 206–07, 222–25, 231–40.

27. *HC*, 51, 57, 115, 191, 197, 199, 205ff., 243–46; *PF,* 51, 114–15, 117–18, 153–54, 178, 228, 258–61; *OR*, 178, 258, 279–85. As to the role of future professors and other publicists, see Kant's *Renewed Question Whether the Human Race Is in Constant Progress toward the Better,* 7:8, 15, 89, 161. See ch 8, n.40.

28. *HC*, 5; *PF,* 39–40f., 47.

29. *HC*, 185–87, 197, 239–41; *PF,* 213–14, 217, 219. See the exchange of letters between Scholem and Arendt, in Arendt, *The Jew as Pariah,* ed. Ron H. Feldman (New York: Grove Press, 1978), 250. For Pericles' remarks, see Thucydides 2.40.4–5, 2.63.2.

30. *PF,* 3–15, 17–40, 178; *HC*, 273–86. See Dana R. Villa, *Arendt and Heidegger: The Fate of the Political* (Princeton: Princeton University Press, 1996), esp. 42–79, 171–207.

Chapter 8. Honorable Greatness Denied (2): The Premises

1. *On the Citizen* VII.2.

2. *Leviathan* I. x, xiv.5, xv.

3. Machiavelli, *Prince,* 15; *Discourses on Livy,* I.55.3–6; Bacon, *Advancement of Learning* II, xxi, 9; *The Essayes or Counsels, Civill and Morall,* Kiernan #29 ("Of the True Greatness of Kingdomes and Estates") and #14 ("Of Nobility").

4. *The Elements of Law, Natural and Politic,* ed. Tönnies, 2d ed. (London: Frank Cass, 1969) I, 9 .1.

5. *Essayes,* "Of Vaine-Glory," #54.

6. *Elements of Law* II.8.3, cf. I.9.21; *On the Citizen* I.5, cf. XV.13.

7. *On the Citizen* III.32.

8. *Leviathan* I.xxi.

9. *On the Citizen,* Dedicatory Epistle.

10. *On the Citizen,* Preface to the Reader, 20, I. 2. Consider John Locke's distinction between the "itch after honor, power, and riches," which is but "fantas-

tical uneasiness" due to "fashion, example, and education," and "uneasiness of hunger, thirst, heat, cold, weariness," which arises from "ordinary necessities." *Essay Concerning Humane Understanding*, ed. Peter H. Nidditch (Oxford: Clarendon Press, 1979), II.21.45.

11. *Leviathan* I.xv.17.

12. *Leviathan* I.xv.21; *Elements of Law* I.17. 1; *On the Citizen*, Preface, 4–8.

13. *Elements of Law* I.14.2; *On the Citizen* III.14, *Leviathan* I.xiii.1–3.

14. Leo Strauss, *Natural Right and History* (Chicago: University of Chicago Press, 1953), 180–81.

15. *On the Citizen* VII.2.

16. *Leviathan* I.xi.1.

17. *Leviathan* I.xi, *On the Citizen* II.32.

18. *Elements of Law* I.9.21.

19. *Elements of Law* I.9.20, I.19.2, *Leviathan* I.6.

20. *Leviathan*, Introduction para. 4.

21. *Leviathan* I.6 ("Of the Interior Beginnings of Voluntary Motions: Commonly Called the PASSIONS, and the Speeches by Which They Are Expressed"), I.10.

22. *Elements of Law* Epistle Dedicatory.

23. *On the Citizen* II.1.

24. *Leviathan* I.xi, *On the Citizen* III.32.

25. Kant, *Metaphysics of Morals* (hereafter *MM*), trans. and ed. Mary Gregor (Cambridge: Cambridge University Press, 1996), 1.29, 2.38.

26. Jean-Jacques Rousseau, *First Discourse*, last paragraph; Kant, Annotations to *Observations on the Sense of the Beautiful and Sublime*, Akademie Ausgabe, 20:44, trans. Pierre Hassner, in "Immanuel Kant," *History of Political Philosophy*, 3d ed., ed. Leo Strauss and Joseph Cropsey (Chicago: University of Chicago Press, 1987), 585–86.

27. Immanuel Kant, *Groundwork of the Metaphysics of Morals* (hereafter *GMM*), trans. H. J. Paton (New York: Harper Torchbooks, 1964), 77.

28. Quoted in Hassner, "Kant," 586.

29. *GMM*, 110–11; cf. *MM*, 3:33, 204.

30. *GMM*, 110–11.

31. *GMM*, 111.

32. *GMM*, 94.

33. *GMM*, 98–100.

34. Susan Meld Shell, "Kant on Democratic Honor," in Michael P. Foley and Douglas Kries, eds., *Gladly to Learn and Gladly to Teach* (Lanham, Md.: Rowman and Littlefield, 2002), 239–55.

35. *MM*, 2:42.

36. *MM*, 2:44, "Remark."

37. *MM*, 2:37.

38. *MM*, 2:39.

39. *GMM*, 100–101.

40. *Renewed Question Whether the Human Race Is in Constant Progress toward*

the Better, VII 8, 15, 89, 161. I draw from passages translated and quoted in Susan Shell's "Honor and the End of History: A Reading of Kant's 'Renewed Question,'" in *Essays in Honor of Burleigh Taylor Watkins* (New York: Lang, 2001), 28–29.

41. *Idea for a Universal History with a Cosmopolitan Purpose*, trans. H. B. Nisbet, in *Kant, Political Writings*, ed. Hans Reiss (Cambridge: Cambridge University Press, 1993), 41. Francis Bacon described the empirical part of his new experimental physics as "natural history." It was the collection of laws of necessary processes, of formulas, that might supply powers for human purposes. See the "Plan" of the *Great Instauration*, as well as *New Organon* II, 4. Bacon authored the extraordinary epigraph of Kant's *Critique of Pure Reason*.

42. *Perpetual Peace*, First Supplement, in *Political Writings*, 112–13.

43. Kant, *Metaphysical Foundations of Natural Science*, trans. and ed. Michael Friedman (Cambridge: Cambridge University Press, 2004), 39, 46, 86–87, and *passim*. The term "model" is Friedman's at vii; cf. viii, xxvii. See Hassner, "Kant," 582, 596.

44. "Kant," 589–90; *MM* 2:38–39.

45. *GMM*, 109.

46. *Critique of Pure Reason*, Transcendental Dialectic, book 1, sect. 1; quoted by Hassner, "Kant," 587.

47. *Observations on the Feeling of the Beautiful and Sublime*, trans. John T. Goldthwait (Berkeley and Los Angeles: University of California Press, 1979), 60. I draw from Susan Meld Shell's "Kant as Spectator: Notes on *Observations on the Feeling of the Beautiful and Sublime*" (hereafter "KS"), *Eighteenth Century Studies* 35, no. 3 (2002): 458–60.

48. While the "nobler impulse" stands out for Kant, Shell concludes, "as aspects of human nature, even the baser instincts cannot lack beauty and dignity." "KS," 459. The paradox seems insuperable. In an early work Kant "reprimands himself" for failing to overcome his preference for noble over base. *Observations*, 73, in Shell, "KS," 459.

49. *MM* 2:42. See Shell, "KS," 7. For Bacon's view: "Excusations, cessions, modesty itself well governed are but arts of ostentation" (*Essayes or Counsels, Civill and Morall*, #54 "Of Vain-Glory"); "A man can scarce allege his own merits with modesty, much less extol them, . . . supplicate or beg; . . . But all these things are graceful in a friend's mouth; . . . where a man cannot fitly play his own part; if he have not a friend, he may quit the stage" (#27, "Of Friendship"); "All fame proceeds from servants" (*Essays*, #55, "Of Honor and Reputation").

50. Unless otherwise noted, quotations are of aphorisms, cited by number, in Nietzsche's *Beyond Good and Evil*, trans. Walter Kaufmann (New York: Vintage Books, 1946). I do not bother with references for well-known Nietzschean doctrines. I have been helped by Bruce Detwiler's *Nietzsche and the Politics of Aristocratic Radicalism* (Chicago: University of Chicago Press, 1990), Werner J. Dannhauser's "Friedrich Nietzsche," in Strauss and Cropsey, eds., *History of Political Philosophy*, 829–50, and Leo Strauss's "Note on the Plan of Nietzsche's *Beyond Good and Evil*," in his *Studies in Platonic Political Philosophy* (Chicago: University of Chicago Press, 1983).

51. Charles de Gaulle, *The Enemy's House Divided*, trans. Robert Eden (Chapel Hill: University of North Carolina Press, 2002), 2–3, 16.

52. *Great Instauration*, Preface; *New Organon* I, 127.

53. "For Nietzsche, nature has become a problem and yet he cannot do without nature." Strauss, "Nietzsche's *Beyond Good and Evil*," 190.

54. *The Enemy's House Divided*, 2.

Index